"Raising Sexually Pure Kids"

Sexual Abstinence, Conservative
Christians and American Politics

"Raising Sexually Pure Kids"
Sexual Abstinence, Conservative Christians and American Politics

Claire Greslé-Favier

Amsterdam - New York, NY 2009

The paper on which this book is printed meets the requirements of "ISO 9706:1994, Information and documentation - Paper for documents - Requirements for permanence".

ISBN: 978-90-420-2678-0
E-Book ISBN: 978-90-420-2679-7
©Editions Rodopi B.V., Amsterdam - New York, NY 2009
Printed in the Netherlands

Table of Contents

Table of Contents

Acknowledgments

In 2004, the American Studies department of the Universität Dortmund welcomed me. Since then they have provided me with the enriching and stimulating environment that allowed me to bring forth this book.

I would like to thank Prof. Walter Grünzweig and Prof. Randi Gunzenhäuser from the Universität Dortmund, as well as Prof. Claudette Fillard from the Université Lumière Lyon II, for their invaluable supervision and their warm encouragement throughout the past years.

I am also very grateful to my colleagues in Dortmund for all their enlightening and challenging feedback.

My final thanks go to my parents and my grandmother for supporting me in so many ways; to my friends for pointing out interesting media resources regarding my topic and sharing with me insights from their own disciplines; and to Andreas for patiently bearing my constant obsessions with abstinence, Americans and their sex lives for more than three years.

Introduction

The time has come to think about sex. To some, sexuality may seem to be an unimportant topic, a frivolous diversion from the more critical problems of poverty, war, disease, racism, famine, or nuclear annihilation. But it is precisely at times such as these, when we live with the possibility of unthinkable destruction, that people are likely to become dangerously crazy about sexuality. Contemporary conflicts over sexual values and erotic conduct have much in common with the religious disputes of earlier centuries. They acquire immense symbolic weight. Disputes over sexual behavior often become the vehicles for displacing social anxieties, and discharging their attendant emotional intensity. Consequently, sexuality should be treated with special respect in time of great social stress.[1]

Over the past decade the European public has become at least superficially aware, through TV shows and newspaper articles, of the promotion of sexual abstinence before marriage by US conservative Christians. This phenomenon is often seen by Europeans, in countries which promote a "Planned Parenthood" type of sexual education like France and Germany, as something ludicrous, another example of American "Puritanism." Western European TV channels and magazines strike viewers by featuring abstinent teenagers explaining their motivations or by presenting fathers pledging to protect their daughters' virginity during formal "Purity Balls."[2] Even to some western European Catholics the idea of asking teenagers to remain abstinent before marriage seems at best unrealistic. Why would chastity work in the United States, a modern society saturated by sexual messages where birth control is easily available, when the Catholic Church has been trying to implement it for centuries with mitigated results even among its own clergy? For people educated in deeply secular countries where sexual matters are considered more private and less legally regulated than in the United States, or even for Americans educated this way, it is indeed very easy to ridicule the conservative and religious communities' promotion of abstinence as a reactionary and necessarily marginal attitude. However, over the past two decades, the idea that sexual abstinence before marriage is desirable has achieved an almost hegemonic status in contemporary debates around sexual education in the United States. After the liberalisation of attitudes towards sexuality during the 1960s and 70s, the US approach to sexual education underwent a conservative backlash led by conservative Christians and the Reagan administration and reinforced by the threat of AIDS in the 1980s.

Today, most US schools are teaching abstinence, be it through "abstinence-only" programs - that promote abstinence without providing information on contraception and abortion except to underline their failure rates and potential negative consequences - or "abstinence-plus" programs - that privilege abstinence but provide information on contraception and abortion and are therefore dismissed as "not being abstinence at all" by most conservatives Christians. A 2006 review of US abstinence and abstinence-only policies and programs published in the *Journal of Adolescent Health* stated that in 2000

> 92% of middle and junior high schools and 96% of high
> schools taught abstinence as the best way to avoid pregnancy,
> HIV, and STDs. Only 21% of junior high and 55% of high
> school teachers taught the correct use of condoms. Between
> 1988 and 1999, sharp declines occurred in the percentage of
> teachers who supported teaching about birth control, abortion,
> and sexual orientation, and in the percentages who actually
> taught these subjects. For example, in 1999, 23% of secondary
> school sexuality education teachers taught abstinence as the
> only way to prevent pregnancy and STDs, compared with only
> 2% who had done so in 1988. In 1999, one-quarter of sex
> education teachers said they were prohibited from teaching
> about contraception.[3]

Even major sex education organizations like Planned Parenthood SIECUS (Sex Information and Education Council of the United States), while disapproving of abstinence-only, privilege abstinence as the best way for teens to prevent pregnancy and STDs. As suggested by journalist Judith Levine in 2001, "today, the embrace of abstinence appears nearly unanimous. The only thing that is left to debate is whether abstinence is the *only* thing to teach."[4] For G. W. Bush and his administration, it was. This, in spite of the fact that most Americans, while privileging an approach to sex education based on abstinence, massively favored the inclusion of information on contraception and abortion in sex education courses.[5] The personal commitment of the president and of the members of his administration[6] dealing with this issue was unprecedented. Never before had a US president committed himself so personally to the reformation of young people's sexual life and sexual choices.

The question of abstinence is sometimes dismissed by scholars as something peripheral, a minor moral agenda of religious conservatives concerned with a trivial matter: sexuality, and therefore of little political relevance. To paraphrase anthropologist Gail Rubin, abstinence is often perceived as a "frivolous diversion" from more critical political problems.[7] However, the enduring commitment of the Bush administration to a strict definition of abstinence-only education highlights the fact that this issue is anything but trivial and conveys important cultural and political messages. Indeed, why did this administration keep supporting programs that many Americans were finding too extreme and which after years of research hinting in that direction were proven inefficient in delaying sexual activity? The amount of money dedicated to abstinence-only programs in the federal budget was not particularly high on a national scale, $171.89 million in fiscal year 2006.[8] However, it did represent a significant sum for programs which were finally found inefficient in reducing STD rates and teen pregnancies and for an administration that cut numerous other welfare spending. In April 2007, an authoritative study commissioned by Congress concluded that sex education programs that focus only on abstinence while excluding information on contraception do not prevent teenagers from having sex before marriage.[9] But these findings did not alter the administration's commitment to abstinence-only, for Harry Wilson, Associate Commissioner at the Department of Health and Human Services (HHS), "this study [was]n't rigorous enough to show whether or not [abstinence-only] education works."[10] Yet at the end of G.W. Bush's last term in office, more and more states started refusing federal funding for abstinence-only education programs as surveys underlined their inefficiency and as the federal requirements got narrower and narrower in its definition of "genuine" abstinence.[11]

What I want to analyze in this book are the types of discourses and the subtexts that justify this unwavering support from the conservative Christian community across a spectrum that goes from fundamentalist preachers to the Bush administration, to underline that abstinence is not a peripheral issue, but is crucial to the sustenance of conservative Christian ideology and political influence, at least during until the end of the Bush presidency. As early as 1998, sociologist Sara Diamond observed that

> some of the evangelical movement's most popular projects are those that seem the most futile. True Love Waits [a prominent pro-abstinence organization], for instance, is a project that

combines the themes of parental rights, support for marriage, and opposition to abortion and sex education.[12]

This constitutes one of the major appeals of the contemporary concept of premarital abstinence, the way it "combines" many of the central demands of conservative Christian ideology. Throughout this work these various demands will be explored, as well as the other functions that discourses promoting premarital abstinence fulfill.

It is my contention that premarital sexual abstinence is not a marginal moral agenda but first and foremost a cultural and political issue of great significance in contemporary US politics. Pro-abstinence discourses coalesce most of the core agendas of conservative Christians and enabled them and the Bush administration, while it was in office, to preserve traditional hierarchies, on the one hand, and on the other hand to maintain the sense of threat necessary to the protection of the status quo and to the enduring commitment of the conservative Christian constituency.

Debates around sexual issues, be it abstinence, abortion, homosexuality or STDs, have been for the past two decades at the core of conservative Christian political agendas. As sociologist Jeffrey Weeks explains, sexuality

> has become a constitutive element in postmodern politics. The politics of the right is preoccupied with sex education, abortion, the threat of the "gay agenda," the dangers of single parenting and the underclass and the need to shore up the family and its "traditional" assignment of gender and childrearing responsibilities. The politics of the left is challenged by the claims of women and erotic minorities for rights, and faced by the need to translate its discourse of fairness and equality into an understanding of sexual change.[13]

This central status of sexual debates in contemporary politics is accounted for by the idea that, as Canadian sexual educator and researcher Alexander McKay underlines "sexuality is important in that its organization significantly shapes the nature of society"[14] or, as Jeffrey Weeks formulated it, "as sex goes, so goes society."[15] This idea is particularly important when considering sexual education for, as Mc Kay argues, the

> nature of sexuality education is so passionately fought over because, as an instrument in the sexual socialization of youth, sexuality education is seen to play a role in the shaping of sexual values and behavioural norms of our culture which in turn are widely perceived to impact significantly on the

character of society as a whole. Sexuality education in the schools is a key battle ground in a wider social conflict about sexuality in particular and the nature of society in general. In other words, the battle over sexuality education is not simply a dispute over the most effective means to promote the sexual and reproductive health of youth, but rather it is, first and foremost, a clash over the shape and direction of society itself.[16]

Contemporary debates over abstinence education are representative of this "clash" between a conservative and religious view of society and a more liberal and secular one. As will be shown throughout this book, this debate does not only take place on a moral level but also involves the organisation of society according to lines of hierarchies within and outside of the family.

Drawing on previous research,[17] McKay differentiates between two opposite visions of sexuality, and consequently of society, that he defines as "restrictive" and "permissive" sexual ideologies respectively. He explains that the "restrictive" sexual ideology generally appeals to "religious traditionalists from various faiths, social political conservatives, and radical feminists."[18] It can be defined as an "act centered sexual ethic" to the extent that it focuses on sexual acts which are considered moral or immoral and not on the individual him/herself.

The "restrictive" sexual ideology originates in early Christianity with the negative vision of sex defended by St Augustine. Based on the interpretation of the Genesis and the fall of Adam and Eve from the Garden of Eden, Augustine considered sexuality as dragging humans down towards earthly desires and away from God and spirituality. With the spread of Christianity to the whole occidental world, this vision would remain the norm for centuries. As summed up by Weeks the "restrictive" or "absolutist" sexual ideology as he himself calls it, claims that

> the disruptive powers of sex can only be controlled by a clear-cut morality, intricately embedded in a particular set of social institutions: marriage, heterosexuality, family life and (at least in the Judaic-Christian tradition), monogamy.[19]

Consequently, the only morally acceptable frame for sexual activity is the heterosexual marriage. Any other forms of sexuality are not morally acceptable and can only have negative outcomes. For example, premarital sex is seen as leading

> to "insecurity and hurt" and "dashed expectations" as well as "emotional problems" including "depression," "neurotic

behavior," and "feelings of inadequacy," not to mention "loss of appetite" and "headaches."[20]

However, some proponents of the "restrictive" sexual ideology nuance the notion of sexuality as only negative and advocate the idea that it can be positive in the context of a committed relationship. This idea makes premarital sex even less acceptable as they also argue that "adolescents lack the maturity to approach sex in an intimate and committed relationship"[21]

The contemporary promotion of abstinence inscribes itself into this tradition. In pro-abstinence discourses premarital sex is systematically described in terms of risks and negative outcomes. An eloquent illustration of this attitude is provided by Levine who explains that

> [c]ommonly, in the professional literature, sex among young people is referred to as a "risk factor," along with binge drinking and gun play, and the loss of virginity as the "onset" of intercourse, as if it were a disease.[22]

In pro-abstinence discourses, teens are systematically described as too immature to assume the potential consequences of their sexuality. They are urged to resist peer and media pressure to engage in an activity which is not appropriate to their age and could ruin their physical and mental health as well as their life prospects. As noted by sociologist Jessica Fields, sexuality researcher Deborah Tolman and other scholars, such discourses erase the notion of pleasure from discourses on teenage sexuality and ignore the potentially beneficial, pleasurable and empowering dimension of risk in human existence.[23] Abstinence education also openly promotes marriage, not only by reasserting it as the only acceptable frame of sexual activity but also by presenting its benefits to the individual. For example, the Department of Health and Human Services explained in 2006, that one of the functions of abstinence-only programs is to equip students with "skills and knowledge that give them a greater capacity to develop [...] healthy marriages in the long-term."[24]

Pro-abstinence discourses were fashioned in opposition to the vision of teenage sexuality developed after the sexual revolution of the 1960s, not only to counteract its acceptance of teen sexuality as legitimate and positive but also to ward off its attacks on the traditional heterosexual patriarchal family cell. Contrary to the "restrictive" sexual ideology, the "permissive" sexual ideology, that characterized US "comprehensive" sex education after the sexual revolution up to the 1980s, saw sexuality as

> a positive, beneficial, joyous phenomena. Its expression is connected to personal health, happiness, self-fulfillment, and

social progress. Sex is said to have multiple meanings; it can be justified as an act of self expression or pleasure, a sign of affection, love or procreative act.[25]

This vision is, McKay argues, mostly promoted by "secular-humanists, social-political liberals, and liberal feminists."[26] The "permissive" sexual ideology is more recent than the "restrictive" one and is linked to the development of a less theological vision of human nature with the growing secularization of the Western world and scientific innovations like Darwinism. This ideology can be defined as a "person centered" sexual ethic. It is not focused on specific acts but promotes sexual diversity and free individual choice attained by informed deliberation "guided by the moral principles of honesty, equality and responsibility."[27] As long as sexual acts are consensual and responsible, they are considered legitimate.

The "permissive" sexual ideology constructed in opposition to the "restrictive" one considers this latter as oppressive. As for the proponents of a "restrictive" sexual ideology, they consider the "permissive" position as morally dangerous and unacceptable, as it questions the principles on which they think a moral and healthy society should be based. The "permissive" position challenges the "clear cut morality" needed to channel the "disruptive powers of sex,"[28] and the major tenets of this morality: marriage and the monogamous heterosexual "traditional" family. It accepts practices like homosexuality, extra-marital sex in general and premarital sex in particular, thus allowing for the creation of alternative family cells based on different types of parenthood. Moreover, its proponents advocate the idea that individuals can decide for themselves what is morally right or wrong, instead of following a religious code of morality emanating from a spiritual authority.

After a growing acceptance of the "permissive" sexual ideology in the 1970s and early 1980s, the United States in the Reagan era saw an increasing backlash on issues of sexuality which in spite of the influence of the Clinton years has continued and been reinforced by the Bush presidency. Though the population at large acknowledges the need to inform teens about means of contraception, abortion and protection from STDs, a relative cultural consensus has been achieved among the adult population on the idea that abstinence for teenagers is the best option.[29] However, in practice few youths remain abstinent throughout their teenage years and the data suggests that even fewer remain abstinent until marriage since "approximately nine out of 10 men (89%) and women (92%) ages 22 to 24 have had sexual intercourse" with the average age of first marriage at "26 for women and 27 for men in 2003"[30]

Studies of abstinence education and pro-abstinence discourses have been so far either focused on the history of the pro-abstinence movement and of the conflicts over sex education in the past decades - like the authoritative book of sociologist Janice M. Irvine, *Talk About Sex: The Battles Over Sex Education in the United States* (2002) - or discussed the subject from a sociological perspective aimed primarily at underlining the potentially negative effects of abstinence-only and abstinence education.[31] So far there has been no study written from an American Studies perspective.

Besides, few scholarly books have been devoted entirely to the topic of sexual abstinence in general and to abstinence education in the United States in particular. In *A History of Celibacy* (1999) Elisabeth Abbot provided a fascinating global history of different types of sexual abstinence from antiquity to today, but gives only an extremely brief overview of abstinence organizations and curricula in the US before the G.W. Bush presidency.

One of the most recent and enlightening study of sex-education, including abstinence-education, is *Risky Lessons: Sexual Education and Social Inequality* (2008) by sociologist Jessica Fields. It is based on her sociological study of sex-education classes in three different schools featuring three different curricula, among them abstinence-only. This work provides an invaluable account and analysis of what is actually taught in the classroom and how the curricula is just one of the defining factors of the lessons conveyed about sex. In fact, Fields explains that by their attitude towards their students' behaviour and reactions to the curricula, as well as through the pedagogical tools they use, teachers send many hidden messages and deliberately avoid sending others. For example, by showing students images of bodies that are always white and slim, the teacher implies that this is the physical norm to which students should conform. Not reacting to a homophobic insult from a student is also a way to evade the issue of sexual diversity. Through this refusal to address the message sent by the student to the classroom, the teacher suggests that homophobia is an acceptable behaviour. Another of Fields' main contention is that sexual education reinforces social and racial inequalities. While the rich and mostly white students of the private school she observed had access to a comprehensive curricula focused on their personal development and sexual well being, poor white students were taught abstinence-only. On the other hand African-American students were offered a comprehensive curriculum, as it was considered unrealistic to expect abstinence from them. Such disparities reinforce traditional stereotype of African-Americans as promiscuous, while the fact that abstinence was taught in sex-segregated classes in a predominantly white school reinforced the vision of white girls as sexually pure and in need of protection.

When Sex Goes to School: Warring Views on Sex - and Sex Education - Since the 1960s (2006), by sociologist Kristin Luker, is another recent book focusing on the debates around sex-education in the United

States. Similar to J.M. Irvine, Luker studies the conflicting views on sex-education in the US in the past four decades. However, instead of taking a historical perspective as Irvine does, Luker centers her analyses on interviews she conducted in different US communities, to understand the motivations behind individuals' commitment to a "conservative" or "liberal" approach to sexuality. Luker's book focuses on debates over sexual education and necessarily involves pro-abstinence discourses however they are not the main focus of her study. Contrary to the present work which focuses on texts by pro-abstinence theorists, the "texts" analysed by Luker are interviews of individuals on both the conservative and liberal sides. Besides, while her book is fairly recent, it does not at all deal with the involvement of the Bush administration in the promotion of abstinence. While this study is not devoid of interest I think that, in spite of its later publishing date, it brings little that was not already present in Irvine's more systematic and thorough analysis, which approached the subject with more historical grounding and less redundancy. Moreover, I disagree with Luker's dismissal of the influence of the Puritan sexual heritage on contemporary American attitudes about sexuality. While the vision of Puritans as "anti-sex" has been reassessed in the past years, and ascribing to them the whole responsibility for contemporary sexual taboos is somewhat misleading, their influence on the emergence of the polarity between marital and extramarital sexuality among others is, I think, significant.

Several books devote very interesting chapters to abstinence education, like Levine's excellent *Harmful to Minors: The Perils of Protecting Children from Sex* (2002), in which she denounces what she sees as the excesses which have resulted from the protection of minors from sexuality, like the pedophile paranoia of the 1980s and 1990s, the condemnation of ever younger sexual "delinquents," or abstinence-only education.

In *Talk About Sex*, Irvine surveys major issues of the sex-education conflict: the attempt to entirely ban sex education before the 1980s; conservative Christians' use of the rhetoric of abstinence; or the opposition to educational materials featuring homosexuality as a legitimate sexual choice. She devotes a significant part of her book to abstinence education and provides an extremely rich analysis of the conservative Christian rhetoric and its evolution in matters of sex education.

Educational policy professor Wanda S. Pillow tackles the issue in a very enlightening chapter of her book, *Unfit Subjects: Educational Policy and the Teen Mother* (2004). She argues that abstinence education, in order to be justified as necessary, requires a continuous "incitement" to the production of negative discourses about teenage sexual activity. She explains that these discourses define sex as "dirty" and "dangerous" to reinforce heteronormativity and traditional gender roles and promote marriage as the best solution to the problem of teenage pregnancy.

In a chapter of his book *The Bush Administration, Sex and the Moral Agenda* (2007), Edward Ashbee, Associate Professor at the Center for the Study of the Americas of the Copenhagen Business School, considers the question of the support of the Bush administration to abstinence-only education. Ashbee's thesis is that, in spite of public perceptions, the G.W. Bush administration in its positions on sexual morality does not so much focus on satisfying the Christian Right as on being attuned to the opinion of mainstream Americans. Overall, Ashbee defends his thesis in a convincing manner however, in the case of abstinence I found that his arguments were based on insufficient evidence. While Ashbee is right in asserting that Americans overall are rather "conservative" regarding sexual matters and that most of them support the emphasis on abstinence in sexual education, he assimilates this support to an overall backing of abstinence-only education. This is problematic insofar as most studies have proven a general demand on the part of American parents for information on contraception and abortion in sex-education classes. Ashbee bases his point on an isolated 2003 survey commissioned by a conservative organization, the Coalition for Adolescent Sexual Health from the polling agency Zogby: [32]

> Although organizations such as SIECUS have made much of these findings [showing parental support of comprehensive sex-education], they should be set in broader context. The questions asked in the Zogby International poll suggest that public opinion is not as clear-cut or unambiguous as commentators might initially be tempted to conclude. If parents are asked as a follow-up about the inclusion of specific forms of instruction or activity[33] in sex education courses, much of the backing that was evident for the programmes when they are talked of in generalized or abstract terms, begins to drop away.[34]

This reference to the Zogby poll enables Ashbee to ground his thesis that the Bush administration in its propagation of abstinence-only education is not disconnected from moderate public opinion and does not run the risk of "alienating" it.[35] However, even if Americans are indeed rather conservative regarding the presentation of sexual information to children, more recent studies[36] have underlined the support of parents to approaches to sex-education that include information on contraception and abortion and their disapproval of abstinence-only education.[37] For example, a 2006 study published in the *Archives of Pediatrics and Adolescent Medicine*, a publication of the American Medical Association, concluded that

US adults, regardless of political ideology, favor a more balanced approach to sex education compared with the abstinence-only programs funded by the federal government. In summary, abstinence-only programs, while a priority of the federal government, are supported by neither a majority of the public nor the scientific community.[38]

Likewise, in 2007 a study conducted in California, one of the only states which consistently refused federal abstinence funding in the past decade, found that opposition to abstinence-only "requirements that prohibit instruction in or promotion of the use of contraceptive methods at any grade level" was overwhelming (96% of parents interviewed) even among self-identified conservatives:

No single subgroup by region, religion, income, education or political party dipped below an 80 percent support level for comprehensive sex education. The lowest level of support was recorded by those who identified themselves as "very conservative," but even they showed overwhelming support at 71 percent. Perhaps most surprising was that 86 percent of those self-identifying as evangelical Christians reported supporting comprehensive sex education.[39]

In view of this, I believe that it is legitimate to assert that the Bush administration, in its support of abstinence-only education, is not in agreement with public opinion and might "alienate" many citizens. In this respect, Ashbee misled his readers. In Ashbee's defense, opposition to abstinence-only education might have been strengthened since 2003 by the publication of scientific studies underlining the inefficiency of abstinence-only programs and the growing opposition of states to the ever more stringent requirements for abstinence-only funding.

A number of scholarly articles have been written about abstinence, in particular sociological studies evaluating the efficiency of abstinence programs.[40] However, none of them focused exclusively on pro-abstinence discourses or envisaged the subject from an American studies perspective. Moreover, their goal was in most cases only to underline the failures of the abstinence-only education approach and not, like the present book, to understand why conservative Christians defend abstinence and what ideological function this issue plays for them. In my view sociologist Jessica Fields has produced, in addition to her book, *Risky Lessons*, the richest and most challenging set of articles on the issue, on her own and together with other scholars. Through case studies, Fields questions the impact of the movement for gay marriage on young people's rights by suggesting that similar to abstinence-only it reasserts the limitation of sexual legitimacy to marriage and consequently further denies the right of youths to sexual expression.[41] In an article co-written with Deborah Tolman she also analyses the construction of teenage sexuality in terms of risk and danger and the provision by schools of abstinence-only education as a protection from these risks. Fields and Tolman argue that such a vision fails to provide young people with the skills and support they need to lead a healthy sexual life, and thus is itself risky. They also oppose the construction of youths as only vulnerable, and advocate the acknowledgment of young people's free choice and the potentially positive dimension of risk.[42] Finally in "Citizenship Lessons in Abstinence-Only Sexuality Education" (2007) co-authored with Celeste Hirschman, Fields underlines the heteronormative dimension of abstinence-only education.

What I think an American Studies perspective can contribute to the study of abstinence, which I found lacking in the mostly sociological approach of available writings on the subject, is a comprehensive analysis of pro-abstinence discourses. Most studies of abstinence so far have focused on criticisms of abstinence programs. Few have analysed extensively the functions and goals of such discourses for the conservative Christian Community and the Bush administration, as well as the way these have used and continue to use abstinence to appeal to conservative Christian audiences. Though these studies shed a relevant and indispensable light on the subject, they have also overlooked some aspects of this issue. The positions defended by conservative Christians have been very much condemned, but their roots and mechanisms have not been investigated thoroughly enough. Moreover, the possibly relevant remarks made by conservatives about sexuality and American society at large have been too often dismissed by proponents of the "permissive" sexual ideological perspective as necessarily "negative." This is why I chose to focus my work on pro-abstinence discourses and not on those that oppose it, to investigate the issue not only from an oppositional perspective but to understand its grounds. The questions I ask and attempt to answer here are not so much to know if abstinence is "good" or "bad" but rather to understand what exactly is at stake in abstinence discourses. Why were they so prominent in the politics of conservative Christians and of the Bush administration in the first decade of the twenty-first century? What political and ideological function they fulfill?

In her studies of the Religious Right's relationship to culture, the media and the market, English professor Linda Kintz has provided a comprehensive analysis of conservative Christian political rhetoric[43] and inspired my approach to the study of abstinence. When I later read the passages media studies professor Heather Hendershot devoted to abstinence in her book, *Shaking the World for Jesus: Media and Conservative*

Evangelical Culture (2004), I was also greatly interested in the way she included the conservative Christian perspective in her analysis. With their cultural studies point of view, these two authors bring a unique perspective towards these issues. While criticising what they consider a problem in conservative Christianity, they both avoid the temptation of describing their subject as "alien" and genuinely seek to understand the attraction of the discourses of conservative Christian leaders for their followers. Throughout my work I have also been inspired by the works of sociologist Jeffrey Weeks and philosophers Michel Foucault, Linda Singer and Antonio Gramsci, to whom I refer at different stages of my text.

In this book, I do underline some of the problematic dimensions of abstinence education; however my goal is first and foremost to understand how pro-abstinence discourses function and which goals their producers seek to achieve through them. I did not attempt to analyse the responses to pro-abstinence discourses in a sociological framework. Rather, I have chosen to focus on texts that I found representative of the different tendencies of pro-abstinence discourses. I did not decide to focus on the discourses of opponents of abstinence either, since I found their arguments already extensively explained by previous studies of the issue.

The need to limit my research to a manageable corpus made me privilege books, articles, speeches and governmental documents over the more fluctuating and less easily synthesised contents of the numerous pro-abstinence websites. I could also have chosen to focus on texts from abstinence curricula, but these would have provided a less comprehensive view of pro-abstinence arguments than the broader approach found in the texts I decided to use. Abstinence curricula are focused on achieving abstinence by a pedagogical method. The texts I selected, on the other hand, provide recommendations to help children remain abstinent and display a wide range of arguments to convince the reader of the necessity of this approach. Moreover they often dwell on a larger array of related ideological issues.

The corpus I have decided to analyse is composed of texts that I considered representative of the various "trends" present in pro-abstinence discourses:

- *Raising Sexually Pure Kids: How to prepare your children for the Act of Marriage*, (1998) by Tim and Beverly LaHaye, a prominent couple of conservative Christian theorists and activists, represents the more "religious trend" of pro-abstinence discourses.
- *Restoring the Teenage Soul: Nurturing Sound Hearts and Minds in a Confused Culture* (1999) and *Epidemic: How Teen Sex is Killing Our Kids*, by pro-abstinence pediatrician Meg Meeker, are

representative of what can be defined as the "medical" trend of pro-abstinence discourse.

- The "political" trend of pro-abstinence discourses is illustrated with texts published by the prominent Washington based conservative think-tank the Heritage Foundation, stating its position on welfare and "family issues" like abstinence, marriage, abortion, etc; and by extracts of the book *Home Invasion: Protecting Your Family In a Culture That's Gone Stark Raving Mad* (2005) by Heritage vice-president, Rebecca Hagelin.

- Finally, the "governmental" trend in pro-abstinence discourses is represented by texts issued by the Bush administration, and former United States governments (speeches, extracts of laws, websites, booklets, etc.) regarding the same issues.

The choice of these texts is of course somewhat accidental. For example while the LaHayes are famous conservative Christian figures, Meg Meeker is known mostly within the pro-abstinence circuit. I discovered her writings through Pat Robertson's TV show the *700 Club* and the Heritage Foundation's recommendation of her books. However, I believe that I have assembled a representative sample of pro-abstinence writings.

This study does not seek to be exhaustive - given the prolixity of pro-abstinence authors such a goal would be unattainable - but tries to offer an analysis of texts representative of the major types of pro-abstinence discourses. I am convinced that this study, though limited, can be very informative. There are many types of pro-abstinence discourses produced by very different instances - radical evangelical preachers or the Bush administration - and I sought to make visible the high level of coherence that this continuum constitutes.

The approach to discourse analysis that I have privileged in this book is thematic. I have tried to identify the recurring themes in the texts of my corpus and then studied the significance of these themes in conservative Christian discourses and politics in general. I then moved on to analyse the interactions between them and the concept of abstinence on the discursive level, how they reinforce each other and how the demand for premarital abstinence gave, in some cases, a new impulse to older agendas. I have also linked these recurring themes to the wider US historical and cultural context and underlined their relation to major American cultural narratives and discursive traditions. Finally, I have analysed how the different producers of the pro-abstinence texts of my corpus formulated and used, openly or not, the demand for abstinence together with the agendas related to it and to what aim.

This book is divided into thirteen chapters. Chapter I constitutes a historical location of abstinence discourses. It provides a brief overview of the different types of sexual abstinence since early Christianity, the varying audiences they targeted, and their social, political and cultural functions.

Chapters II to V describe the corpus of texts investigated here and present their authors.

The purpose of Chapter VI to Chapter XI is to identify the recurring conservative Christian themes present in pro-abstinence discourses and to understand how abstinence interacts with other discourses in this culture. Chapters VI and VII focus on abstinence and religion through the question of creationism in pro-abstinence discourses and the dichotomous vision of sexuality constructed by them in order to actualize conservative Christian's understanding of their sexuality. Chapters VIII and IX are centered on the theme of the family in pro-abstinence discourses. The first investigates how these discourses reassert the traditional patriarchal family cell as the ideal environment for "raising virtuous children," while the second section explores how they advocate the conservative Christian demand for "parental rights." Finally, Chapters X and XI highlight in what manner the demand for abstinence constitutes a discursive tool in the promotion of a conservative vision of poverty, work and the welfare society and studies the use of the narrative of the "culture war" by pro-abstinence writers.

Chapters XII and XIII engage in a more critical appraisal of the political mechanisms in action through pro-abstinence discourses, and seek to understand the subtexts or "hidden agendas" behind the defense of abstinence for young people's sake. The questions asked in these two chapters are: why did the demand for sexual abstinence become particularly visible in the late 20th and early 21st century? How does the theme of abstinence blur the boundaries between religious and political discourses? What function did pro-abstinence discourses play on the one hand for conservative Christians and on the other hand for the Bush administration in the past decade? Did pro-abstinence discourses by the Bush administration and by conservative Christians reinforce traditional adult-child hierarchies, and how? And how far did they invest teens with the symbolical weight of the nation's sexual morality?

The debate over abstinence education might become less heated in the coming years with the election of president Barack Obama. Yet I believe it is crucial to understand why this issue, which had significantly subsided with the sexual revolution, progressively reappeared to achieve such political and cultural prominence in the American context at the dawn of the twenty-first century. Especially, since the theme of sexual abstinence education might be yet again revived in the future to serve similar or new ideological purposes.

Notes

[1] G Rubin, 'Thinking Sex: Notes for a Radical Theory of the Politics of Sexuality' in C Vance (ed.), *Pleasure and Danger: Exploring Female Sexuality*, Routledge and Kegan Paul, Boston, 1984, p.267.

[2] In its issue of May 2007 the French edition of the women magazine *Glamour* featured the adaptation of an article on "Purity Balls" from the magazine's US edition, see J Baumgardner and N Dépret, 'Le bal de la virginité,' *Glamour* (French Edition), May 2007, 38, pp.50-54.

[3] J Santelli et al., 'Abstinence and Abstinence-Only Education: A Review of U.S. Policies and Programs," in *Journal of Adolescent Health*, 2006, 38 (1): 72-81, p.77.

[4] J Levine, *Harmful to Minors: The Perils of Protecting Children from Sex*, University of Minnesota Press, Minneapolis and London, 2001, p.92, emphasis in the original.

[5] National Health Information Center, 'Most Americans Favor Comprehensive Sex Education,' in *Family Health and Relationships Newsletter*, 20 November 2006, viewed on 8 May 2007, <http://www.healthfinder.gov/newsletters/relation112006.asp>

[6] For example Eric Keroack, former medical director of an anti-abortion and anti-contraception group, was deputy assistant secretary for population affairs of the HHS (US Department of Health and Human Services) from 2006 to 2007. From 2001 to 2007, abstinence-proponent and prominent conservative Wade Horn was Secretary for Children and Families at the HHS and oversaw the administration of abstinence programs; and Mike Leavitt, former Governor of Utah, who also displayed a strong anti-abortion and pro-abstinence stance was appointed by President Bush as Secretary of the HHS (2005-today).

[7] Rubin, op. cit., p.267.

[8] Republican Study Committee, 'Title X Funding and Abstinence Funding,' April 2006, viewed on 8 May 2007, <http://www.house.gov/hensarling/rsc/doc/HC_061306_TitleXvs.Abstinence Funding.doc>

[9] Mathematica Policy Research, Inc., *Impacts of Four Title V, Section 510 Abstinence Education Programs, Final Report*, April 2007, viewed on 8 May 2007, <http://www.mathematica-mpr.com/publications/PDFs/impactabstinence.pdf>

[10] L Sessions Stepp, 'Study Casts Doubt on Abstinence-Only Programs,' *The WashingtonPost.com.* 14 April 2007, viewed on 8 May 2007, <http://www.washingtonpost.com/wp-dyn/content/article/2007/04/13/AR2007041301003.html?nav=rss_health>

[11] See P J Huffstutter, 'States Abstain From Federal Sex-Ed Funds,' *LATimes.com*. 8 April 2007, viewed on 8 May 2007, <http://www.latimes.com/news/education/la-na-abstinence8apr08,1,1290457,full.story?ctrack=2&cset=true>

[12] S Diamond, *Not by Politics Alone: The Enduring Influence of the Christian Right*, The Guilford Press, New York, 1998, p.129.

[13] J Weeks, *Invented Moralities: Sexual Values in an Age of Uncertainty*, Polity Press, Cambridge, 1995, p.83.

[14] A McKay, *Sexual Ideology and Schooling: Towards Democratic Sexuality Education*, State of New York University Press, Albany, 1999, p.19.

[15] J Weeks, *Sexuality*, Ellis Horwood Limited, Chichester, 1986, p.36.

[16] McKay, op. cit., p.13.

[17] See M S Davis, *Smut: Erotic Reality/Obscene Ideology*, University of Chicago Press, Chicago, 1983; J Weeks, *Sexuality and its Discontents: Meanings, Myths, and Modern Sexualities*, Routledge and Kegan Paul, London, 1985 and J Weeks, *Sexuality*, Ellis Horwood Limited, Chichester, 1986; S Seideman, *Embattled Eros: Sexual Politics and Ethics in Contemporary America*, Routledge, New York, 1992.

[18] McKay, op. cit., p.38.

[19] Weeks, *Sexuality*, Ellis Horwood Limited, Chichester, 1986, p. 100.

[20] Davis, op. cit., p.209, cited in McKay, op. cit.

[21] Seidman, op. cit., , p.6, cited in McKay, op. cit.

[22] Levine, op. cit., pp. xxvi-xxvii.

[23] J Fields and DL Tolman, 'Risky Business: Sexuality Education and Research in U.S. Schools,' in *Research and Social Policy: Journal of NSRC*, September 2006, 3 (4), pp. 63-76, p.64.

[24] U.S. Department of Health and Human Services Administration for Children and Families, 'Announcement for Funding Opportunity Under CBAE, Funding Opportunity Number: HHS-2006-ACF-ACYF-AE-0099,' 2006a, viewed on 22 March 2007, <http://www.acf.hhs.gov/grants/pdf/HHS-2006-ACF-ACYF-AE-0099.pdf>

[25] Seidman, op.cit., pp. 5-6, cited in MacKay, op. cit.

[26] McKay, op. cit.,p.38.

[27] ibid., p.57.

[28] Weeks, op. cit., p. 100.

[29] See B Albert, 'American Opinion on Teen Pregnancy and Related Issues 2003,' 7 February 2004, viewed 11 May 2007, <https://www.teenpregnancy.org/works/pdf/American_Opinion.pdf>, C Dailard, 'Sex Education: Politicians, Parents, Teachers and Teens,' February 2001, viewed on 5 February 2009, <http://www.guttmacher.org/pubs/tgr/04/1/gr040109.html>

[30] Kaiser Family Foundation, 'Sexual Health Statistics for Teenagers and Young Adults in the United States,' September 2006, viewed on 11 May 2007, <http://www.kff.org/womenshealth/upload/3040-03.pdf>

[31] See Levine, op. cit.; J Fields, 'Same-Sex Marriage, Sodomy Laws, and the Sexual Lives of Young People,' *Sexuality Research and Social Policy: Journal of NSRC*, September 2004, 1 (3), pp. 11-23; Fields and Tolman 2006; J Fields and C Hirschman, 'Citizenship Lessons in Abstinence-Only Sexuality Education,' *American Journal of Sexuality Education*, 2007, 2 (2), pp. 3-25; W S Pillow, *Unfit Subjects: Educational Policy and the Teen Mother*, RoutledgeFalmer, New York and London, 2004; B Finlay, *George W. Bush and the War on Women: Turning Back the Clock on Progress*, Zed Books, London and New York, 2006.

[32] Coalition for Adolescent Sexual Health, 'Zogby International 2003 Survey on Parents' Reactions To Proposed Sex Education Messages In The Classroom,' 3 February 2003, viewed on 13 May 2005, <www.whatparentsthink.com/pdfs/z_p1_sokfbsdbq.pdf>

[33] In this case Ashbee refers to the disapproval by parents of demonstration and practice of condom use on, for instance, wooden models or to the discussion of masturbation and orgasms.

[34] E Ashbee, *The Bush Administration, Sex and the Moral Agenda*, Manchester University Press, Manchester and New York, 2007, p.128.

[35] ibid., p.128.

[36] Kaiser Family Foundation, National Public Radio and the Kennedy School of Government, 'Sex Education in America: General Public/Parents Survey,' 2004, viewed on 9 February 2007, <http://www.kff.org/newsmedia/upload/Sex-Education-in-America-General-Public-Parents-Survey-Toplines.pdf>; A Bleakley, M Hennessy and M Fishbein, 'Public Opinion on Sex Education in US Schools,' *Archives of Pediatrics and Adolescent Medicine*, November 2006, (160), pp. 1151-1156; Harris Interactive, 'Majorities of U.S. Adults Do Not Believe Abstinence Programs are Effective in Preventing or Reducing HIV/AIDS, Unwanted Pregnancies or Extra-Marital Sex,' 11 January 2006, viewed on 23 June 2007, <http://www.harrisinteractive.com/harris_poll/index.asp?PID=629>; Public Health Institute, 'Regardless of Religion, Politics or Location, New Poll Shows Overwhelming Parental Support for Comprehensive Sex Ed,' 23 May 2007, viewed on 25 May 2007, <http://askmerrill.ml.com/markets_news_story/1,2263,%7B8A40E614-F1C3-47CB-843B-6DEF0E770DC8%7D,00.html>

[37] The latest poll on the issue conducted by the firm Lake Research and released on June 7, 2007 found out that 88% of the 1,011 adults polled in May 2007 "agreed that public schools should teach sex education that

includes information on abstinence and contraception," C Wetzstein, 'Poll finds majority back birth control; Access sought without 'delay,'' *The Washington Times*, June 8, 2007a, viewed on 24 June 2007, <http://www.religiousconsultation.org/News_Tracker/poll_finds_majority_ba ck_birth_control.htm>

[38] Bleakley et al., op. cit., p. 1151.

[39] Public Health Institute, 2007.

[40] P S Bearman and H Brückner, 'Promising the Future: Virginity Pledges and the Transition to First Intercourse,' *American Journal of Sociology*, 2001, 106 (4), pp. 859-912; D Kirby, 'Do Abstinence-Only Programs Delay the Initiation of Sex Among Young People and Reduce Teen Pregnancy?,' October 2002, viewed on 23 March 2007, <http://www.teenpregnancy.org/resources/data/pdf/abstinence_eval.pdf>; Santelli et al., 2006; Mathematica Policy Research, 2007.

[41] Fields, op. cit., 2004.

[42] Fields and Tolman, op.cit., 2006.

[43] L Kintz, *Between Jesus and the Market: The Emotions that Matter in Right-Wing America*, Duke University Press, Durham and London, 1997; L Kintz and J Lesage (eds), *Media, Culture and the Religious Right*, University of Minnesota Press, Minneapolis, 1998.

Chapter 1
Pro-"Sexual Abstinence Before Marriage"
Discourses in US History

Sexual abstinence before marriage can seem, at first sight, a necessary requirement of our forefathers' sexual lives. The absence of reliable contraception and the ideal of the virginity of the bride to guarantee the legitimacy of her husband's offspring were reason enough to desire it. However, what were pro-abstinence before marriage discourses concerned with in the past? By whom were they formulated? At whom were they targeted, and why? At which point was sexuality considered legitimate? This historical chapter will attempt to answer these questions in order to situate contemporary discourses on abstinence in their historical context, and to underline the similarities they share with, as well as the ways in which they differ from previous discourses on this issue.

1.   Lifelong Abstinence vs. Abstinence Before Marriage

The requirement of abstinence is strongly grounded in religion, therefore it is important to distinguish between the two different types of sexual abstinence present in the Christian tradition: lifelong celibacy and premarital abstinence. The crucial difference between those two types of celibacies lies in their respective relationship to the concept of family. Whereas, as this book underlines, premarital abstinence reasserts the necessity of marriage and family, lifelong celibacy, on the contrary, questions it.

Lifelong celibacy, which is still demanded from the Catholic clergy, reflects the traditional catholic vision that sexuality is innately sinful and that even within marriage it draws the believer away from God. Since early Christianity, sexuality has been seen as a link to the earthly realm that needed to be renounced to achieve spiritual immortality. As feminist theologian Rosemary Radford Ruether explains in her work *Christianity and the Making of the Modern Family*,

> [t]he renunciation of sex was seen as a key expression of world renunciation, but not necessarily because sex was the most urgent need of the body; for many monks, hunger, the craving of the belly, was a more insistent bodily demand, and less easy to control. Rather, sex tied a person to marriage and family [...]. Through sex and marriage, "the world" as a social system of power and possessions was reproduced. To renounce marriage was to renounce that

"world" in all its social, economic, and political implications.[1]

Early Christianity, with its demand for lifelong celibacy, was consequently very much anti-family and privileged the spiritual bonding of Christian brotherhood over "blood" ties. It thus erased social and ethnic differences, which made it a deeply subversive movement. A telling example of this potential can be found in the lives of numerous female saints who were supported by other Christians in refusing the marriages forced on them by their families in order to answer their spiritual calling and join a religious community.[2] Later on, female religious communities would also provide women with a significant sphere of power and freedom; however, they would also be used to alienate them. With the spread of Christianity, the subversive elements of the Christian message were significantly weakened. As for celibacy, it lost its equalising dimension and began to be used to enforce hierarchic differences in the community with its institutionalisation by the clergy. The celibate clergy was thus asserted as standing higher on the spiritual scale than its non-abstinent parishioners. Yet as Radford Ruether underlines, though channelled by the Church, this higher status of celibate priesthood would continue to carry (up to the present day in Catholic communities) the subversive "anti-family" message "that marriage is a second-class choice for Christians. Those who aspire to perfection should renounce sex, marriage, and reproduction for a chaste single life."[3]

The Reformation staunchly opposed this vision of sexual abstinence. Still inscribing himself in the Augustinian tradition that saw sexuality as necessarily sinful after the Fall, Luther nevertheless condemned lifelong celibacy. Radford Ruether states his position on the issue as follow:

> For Luther, marriage had been given to men and women by God in Paradise as the basic unit of society for companionship and procreation. Since the Fall, all - that is, all *men* - had been affected with sinful lust. Thus the celibate ideal was both wrong and impossible, as it went against both created and fallen nature. All *should* marry because God's intention from the beginning had been to unite men and women in marital union and bid them to procreate. Almost all *must* marry because the lustful urges that had arisen from the Fall could be contained without sin only in marriage. Without marriage, lust would quickly lead to fornication for all but an exceptional few (again, men) who could be celibate without falling into sexual sin.[4]

She further explains that Luther saw the celibate ideal as "an insult to God", who had intended men and women to live together and procreate, and could only lead to fornication, given men's lustful nature. He saw proof of this in all the monks who pretended to be celibate but were not.[5] Indeed, the Church always met great difficulties in imposing chastity on its clergy, particularly on the great numbers who did not choose this path out of conviction but rather by coercion or on financial grounds.

Lutherans also defined a new way to mark the moment when a couple was declared married. For example, contrary to medieval custom, they rejected clandestine marriages or marriages that had not been consecrated by the church and required parental acceptance and public blessing. Thus "they rejected the canonical view that consent of the couple alone was essential for a marriage's validity."[6] Moreover, to former rituals of marriage, which predominantly belonged to folk traditions and the family, which they saw as "a source of sinful waste, gluttony, drunkenness and lascivious dancing"[7] they opposed a sober rite which was used to instruct the couple in the doctrine of marriage. In this context, as sex could be justified only within marriage and would be inevitably sinful outside of it, abstinence was seen as the required standard for unmarried youths, who when coming of age would be encouraged to marry in order to fulfill God's mandate of reproduction and to channel their lust.

2.   Pro-Abstinence Discourses from Colonial America to the Early 19th Century

In his book *Sexual Revolution in Early America*, historian Richard Godbeer gives an enlightening account of debates around sexuality in the colonial period. He first explains that at the time of the exploration of the New World, England was the stage of heated debates about sexuality. Sexual impropriety was used as a metaphor for sin and chaos, and represented the fears about an uncertain future harbored by Englishmen after the end of the long reign of Queen Elisabeth I. Like conservative Christians today, many English social critics of the time saw premarital sex as an open door to disorder and immorality.

Godbeer argues that the Puritan settlers brought those concerns with them to the New World, where they took on a new dimension.

> Sexual mores took on additional significance in a colonial setting: imposing moral order was rendered both more urgent and more far-fetched by the primitive surroundings in which colonists found themselves, "a desolate wilderness" located "at the end of the world." Such an environment seemed to encourage debased, even barbaric, tendencies among those who migrated to North America, raising the grim prospect of cultural degeneration. That danger was compounded in the eyes of many

contemporaries by the presence of apparently savage Indians and Africans, who threatened to contaminate the colonist and further compromise their civility.[8]

The debate on premarital sex in England and in the New World revolved around the opposition between the vision of religious and state authorities, and traditional views on where the boundary between licit and illicit sex was drawn. Godbeer explains that for a conjugal union to be valid, English law traditionally only required that a couple declare themselves husband and wife, even without public ceremony or witnesses. By the late 16th century the religious ceremony was well established in England; however, the particular context of colonial America revived the practice of informal marriages. The shortage of ministers and magistrates, in particular, encouraged this practice. Despite the efforts of colonial authorities to enforce marriage and sexual norms of propriety, numerous settlers and self-identified Puritans attached more meaning to the approval of their relationships by their neighbors and community than by the authorities. Moreover, as Godbeer explains, serial monogamy caused by widowhood or desertion was a widespread practice in colonial America, thus further calling into question the permanence of marriage and the validity of public ceremonies. Yet another point of disagreement between the American population and its leaders was the propriety of premarital sex. In the view of many settlers, as had been long been condoned by the English tradition, premarital sex was seen as legitimate when the couple was committed to marry. This went against the position of New England authorities, which like the British ones, tried to enforce the idea that official marriage was a prerequisite for marital sexuality. In a statement that echoes contemporary debates on abstinence, Godbeer comments that

> [t]he campaigns waged in British America by those who sought moral reformation amounted to a culture war, pitting different conceptions of sexual and marital etiquette against each other. Popular customs and attitudes persisted throughout the seventeenth and eighteenth centuries, despite attempts by church and state to impose quite different ideals. [...] Words such as marriage meant different things to different people: whereas clergymen understood marriage to involve a public ceremony in the presence of an authorized official, some settlers saw neither public ritual nor official validation as a prerequisite for marital respectability.[9]

Hence the Puritan leaders who argued for a moral reformation had to strike a compromise with the diverging vision of other settlers, and accommodate to constraints such as the shortage of church and public officials to celebrate formal marriages. Still, throughout the Puritan era and until the 18th century, church and public authorities tried to alter public acceptance of premarital sexuality through speeches, prosecutions and public punishment. It is only towards the end of the 18th century that local courts, more concerned about commercial and financial issues, progressively ceased to deal with moral enforcement, leaving this to families and neighbors.

Through customs like "bundling" that allowed young people to experience physical contact before marriage under parental supervision, premarital sexual desires were largely condoned by public opinion, in spite of the attacks of the clergy against it. Bundling was seen by many families as preferable, as it allowed them to know who was involved with their daughters and who could be forced to marry them in case of pregnancy. Along with the loosening of Puritan influence and of parental authority, the 18th century saw a steady increase in premarital pregnancy. As family, church and community control became more and more difficult to enforce, public opinion became sensitive to the greater risks faced by young women who could not expect that marriage would necessarily follow a premarital pregnancy. Moreover, whereas in the past sex ratios favoring women had made it easier for them to marry and remarry, the inversion of these ratios made it increasingly more difficult. With the growing urbanisation and the departure of young people from the country to factories, the risks faced by women would only increase.

Whereas earlier they had been concerned with the morality of both sexes, public discourses at that time started to focus on female chastity. Moreover, as Godbeer argues:

> Widespread rape during the Revolutionary War had exacerbated public anxiety about the sexual dangers facing young women, while the emphasis within republican ideology upon women's role as moral exemplars reaffirmed the need to protect female virtue [...] the sustenance of public and private virtue became tightly interwoven during the closing decades of the century, which in turn gave new significance to discussion of courtship and sexual politics.[10]

Hence women, now considered more "moral" and self-controlled than men, were deemed indispensable in helping men achieve self-control and maintain moral order in a new republic where, without the authority of the king, people might focus on instant and personal gratification only. Though this vision did not immediately engender the idea that women were devoid of sexual desire, historian Nancy Cott argues that inevitably "passionlessness was on the other side of the coin which paid, so to speak, for women's admission to moral equality."[11] Thus the nineteenth century middle-class developed the ideal of female "passionlessness" and moral superiority with its correlate the "fallen woman." As historians D'Emilio and Freedman underlined

> [i]n the past, as long as she repented, the woman who once sinned - like a male transgressor - could be reintegrated into the community. Now, however because woman allegedly occupied a higher moral plane than man, her fall was so great that it tainted her for life.[12]

Though this double standard would continue to lead to heavier consequences of premarital promiscuity for women, it was primarily the males on which pro-abstinence discourses focused during the nineteenth century, as will be shown in the coming section.

3.   Abstinence Discourses in the Victorian Era

In his book *Teaching Sex: The Shaping of Adolescence in the 20th Century*, historian J. P. Moran explains that the idea of female passionlessness had the correlating notion that chastity was an easy task for women, as they went directly from the parental home to their husbands'. On the contrary, men who were considered to have overpowering sexual urges and who faced a longer period of independence needed all the possible help to remain chaste. Consequently, most nineteenth century pro-abstinence discourses, while applicable to women, were primarily targeted at men.

In her *History of Celibacy* historian Elizabeth Abbott presents the British arguments in favor of male chastity:

> In late-Victorian England, proponents of respectable gentlemanly chastity elaborated a nonmedical rationale, based on a current economic model. It proceeded from a general idealization of self-control in all spheres and argued that, like fiscal continence, sexual continence was good and could be achieved through self-control and sublimation, preferably by industrious use of time. The result of this sort of celibacy would be the accumulation of capital. Incontinence, on the other hand, was bad and provoked too early marriages and poverty.[13]

Along similar lines "the Male Purity Movement", an original American discourse on male chastity, was elaborated in the 1830s by men like Presbyterian minister Sylvester Graham, creator of the Graham cracker, educator William Alcott, and medical doctor S. B. Woodward. Abbott argues that those authors of advice books advocating chastity were concerned about the changes caused in American society by the greater number of male youths who left the countryside and the authority of their parents to work in urban factories. The leaders of the "Male Purity Movement" feared that the newfound independence of those youths would lead to the erosion of "discipline, manhood and morality."[14] To help young men left to themselves and exposed to the multiple and particularly sexual temptations of the modern city that would inevitably lead them to immorality and poverty, the Male Purity Movement advocated a strict code of behavior. They believed that chastity, as Moran explains, was critical to character building, which was achieved "by mastering in all areas of life [the] too-human propensity for the easy path and immediate gratification."[15] In their view, complete chastity before marriage was a matter of will and self-control. If it was not adhered to, there would be dire consequences. The Male Purity movement

> preached temperance, vegetarianism, moral reform, and chastity before marriage. Alcohol and rich, spiced foods overstimulated and led to eroticism, and eroticism, often self-administered, corrupted, caused mental illness, disease, and the decay of the entire society.[16]

Sexuality was not judged as completely negative but the representatives of the Male Purity movement contended that "semen should be expended solely for propagating children and otherwise stored up as energy to be directed to the higher things in life."[17] This argument was rooted in the idea, dating back to the Greek physician Hippocrates, that semen was a vital fluid, like blood, stored only in limited amount in the body and which, if squandered, would lead to degeneracy and death. Hence, masturbation was considered lethal, as well as leading to insanity. As for sexual intercourse, it was acceptable only within marriage and then only a limited number of times a year (about once a month) as more would put the man "at risk of early death because each ounce of lost semen equaled four ounces [...] of precious blood."[18] Finally, at around forty-five years of age, sexual activity should be altogether renounced, as enough sperm had been lost. To help men through this difficult practice of self-control the Male Purity Movement advocated the consumption of bland food, among others Graham crackers and Dr. John Harvey Kellogg's breakfast cereal to "subdue eroticism."[19] This movement remained successful only until the 1860s, but the warnings against masturbation persisted well into the 20th century.

Another short-lived vision of sexuality and self-control that flourished in the late 19th and early 20th century also used chastity as a means to differentiate between "civilised" Anglo-Saxons and "uncivilised" immigrants. This vision urged sexual control even within marriage as to use sex "for mere pleasure was supremely selfish and betrayed the continued presence of the brute within the man."[20] The ideal of sexual respectability was thus used to create a new aristocracy and came to be seen as an inherent Anglo-Saxon quality, the sign of racial superiority. On the contrary sexual indulgence was seen as leading to racial degeneracy.

Though reasons to justify the need for premarital chastity would evolve throughout the 20th century, it continued to be the standard of behavior expected from young people.

4.   20th Century Abstinence Discourses

The concept of adolescence as a separate period in life was created at the beginning of the twentieth century by the psychologist G. Stanley Hall. Moran explains that although Hall condemned the sexual repression of the 19th century and did not consider children and adolescents as sexually "innocent", in his view, chastity still played a crucial role in this phase of human development. In view of the fact that puberty occurred earlier and marriage later, Hall believed that the prolonged period of chastity thus forced on youths was to be used to build character and virtue.

This idea was reinforced by the campaign against venereal diseases and prostitution led by Social Hygienists in the first two decades of the twentieth century. Moran writes that for Social Hygienists, the epidemic of venereal diseases needed to be counteracted by a return to chastity, which had been undermined by the corrupting influence of modern society and education. If children were educated in a scientific way, they thought, they would be able to make sound health choices and remain chaste before marriage. But their wish to bring sex education to the schools was met by a considerable opposition from groups who thought that children were innately innocent and would be corrupted by information on sexuality. The Social Hygienists, in a pattern reproduced decades later by pro-abstinence authors Meg Meeker and Tim and Beverly LaHaye, opposed this by arguing that given the corrupted state of the modern world, the question was not any longer if children would get sexual information but rather, from whom. A timely scientific sexual education would thus do much less damage than silence and information obtained secretly from unreliable and immoral sources.

The teachings offered by the Social Hygienists were limited to reproduction and venereal diseases. One of their goals was to dispel "the fallacy of male sexual necessity"[21] - the idea that not having sex might endanger men's health or "hurt" them physically - which in their view fueled prostitution. For them, the same standards of morality applied to women and men, though they focused their efforts more heavily on the latter, still convinced that chastity was harder for men to achieve.

One of the main challenges faced by this "scientific" movement was the difficulty to ground the need for chastity outside of religion. This could only be done as long as chastity was considered the norm by society, but this would change in the 1920s. The main argument in favor of sexual education thus became the fear of venereal diseases. This fear was reinforced during the First World War, as a result of the high rate of venereal diseases discovered in the military and, later on, the civilian population. However, the methods used to answer this problem were not only education and chastity but also the medical protection provided to soldiers. Progressively, the appearance of efficient cures for venereal diseases would make it a poor argument for promoting chastity. Though most Americans in the 1920s and later were still averse to teenage sexuality, the liberation of women and youths as well as the increase in the use of contraceptives and in divorce made it more and more irrelevant to demand chastity from the population at large.

Consequently, a new argument in favor of premarital abstinence had to be found. This argument used the recent expectations of sexual fulfillment within marriage that came out from the differentiation between reproduction and sexuality and the rise of psychoanalysis. Abstinence proponents thus argued that premarital sex endangered sexual and emotional adjustment within marriage. This notion, held in the Family Life Education classes of the 1950s, is still at the core of contemporary pro-abstinence discourses and was in the 1960s still supported by the feminist Mary Calderone, creator of the liberal Sexuality Information and Education Council of the United States (SEICUS).

Created in 1964, SIECUS' major objective was to make information on sexuality widely available. It promoted a more positive view of sex and tried to underline the importance of pleasure and well being in this experience. However, as Moran underlines, breaking from the tradition of sex education as disease prevention was a difficult task, as STDs still provided the major ground for sex education, which often amounted to little more than information about the negative consequences of premarital sexuality.

Moran therefore highlights the irony of the attacks launched by conservative Christians (the LaHayes among them) on SIECUS which they saw as promoting promiscuity and providing "intercourse education", as they dubbed it, in spite of the fact that

> SIECUS had risen to popularity largely on the strength of its hostility to teenage promiscuity, venereal disease, pregnancy, and all-around misbehavior. Like sex education curricula in general, SIECUS's materials were heavily imbued with sexual warnings, moralistic stories, and statements of support for conventional morality.[22]

Conservative Christian attacks, while clearly exaggerated, were strategically extremely efficient and contributed to the strengthening of the Religious or "New" Right through a shift in emphasis from communism to "family" and "morality" issues.

With the advent of the sexual revolution, the 1970s saw a shift in public opinion on the issue of premarital sex. More and more Americans were endorsing premarital sex and its correlate, cohabitation, though, as Moran underlines, in lesser numbers when asked specifically about teenagers. Marriage was "losing its privileged position as the sole site for sexual relations."[23] At the same time SIECUS became part of a movement to protect teenagers' access to contraception and sex information. To support this cause, sexual liberals created the myth of a teen pregnancy epidemic, arguing that to protect young women, and by extension society, from poverty, the inevitable outcome of teen pregnancy, contraception and abortion should be made easily accessible. However, this epidemic was turned against its creators, as conservatives used it to emphasise that contraception and abortion were not the remedy but the cause of the problem, as they encouraged teens who should not be sexually active to be so.

With the AIDS epidemic, the 1980s brought a new task for sexual educators. Moran argues that from that time onwards, conservatives could not ignore the need for sexual information any more and had to define a new strategy through abstinence curricula. Though conservatives had long claimed that sex education programmes encouraged sexual activity, they did not effect a revolution with their own programmes as "a 1989 survey found that nine out of ten educators were [already] teaching that abstinence is the best alternative for preventing pregnancy and STDs."[24] Moreover, as Moran underlines:

> [...] despite their desire to teach abstinence only because it is right morally, conservative educators harked back to the earliest sex hygienists, who could not resist pointing out that God had conveniently arranged life so that morality and hygiene were indistinguishable.[25]

This desire can also be found in the LaHayes' writings which use the fear of STDs and pregnancy to convince young Christians of being abstinent, in spite of the fact that the religious argument should suffice. The opposition of some conservative Christian groups, like the Family Research Council (FRC) to the Gardisal vaccine, which helps prevent Human Papillomavirus (HPV, a sexually transmitted virus which causes a majority of cervical cancers), also witnesses the extent to which pro-abstinence discourses rely on STDs. This point was underlined in 2005 by the scientific magazine the *New*

Scientist, in an interview of FRC spokesperson B. Maher on the Gardisal vaccine.

> "Abstinence is the best way to prevent HPV," sa[id] Bridget Maher of the Family Research Council, a leading Christian lobby group that has made much of the fact that, because it can spread by skin contact, condoms are not as effective against HPV as they are against other viruses such as HIV. "Giving the HPV vaccine to young women could be potentially harmful, because they may see it as a licence to engage in premarital sex," Maher claim[ed.][26]

Thus Maher suggested that without the threat of HPV, which ruled out condoms as an efficient protection against STDs, abstinence education would become inefficient. Paradoxically, by thus presenting STDs as the major reason to abstain, some conservative Christians undermine their own stance on premarital sex as morally wrong and condemned by God, suggesting that this latter point might not be enough to justify abstinence.

But the question remains open as to whether or not sex education of any kind can in any way convince teens to be abstinent or to protect themselves. Moran concludes his book by the insightful contention that sexual education programmes, whatever their strategy, have limited chances of succeeding, as teens' sexual behaviors are mostly determined by their social environment, and very little by sexual education.

> The sex educator's expectation that students will respond rationally to classroom knowledge is a peculiarly middle-class ideal. [...] Their faith in education is generally justified, however only insofar as the students share their social background. Because young people of higher socioeconomic status are more oriented toward the future than their less advantaged peers, they may be more likely to change their behavior in response to new knowledge. [...] To students who lack this future orientation, who find the question of where they will be in five or ten years a matter of fatalism or indifference, an education based on future consequences has little meaning. If receptivity to sex education is socially conditioned, then an educational programme by itself will have little tangible effect on those students most at risk for the ills associated with adolescent behavior.[27]

Moreover, in Moran's view, the American vision of teenage sexuality is one that is far from being unproblematic, by causing a wider dissemination of sex education programmes, the "epidemics" of teenage pregnancy and AIDS multiplied the possible battlegrounds for the culture wars, but they did little to change the terms of the debate over sex in the schools. Sex educators have always shown, for example, a propensity for conflating moral issues with matters of health and illness, and sex educators and their opponents in the AIDS era continue to mix morality with medicine. In this approach, they reflect a general American tendency in the twentieth century to conceive of sexuality and adolescence primarily in terms of danger. Teenage pregnancy and the AIDS epidemic have buttressed a peculiarly American disposition to view adolescent sexuality as a hazard, and intensified the impulse for educators to regulate adolescent desire.[28]

The right of teenagers to sexual activity is indeed far from being established in America, and teenage sexuality is increasingly surrounded by notions of danger and irresponsibility. As underlined by sexuality researcher Deborah Tolman and sociologist Jessica Fields, most abstinence-only programmes present the consequences of sexual behavior as

inevitable and innumerable: ruined reputations, broken hearts, humiliation, HIV/AIDS, unwanted pregnancies, genital herpes, and death. This narrative, common among abstinence-only educators, casts sexuality only in terms of dire consequences. According to this cautionary tale, sexual behavior is fundamentally and essentially risky for youth, and any instruction suggesting the possibility of anything other than a painful outcome is irresponsible and dangerous.[29]

Teenage sexual behaviors are the focus of fears that overlook the fact that youth behaviours might not be that separate from those of adults (as many adults would like to think) and mirror tendencies already present in the population at large.

As professor of English James R. Kincaid noted in the late 1990s in his book, *Erotic Innocence: The Culture of Child Molesting*, contemporary American culture is still pervaded by the 19th-century concept of childhood as an asexual period clearly separate from adulthood. This became particularly visible in the child molesting paranoia of the 1980s and 1990s, spread through the media and spectacular trials like the McMartin preschool case

(1983-1990) or the Megan Kanka case in 1994. It popularised the vision of innocent children as being permanently surrounded with predators coming from outside and within the family, such as molesters, pornographers, satanists, abductors, incestuous fathers, etc. In Kincaid's view this paranoia, though apparently focused on protecting children was in fact focused on a fantasised innocent child rather than any real children, who are today at much greater risk of starvation and poverty than sexual abuse. This construction of the innocent child was so powerful that it even extended to individuals who barely qualified as children anymore. Referring to the trial of a school teacher who allegedly had sexual intercourse with one of her pupils, Kincaid explains that through the discourse surrounding the case, the "victim", 16-year-old Alan,

> [a] smart and active older adolescent is shrunk into a child, a generic "essence-of-child," by this cultural story, remolded as passive, innocent, and guileless. His actual age, activities, particularities are melted away to fit our needs. Alan's sexual activity in particular is fashioned as unwilled, forced unto him or drawn from him "unnaturally."[30]

Instead of acknowledging the possibility that a sixteen-year-old might be sexually attracted to an older teacher, the "cultural story" preferred to refashion Alan as a "victim," an innocent child in spite of his age and personality. Discourses of child-molestation force this sexual innocence on children. This, in spite of all the evidence that children are not "innocent" and can hardly be in an "oversexualised" society that makes them a privileged object of erotic projection. As will be shown further on, pro-abstinence discourses also use the image of the innocent child and the fear of molestation extensively, and though they acknowledge the fact that the adolescent has sexual urges, they try to maintain part of his/her innocence by refusing him/her the right to act sexually.

But what purposes does such a distinction - extensively used by conservatives - serve, between sexual adulthood and asexual childhood? Kincaid argues, among other explanations, that "recognising children as sexual beings means recognising one's own children that way, which in turn may force us far too close to incestuous ponderings."[31] Though relevant, this explanation can only account in a very limited way for the insistence laid by abstinence proponents in particular and conservatives in general on picturing children as sexually innocent. Hence, it is important to note that the innocent child serves wider functions than merely sexual ones.

The idea of children as innocent appeared during the Romantic era with Rousseau's notion of children as pure and uncorrupted by the adult world. Kincaid explains that thus

> the modern child was deployed as a political and philosophical agent, a weapon to assault what had been taken as virtues: adulthood, sophistication, rational moderation, judicious adjustments to the ways of the world.[32]

It is only in the early twentieth century that this innocence clearly became sexual, and though Freud and Hall started recognising the sexual dimension of children, they respectively tempered it by the notion of latency, or by explaining that sexual activity during adolescence was dangerous to healthy physical and mental development. As previously mentioned, this vision of teenage sexuality as hazardous still pervades American culture.

Another function of childhood's innocence is its ability to justify censorship and repression, as witnessed by the campaigns to censure pornography on paper or on the web, explicit TV programmes or schoolbooks, as well as campaigns to allow public access to pedophiles' police files.

This issue of power, power to protect or power to control the beginning of sexual activity and its legitimacy is at the heart of pro-abstinence discourses throughout the centuries. Through abstinence-before-marriage, control is established over all beings who do not inscribe themselves in the frame of heterosexual matrimony, be it unmarried youths, gays, or cohabiting couples. Conversely, lifelong abstinence in early Christian times could provide an escape from this type of control. Abstinence also served and continues to serve to reinforce a number of hierarchic relationships. In the Catholic Church, for example, it serves to assert the authority of the celibate priest over his flock. For all religious authorities, defining religious marriage as the prerequisite for sexual activity ensures their role as social authorities and moral arbiters. Moreover, abstinence education and the differentiation it makes between adults and children also reinforces the power of adults to protect innocent youths from immorality, physical and mental corruption, STDs, pregnancy or abuse, as well as emotional and academic failure. Finally, in some cases abstinence education is also used to promote gender stereotypes and hierarchies by affirming, for example, men's allegedly greater sexual needs and status as breadwinners and women's foremost focus on romance and motherhood.

While today's pro-abstinence discourses draw on and are rooted in a long tradition of promotion of premarital chastity, the contemporary defense of sexual abstinence by conservative Christians and the Bush administration displays some unique features.

In the past three decades, the political lobbying of conservative Christians was not limited to abstinence, but also included opposition to abortion, gay rights, and pornography, yet it was nonetheless an innovation in abstinence advocacy in US history. The influence of churches in imposing sexual norms has been eroding since the 18th century, and in the 19th century the promotion of abstinence had mostly been the work of social reformers and medical authorities. But in the past three decades, in reaction to the sexual revolution, conservative Christians brought back religion in the field of abstinence promotion. In spite of a traditional refusal of political involvement, fundamentalist Christians started lobbying Congress, thus initiating a new trend in politics and in abstinence advocacy.

Though the past three decades, beginning with the Reagan era, saw important victories for conservative Christians regarding sexual matters, the Bush administration marked an exceptional presidential commitment to conservative Christian sexual norms. In fact, the open support of this administration to conservative Christian sexual agendas, like the opposition to abortion, gay rights and premarital sex, as well as the apparently high personal commitment of the president and many of his appointees to these issues, exceeded those of previous Republican administrations. In the case of abstinence-only education, such support at the presidential level can be said to be unique and might remain so. It was even pushed so far as to deny the rejection by the majority of the US population of abstinence-only education and to deliberately ignore and dismiss the scientific proofs of its inefficiency as a public health and welfare policy.

Whereas previous generations of abstinence education proponents were faced with the challenge of having to find new grounds for defending their cause when faced with medical progress and ideological changes, the contemporary abstinence movement is the first to be faced with hard empirical evidence of the inefficiency of its approach. What remains to be seen is the viability of abstinence as a method of sex-education in spite of this evidence.

Notes

[1] R Radford Ruether, *Christianity and the Making of the Modern Family*, SCM Press, London, 2001, p.38.
[2] Ibid., p.34 and E Abbott, *A History of Celibacy*, Da Capo Press, Cambridge, 2001.
[3] Radford Ruether, op. cit., p.35.
[4] ibid., p.74.
[5] ibid., p.75.
[6] ibid., p.78.
[7] ibid., p.78.

[8] R Godbeer, *Sexual Revolution in Early America*, Johns Hopkins University Press, Baltimore and London, 2002, p.4.

[9] ibid., p.9.

[10] ibid., p.279.

[11] N F Cott, 'Passionlessness: An Interpretation of Victorian Sexual Ideology, 1790-1850' in N F Cott and E H Pleck (eds), *A Heritage of Her Own*, Simon and Schuster, New York, 1979, quoted in J D'Emilio and E B Freedman, *Intimate Matters: A History of Sexuality in America*, The University of Chicago Press, Chicago and London, 1997, p.45.

[12] D'Emilio and Freedman, op. cit., p.70.

[13] Abbott, op. cit., p.201.

[14] ibid., p.203.

[15] J P Moran, *Teaching Sex: The Shaping of Adolescence in the 20th Century*, Harvard University Press, Cambridge and London, 2000, p.7.

[16] Abbott, op. cit., p.203.

[17] ibid., p.204.

[18] ibid., p.204.

[19] ibid., p.204.

[20] Moran, op. cit., p.6.

[21] ibid., p.49.

[22] ibid., p.186.

[23] ibid., p.198.

[24] ibid., p.214.

[25] ibid., p.215.

[26] D MacKenzie, 'Will Cancer Vaccine Get to All Women?' in *NewScientist.com*, 18 April 2005, viewed on 22 June 2007, <http://www.newscientist.com/channel/sex/mg18624954.500>

[27] Moran, op. cit., pp.222-223.

[28] ibid., p.216.

[29] Fields and Tolman, op. cit., p. 67.

[30] J R Kincaid, *Erotic Innocence: The Culture of Child Molesting*, Duke University Press, Durham and London, 1998, p. 31.

[31] J R Kincaid, *Child-Loving: The Erotic Child and Victorian Culture*, Routledge, New-York and London, 1994, p.26.

[32] Kincaid, *Erotic Innocence: The Culture of Child Molesting*, Duke University Press, Durham and London, 1998, p.15.

Chapter 2
"Religious" Pro-Abstinence Discourses: The LaHayes

The next four chapters present the corpus of pro-abstinence discourses investigated in this work to facilitate the understanding of the core of the book, which analyses all these texts in parallel. To explain from which angle these texts are written, each of these chapters looks at their authors, their authors' background, as well as the texts' structures and major themes. For each type of text, an overview of the issues they tackle is provided, most of which are underlined generally and analysed in details further on. The presentation of these texts is organised from the more "marginal" to the more "mainstream" types of pro-abstinence discourses. Though these discourses differ in the emphasis they put on religion, moral values, public health or welfare related issues, each chapter underlines how they all are, in their support of abstinence, taking part in similar discursive strategies.

Before turning to the presentation of the first texts, it is necessary to define some of the vocabulary employed by their authors, in particular the LaHayes, who inscribe themselves in a fundamentalist religious tradition. The LaHayes are "fundamentalist Christians" and also define themselves as "evangelicals." Those two terms, though they have become familiar through the media in the past thirty years, are difficult to define and can be confusing, as they do not stand for homogeneous groups and tend to overlap. To clarify them I will use the definition given by Nancy T. Ammerman, who presents American fundamentalism in an extremely clear and functional manner.

The term "fundamentalist" comes from a series of essays entitled *The Fundamentals*, published between 1910 and 1915, which sought to defend traditional protestant beliefs against the attacks of modern society and modern scholarship best represented by Darwinism and the 19th century German critique of the Bible.

Evangelicals, on the other hand, define themselves through their personal relationship to Christ. For them "only an individual decision to follow Jesus will suffice for salvation."[1] Evangelicals also have to be witnesses and proselytes of the necessity to change one's life and receive Christ intimately in order to "win souls" on his behalf. This experience of religious conversion is often defined as being "born again."

Throughout the first half of the 20th century, very similar realities were subsumed under the terms "fundamentalist" and "evangelical."[2] However, as Ammerman explains,

> as orthodox people began to organise for survival in a world dominated by the nonorthodox, two significantly different strategies emerged. Seeking a broad cultural base for their gospel, one group saw benefits in learning to get

along with outsiders. They did not wish to adopt the outsiders' ways, but they wanted to be respected. They began, especially after World War II, to take the name "evangelical" for themselves. Billy Graham can be seen as their primary representative. The other group insisted that getting along was no virtue, and they advocated active opposition to liberalism, secularism, and communism. This group retained the name "fundamentalist."[3]

Following Ammerman the central features of fundamentalism in North America can be summed up as follows:
- Evangelism: similar to evangelicals, fundamentalists are "saved" or "born-again" and attempt to "save" as many souls as they can.
- Inerrancy: fundamentalists believe that salvation can only be achieved through faith in an "inerrant Bible."[4] Inerrancy is defined by the *Evangelical Dictionary of Theology* as the belief that when

all the facts become known, they will demonstrate that the Bible in its original autographs and correctly interpreted is entirely true and never false in all it affirms, whether relative to doctrine or ethics or the social, physical or life sciences.[5]

Consequently, "the Bible can be trusted to provide an accurate description of science and history, as well as morality and religion"[6] or of the creation of the world.
- Premillennialism: fundamentalists also look to the Bible for signs of their destiny, especially in the prophecies. Ammerman explains that most contemporary fundamentalists are "pre-Tribulation dispensational premillenarists," a theological approach centred on the idea of the Rapture[7] and which will be explained in greater detail further on.
- Separatism: "fundamentalists insist on uniformity of belief within the ranks and on separation from others whose beliefs and lives are suspect."[8] They tend to live in rather close communities to avoid being "contaminated" by non-believers and adhere to strict rules of behavior. However, the requirement to save "souls" forces them to reach out to non-Christians in an attempt to convert them.

Throughout this book I have chosen to use the term "conservative Christians" to describe the ideological group to which most pro-abstinence writers and their audience belong. This term, also used by sociologist William Martin in his book, *With God on Our Side, The Rise of the Religious Right in America* (1996) as well as by professor of English Julia Lesage and media specialist Eithne Johnson in the collective volume *Media Culture and the Religious Right* (1998), includes both evangelicals and fundamentalist Christians. My choice was motivated by the fact that it is more inclusive than terms like "Religious Right" or "Christian Right" which both refer to the political and social movements derived from the worldview shared by conservative Christians.

The texts presented in this chapter were written by Tim and Beverly LaHaye, a couple of conservative Christian activists, who are well known for their writings on sexuality targeted at their fellow believers.

Tim LaHaye was born in 1926 in Detroit, Michigan. In 1950, he received a BA from the Christian Bob Jones University. According to the Tim LaHaye Ministries website, he also "holds a Doctor of Ministry degree from Western Theological Seminary and a Doctor of Literature degree from Liberty University"[9] founded by the late Moral Majority founder and conservative minister Jerry Falwell. In 1958, the LaHayes settled in San Diego where Tim LaHaye was, for twenty-five years, the pastor of Scott Memorial Church.

Tim LaHaye is the founder of a number of organizations and Christian initiatives among them, Family Life Seminars, Inc., that focuses on family counseling. He

> founded two accredited Christian high schools, a school system of 10 Christian schools, Christian Heritage College, and assisted Dr. Henry Morris in the founding of the Institute for Creation Research, the nation's foremost exponent of creationist materials.[10]

His wife and he are both currently sitting on the board of trustees of Liberty University..

LaHaye also created the Time LaHaye Ministries and the Pre-Trib Research Center, which seeks to "encourag[e] the research, teaching, propagation, and defense of the pretribulational rapture and related Bible prophecy doctrines."[11] Pretribulationists' beliefs are mainly based on a reading of the Book of Daniel in the Old Testament and of the Book of Revelation in the New Testament. The apocalyptic vision they derive from those texts goes as follows: before the second coming of Christ, the Christians then alive will be "raptured," meaning, bodily transported to heaven. Christians who converted after "the Rapture" will have to go through a period of trial, persecution and intense suffering called the Tribulation, which should last from three and a half to seven years, depending on the interpretations. After this time will be Christ's second coming. English professor Linda Kintz helps us understand the appeal of this apocalyptic reading of the Bible for conservative Christians like LaHaye:

The generic apocalyptic narrative includes an eschatology, a discourse about the events that will lead up to the last days. Michael O'Leary argues that apocalyptic narratives share certain characteristics: a sense of history as a divinely predetermined totality, a sense of pessimism about the present and the conviction of an imminent crisis, and a belief in the judgment of evil and the triumph of good.[12] They also imply the eventual triumph of a transcendent theological meaning which provides a rhetorical solution to the problem of evil on both a rational and a mythical level. And as Elaine Pagels argues, 'the faith that Christ has conquered Satan assures Christians that in their own struggles the stakes are eternal, and victory is certain. Those who participate in this cosmic drama cannot lose.'[13,14]

These elements are important to understand LaHaye's pessimistic vision of contemporary culture which, as we will see later, he rejects as "permissive" and "immoral."

To help change this culture, Tim LaHaye also became very involved politically. He was, for example, one of the founding board members of the Moral Majority created in 1979 by Jerry Falwell, and of the very secretive conservative organization, the Council for National Policy (CNP). He also founded the now-defunct American Coalition for Traditional Values (ACTV), which received, during the 1984 presidential campaign, "a $1 million grant from a White House fundraiser to conduct a voter registration drive that added several thousand new voters to the Republican rolls."[15] In 1986, Tim LaHaye dissolved the ACTV following "the revelation by *Mother Jones* magazine that one of the organization's biggest supporter was the Reverend Sun Myung Moon's Unification Church [which] damaged its credibility."[16]

Yet it is as a bestselling author that Tim LaHaye is today most famous. His wealth and his still-growing fame stem from the pretribulational *Left Behind* series of novels that he co-authored with professional writer Jerry Jenkins. In an interview to *People Magazine*, LaHaye explained that the idea of these books came to him as "sitting on airplanes and watching the pilots, I'd think to myself, 'What if the Rapture occurred on an airplane?'"[17] From this question, LaHaye imagined an apocalyptic storyline based on an account of the Rapture and of the Tribulation. It was then used by Jenkins, who from the general ideas proposed by LaHaye for each volume, wrote a "biblical" thriller set in modernity with cell phones and high-technology. According to *Newsweek* the LaHaye-Jenkins duo outsells Stephen King and John Grisham and its last volume sold almost 2 million copies even before its March publication; it's still tied for No. 2 on *The New York Times*'s list - which doesn't count sales at Christian bookstores. In all, the *"Left Behind"* books have sold more than 62 million copies.[18]

For clues of who those 62 million readers are, *Newsweek* journalist D. Gates explains that 71 percent of the readers are from "the South and Midwest, and just 6 percent from the Northeast [...]. The 'core buyer' is a 44-year-old born-again Christian woman, married with kids, living in the South."[19] It is difficult to assess the extent to which the readers of LaHaye's books share his beliefs, but the commercial success is indisputable. The series even generated derived products like a children's version, movies and a video game.

Tim LaHaye is also renowned, though to a lesser extent, for numerous other non-fiction writings about family life, self-control, or books against feminism, leftist ideas, or homosexuality as well as Bible commentaries. His first important publishing success was the sex-advice book he co-authored with his wife in 1976, *The Act of Marriage: The Beauty of Sexual Love*. According to the book's publishing house, Zondervan, the sex-advice books by the LaHayes have been so far purchased by 2,250,000 readers. In this book, the LaHayes advise Christians on how to achieve a fulfilling sex life. Though this stance might appear unusually progressive for fundamentalist Christians, the LaHayes' advice only concerns marital sexuality and constantly reasserts the traditional patriarchal structure of the family. The vision of the couple relationship that the LaHayes derive from their literal reading of the Bible is well represented by the following passage from *The Act of Marriage*:

> God designed man to be the aggressor, provider, and leader of his family. Somehow that is tied to his sex-drive. The woman who resents her husband's sex drive while enjoying his aggressive leadership had better face the fact that she cannot have one without the other.[20]

However, the issue of leadership in the life of the married couple of Tim and Beverly LaHaye does not seem to be as straightforward as this quote seems to infer. Beverly and Tim LaHaye have been married for more than fifty years and have had four children together. But Beverly LaHaye is not merely the wife of Tim LaHaye, or the mother of his children, as the positions they defend in their writings might suggest. She is author and co-author of approximately twenty books like *The Spirit Controlled Woman* (1976), *Who Will Save Our Children?* (1991), *The Desires of A Woman's Heart* (1993) and *The Strength of a Godly Woman* (2001), or *The Act of*

Marriage and *Raising Sexually Pure Kids*, which she wrote with her husband. She is also the prominent founder and life president of the conservative women's organization, Concerned Women for America (CWA), which focuses on the defense of six "core issues":

> *Family:* CWA believes that marriage consists of one man and one woman. We seek to protect and support the Biblical design of marriage and the gift of children.
> *Sanctity of human life:* CWA supports the protection of all innocent human life from conception until natural death. This includes the consequences resulting from abortion.
> *Education:* CWA supports reform of public education by returning authority to parents.
> *Pornography:* CWA endeavors to fight all pornography and obscenity.
> *Religious liberty:* CWA supports the God-given rights of individuals in the United States and other nations to pray, worship and express their beliefs without fear of discrimination or persecution.
> *National sovereignty:* CWA believes that neither the United Nations nor any other international organization should have authority over the United States in any area. We also believe the United States has the right and duty to protect and secure our national borders.[21]

This last point may appear less in keeping with the more religious and moral concerns of conservative Christians. In fact, it derives from the belief recurrently promoted by Tim LaHaye in his writings, that the UN might have a "corrupting" influence on the nation, for example by requiring it to conform itself to a definition of the human rights that would include abortion or euthanasia, or demanding more secularism from federal institutions.

Some of the particularly controversial issues defended by CWA are: its opposition to the Equal Rights Amendment (ERA) and its defense of the literal biblical vision of man as "the head" of his wife and family; its anti-abortion positions; its support of programs that aim at bringing homosexuals to heterosexuality through faith and prayer; and its condemnation of books like the *Harry Potter* series which, according to the organization, draws children to witchcraft and paganism.

At the root of the creation of CWA is, according the organization's website, Beverly LaHaye's reaction to a television interview of the feminist Betty Friedan, in which Friedan apparently said that she represented a great number of women in America, a claim with which Beverly LaHaye could not agree. She argued that "Betty Friedan d[id]n't speak for me and I bet she d[id]n't speak for the majority of women in this country."[22] LaHaye thus, as retold by feminist writer Susan Faludi, vowed "to rally other 'submissive' women who believe, like her, that 'the women's liberation movement is destroying the family and threatening the survival of our nation.'"[23]

While it is not devoid of bias, the presentation Faludi provides of LaHaye nonetheless reveals interesting aspects of her life and personality. For example, she underlines the fact that hearing the remark of Betty Friedan in 1978 is not what started Beverly LaHaye's "anti-feminist" activism. At that time, she was already a prominent speaker in the Christian community. She was directing the Family Life Seminars with her husband, hosting a television and radio show, and in 1976 she had written her first self-help book *The Spirit Controlled Woman*, as well as *The Act of Marriage*, together with her husband. According to Faludi she also worked for years as a teletype operator for Merrill Lynch when her children were still small, and hired a black single mother to take care of her household. Today, Beverly LaHaye is one of the most successful female leaders on the conservative scene. Her organization claims over 500,000 members. She directs CWA, presents a radio show, writes, sits on the board of Liberty University, and defends conservative values on television and in numerous meetings. This is a far cry from the picture she promotes of the traditional housewife and closer to that of the successful career woman whom she targets as the "enemy" of the traditional family.

This apparent paradox is reinforced by Faludi as she quotes passages of Beverly LaHaye's *The Spirit Controlled Woman* that echo the concerns over female self-fulfillment within and without the family raised by Betty Friedan in *The Feminine Mystique*.[24] The realisation that women might need more than their household and family to be fulfilled brought Friedan and numerous American women to feminism, however Beverly LaHaye found another way to emancipate herself. She decided to commit herself to "traditional family values" and created CWA, an activism that could not be objected to by conservative males as it was of tremendous help to their politics. Indeed, as Linda Kintz suggests:

> [...] this valorisation of mothering within a religious community whose members increasingly participate in political activism [...] also ensures that there are women available for such activist work.[25]

Leading conservative Christian organizations like CWA, the Christian Coalition, or the "trendier" Independent Women's Forum have shown a remarkable capacity to use the potential for personal investment of these housewives in conservative causes and have thus developed an efficient national grassroots support. Such organisations feature programs to train activists in public relation and political strategy so that they can run for local positions, especially school boards. As mentioned before, this especially concerns women who do not work, as they have more time for this kind of investment. Moreover, by dealing with issues of more direct concern to themselves and their families, it is easier for traditional housewives to justify investing so much time in activities outside the home. Activism becomes an extension of their nurturing and mothering tasks, as they do so to protect their children and families.[26] With her organisation's particular focus on women, Beverly LaHaye has successfully tapped into this extensive resource of committed activists and potential readers of her female-targeted Christian writings.

In 1976, with *The Act of Marriage*[27] the LaHayes became the most visible advocates of what sociologist Janice M. Irvine calls "the sexualisation of Christian evangelicalism."[28] The idea of a book of sexual advice written by fundamentalist Christians may seem unusual as religious fundamentalism is often associated with a negative view of sexuality. However, if this negative vision is still promoted by some conservative Christians, others like the LaHayes saw the need, after the sexual revolution to renew their discourse on this question. As Irvine explains, in the 1970s evangelicals

> and by extension the Christian Right, entered a new phase in sexual politics. Instead of a movement only opposed to the sexual culture, conservative evangelicals and fundamentalists also developed a proactive movement for sexual change. In the sixties sex education battles these groups had spoken against sex with the angry voices of censors. By the mid-seventies, however, many of them had found a different voice that celebrated sexuality. They began to speak about sex not simply to oppose social change, but also as therapists, educators, even sexual confidants. And they built their own alternative sexual industry.[29]

As mentioned earlier, the growing interest of conservative Christian writers for sexual fulfillment constituted a mechanism of defense. If sex was being talked about everywhere, Christians also needed to provide believers with religiously appropriate sources of information on sexuality to counter the "immoral" influence of secular sources. Sex needed to be talked about by Christians, for Christians, before believers, and especially children, got information on sexuality from "depraved" secular sources. As explained by the LaHayes in the opening of *The Act of Marriage*,

> [m]ost Christian books on [sexuality] skirt the real issues
> and leave too much to the imagination; such evasiveness is
> not adequately instructive. Secular books, on the other
> hand, often go overboard telling it like it is in crude
> language repulsive to those who need help. In addition,
> such books usually advocate practices considered improper
> by biblical standards.[30]

To prevent such practices from spreading in the evangelical community, fundamentalist Christian leaders needed to send a clear message of what is "proper" or not, and be open enough in their discourses on sex to leave no space to the "imagination," or gaps that might be filled by secular literature. Therefore the LaHayes decided to accept the offer of a publisher to write a book of sexual advice for Christians. With this book they became forerunners of a new trend in fundamentalist discourses about sexuality and thus paradoxically took part in the sexual revolution that they, still today, so staunchly reject. In the steps of another evangelical sex-advisor, Marabel Morgan, the LaHayes defended in their book the revolutionary idea that sexual pleasure was not evil and was in fact intended by God for Christians to enjoy.

> God is the creator of sex. He set our human drives in
> motion, not to torture men and women, but to bring them
> enjoyment and fulfilment. [...] What kind of God would go
> out of His way to equip His special creatures for an
> activity, give them the necessary drives to consummate it,
> and then forbid its use? Certainly not the loving God
> presented so clearly in the Bible. [...] When we look at it
> objectively, we realize that sex was given at least partly for
> marital enjoyment.[31]

This shift towards a positive vision of sex and the focus on the development of more egalitarian sexual relationships in the couple can, according to Linda Kintz, be explained as a way to provide greater incentive to marriage. The guarantee of a fulfilling sex life is used to attract to matrimony men who, in the LaHayes' view, might not be so prone to it, and to maintain within it women who no longer systematically depend on their husbands for economic survival.[32] Therefore, the LaHayes also dwell on female sexual satisfaction and the qualities men require to develop and optimise it. They acknowledge the fact that, for too long, women's need and capacity for pleasure was underestimated. The LaHayes contradict popular stereotypes of marriage as a routine that inhibits sexual drives, on the contrary, they argue, through the spiritual communion with God it provides, marriage enhances pleasure. Christians can therefore find great benefits in getting and remaining married. The LaHayes even assert that Christian couples have better sex, since they are not "obsessed" by it like other people.[33]

In their attempt to provide Christians with sex advice open and clear enough to really help them with the difficulties they might encounter, they deal with subjects like frigidity, impotence or menopause as well as "sane family planning." They also describe sexual organs and processes with drawings, using scientific terms and, for example, advise women on muscular training to help strengthen their vaginal muscles after pregnancy or when they become older.

Not surprisingly, the LaHayes' book generated controversy in their community. Some Christians criticized them for what was seen as an "unseemly emphasis on sex."[34] Indeed, as Tim LaHaye explains in the introduction to *The Act of Marriage*, the decision to write the book was not a light one, and a number of their friends advised them against it. Yet, after prayers and what they interpreted as signs from God, they decided to do it. Irvine agrees that there was

> danger in speaking openly about sexuality, and indeed LaHaye did incur some criticism for being too liberal by refusing to outright condemn birth control for married couples. But ultimately he did not ruin his reputation. That he and his wife Beverly remain prominent Christian right leaders speaks [...] to the cultural legitimacy that sex counseling acquired among evangelicals and fundamentalists.[35]

Other criticisms came from sexual liberals who opposed the very patriarchal vision of the couple defended by the LaHayes. Indeed, while some of their positions, on female sexual pleasure or birth control for example, can appear quite progressive, the framework of sexuality that they advocate still remains traditional and heteronormative. Men are still defined as having more important sexual needs that women have to fulfill in order to "reward" them for their breadwinning duties.

For the LaHayes, sexuality is defined in a binary manner: on the one-hand marital sexuality that is "holy" and intended by God for the purpose of reproduction but also for the enjoyment and the strengthening of matrimonial ties; and on the other hand all the other expressions of sexuality, extra-marital, homosexual, pre-marital, which are defined as "evil." Quoting the Bible extensively, the LaHayes propagate a patriarchal view of the family in which men are "leaders" whose wives and children should obey. The world that they represent in their writings is limited to white middle class traditional Christian families who attend church regularly and live in socially and culturally homogenous neighborhoods. The aim of life in this context is to worship God and have a family, since the Lord asked believers to "be fruitful and multiply" (Genesis 1:28), while women take care of their children and their husbands in particular by fulfilling the latter's sexual demands.

Raising Sexually Pure Kids: How to Prepare Your Children for the Act of Marriage was originally published in 1993 as *Against the Tide: Raising Sexually Pure Kids in an Anything-Goes World* and was revised in 1998. It follows in the tracks of *The Act of Marriage*, and presents parents with practical advice to raise their children according to the principle of premarital sexual abstinence. As is the case with their previous book, the aim behind writing *Raising Sexually Pure Kids* is to counteract the influence of "secular" sexual values. The LaHayes argue that today

> more than ever before, children need their parents to accept their role of family sex education instructors. This book will equip you for that role. The best way to ensure that your children share your moral values is to teach those values to them. Then they can be fortified by your church and other Christian influences. But good sex education should always begin at home. Some one (sic.) is going to teach your children about sex. This book is designed to equip you, the most important person in your child's life, to be that teacher.[36]

In this case, teaching teenagers and children about sex is not done primarily to help them understand the changes taking place in their bodies, but rather to counteract the other discourses that modern society exposes them to by putting parents back in control of their children's sexual education. Hence, the LaHayes conceived this book to provide parents with extensive medical, scientific and moral information so they can be the best possible "Christian" sex educator for their children.[37]

As suggested in one of the sections of *Raising Sexually Pure Kids'* table of contents,[38] parents should try to learn as much as they can about sexuality so that "they know more than their children" and remain an uncontested authority on the subject. A task which, the LaHayes are aware, becomes more and more difficult in a multimedia society, but is therefore even more necessary. Christian parents have to overcome the prejudices they might have about teaching their children about sex, in spite of the feeling that talking about it might encourage children to experience it. The strategy of the LaHayes goes against this commonly-held notion by promoting discourse as a means of prevention. For them, as children will inevitably be exposed to sexual images in the media or in public schools, avoiding sexuality at home is not an efficient strategy any more, as it gives free hand to "immoral" discourses. On the contrary, parents should oppose these "immoral" messages by a stronger discourse which will teach their children an alternative "Christian" vision of sexuality that can be opposed to the secular vision as the only "appropriate" one. The LaHaye's book therefore devises a strategy to enable parents to do so.

Raising Sexually Pure Kids is divided into four major parts. The first part, "A Call to Virtue",[39] deals with the ideological positions of the LaHayes and defines the approach and aims of the book. It provides an outline of the general advice on children's sexual, moral and religious education that they develop, for example: "provide them two loving role models," "start early teaching your children about sex," "keep them out of public school sex education classes," "teach them moral values," "keep them active in your church youth group," "help your children select their friends," "warn your children about the joys and dangers of sexual attraction," "provide them with clear guidelines for dating," "help them make a formal commitment to virtue," "watch for signs of sexual involvement," "don't make them delay marriage too long" or "surround them with prayer."

The second part of the book, "What Young Children Need to Know About Sex,"[40] provides guidelines and pedagogical materials, like drawings, to teach children about sexuality from the moment they start asking questions to thirteen years of age. It is mostly devoted to technical aspects of procreation, the reproductive organs, sexual intercourse, puberty and menstruation. It also deals with more complex issues like "sexual identity" that is, the one that "God gave you at birth [which] is determined by your sexual parts,"[41] since for the LaHayes "heterosexuality is God's design; homosexuality an abomination or a perversion of that design."[42] Masturbation and nocturnal emissions are also dealt with. The most important advice that the LaHayes give in this chapter is to be open to children's questionss and never to reject them but rather answer them in the most honest and straightforward way. They give examples of possible questions children might have and possible ways to answer them with respect to Christian appropriateness.

"How To Teach Your Teens To Be Sexually Pure"[43] is the third and most important part of *Raising Sexually Pure Kids*. Going beyond "sexual education," it deals with "abstinence education" and the strategies parents can develop to preserve teens' "purity" until marriage. Chapter VII again takes on the methods of sexual education but in a clearly gendered way. It is articulated around two sections, "Father's Questions To Sons" and "Mother's Questions To Daughters," which present the main sexual issues teenagers have to deal with at puberty, like sexual arousal, masturbation (only for boys) or teen pregnancy. Each of these sections is followed by another one: "Reasons You Can Give Your Son for Waiting to Have Sex" and its equivalent for daughters. Here again the emphasis is on dialogue. An emphasis which sometimes sounds very much like the one propagated by secular "liberal" sexual educators and psychologists. Parents are advised to talk with their children about sex as well as morality and abstinence. They should not wait too long, or they might be too late. Even if this is so, they should not give up the dialogue and should remain open. Parents should be relaxed, to make teenagers feel comfortable. They should not criticise but listen to what teens have to say to make them feel that they can open up without running the risk of being judged. The LaHayes also advise parents to be shockproof, as teenagers can be deliberately provocative, to test limits. Rather than criticising teenagers' pronouncements, parents should ask them if what they say is really what they think or feel about this question. Parents should initiate the dialogue on sexuality, since their children might be afraid to do so.[44] For the LaHayes, keeping the "conversational door" open is of utmost importance to pass on to children the moral values one wants to see them applying to their sexual life.[45] Part of this ongoing dialogue is the "commitment to virtue" that the LaHayes advise parents to make their children take in Chapter VIII.

This "commitment to virtue" or "virginity/chastity pledge" is an important concept in pro-abstinence rhetoric. It is used by numerous pro-abstinence educators and organisations like, for example, True Love Waits, the abstinence program of the Southern Baptist Convention. The LaHayes recommend that when children turn fifteen or sixteen, depending on the age decided on as appropriate to start dating, parents should make them take this pledge. They suggest that the parent of the same sex as the child bring him or her to a restaurant for a "big night" that will remain special for both of them. This exceptional and pleasurable time will be set aside to discuss sex and make sure that the child knows everything s/he needs to know about it and that s/he shares his parents' values on the subject. This time should also be a time of prayer, during which the parent presents his/her child with the reasons for waiting to have sex, and makes him/her take a commitment before God to remain virtuous until marriage. This commitment can be symbolised by a "virtue ring" or "pendant" that the parent gives the child. This piece of jewelry will become a "keepsake" that the child will be able to give his/her future spouse on his wedding night to underline his successful commitment.

To parents who might think that this is a lot of fuss for something that should not require discussion, the LaHayes explain that:

> A commitment to virtue is so important today because of
> the enormous pressures young people face. Many of these
> pressures are much stronger and different than the
> pressures we faced when we were their age. Today's kids

are encouraged to throw away their virtue and express their sexuality. We believe that a formal commitment to virtue is both needed and a powerful tool that can help safeguard your teen from premarital sexual involvement. When emotions get out of control and threaten to overpower common sense, a strong resolve or commitment to virtue can prevent your teen (and your family) from experiencing enormous heartaches.[46]

An interesting detail here, characteristic of conservative rhetoric, is the idealisation of the past that is made and the demonisation of the present. The LaHayes were past seventy when they wrote this book, but the parents they are writing for, on the contrary, must have been teenagers in the 1970s. Though it cannot be denied that today's society is filled with sexual messages, the way they overlook the charged sexual atmosphere of the 1970s seems more rhetorical than realistic. Referring to an ideal time gone by is a constant trope of conservative discourses, a way to underline the "immorality" and "permissiveness" of the present. The insistence on a present state of moral decay echoes apocalyptic narratives that are very important for fundamentalists in general and Tim LaHaye in particular. Moreover, as quoted further above, the apocalyptic narrative features "a sense of pessimism about the present and the conviction of an imminent crisis, and a belief in the judgment of evil and the triumph of good."[47] By demonising the present, fundamentalists confirm their belief that the Judgment is close.

        In such a decadent world, the LaHayes are aware that not every child, especially if they have not been "born again" yet, will remain virtuous. One of the problems of the chastity pledge is that it excludes children who were already sexually active. Therefore, abstinence proponents needed to devise a strategy for these children so that they do not go on being sexually active thinking that the "sin" being already done they had nothing to lose anymore. That is why, the LaHayes explain, it is never too late to become "virtuous again," labeled by other abstinence proponents as "secondary/born-again virginity." Teens who "repent" and take a "secondary virginity pledge" "can become virgins again in the sight of God. Once they're forgiven, it is as though they have never sinned."[48] However, those teens might still have to struggle with guilt, as "admittedly, God can and does completely forgive their sin of fornication, but it is impossible to return their virtue. When it's gone, it's gone."[49] This idea of "secondary virginity" is therefore an ambiguous one as, on the one hand, "sinful" children should not be abandoned, but on the other hand, secondary virginity still has to be presented in a negative light so that it remains an "emergency" option.

To avoid the need for secondary virginity, the LaHayes provide a chapter with clear "Guidelines for Dating" that parents should apply to teenagers. To a "liberal" eye, most of this advice seems old-fashioned and extremely strict, exerting a control over teens' lives that some would consider illegitimate and dangerous. It has to be acknowledged that some appear very difficult to apply in contemporary US society. Their recommendations range from the proper age for dating, fifteen years old and over, to the interdiction of "French kissing" as it would, according to the LaHayes, inevitably lead to more physical intimacy. They also advise parents of daughters "to schedule a predating interview with Dad"[50] with the boy who asks her out. Parents should always know where their kids are and what they are doing. Teens should never be left in a house alone without an adult. The section "avoid all petting, caressing or other physical expressions of affection that lead to sexual arousal"[51] includes many details, so teenagers can be ready for any possible situation that might threaten their commitment to virtue. Until high-school graduation, teens are only allowed to double-date, to prevent too much intimacy. Moreover, Christian teens should only date other "Christians," for as the LaHayes explain:

> One cardinal principle clearly stated in the Word of God is: "Do not be yoked together with unbelievers" (2 Corinthians 6:14). Dating is a yoke of fellowship that can eventually lead to marriage. We can help our young people avoid the emotional trauma of ever having to decide, 'Should I marry this unsaved person I am very much in love with or should we break up?' by refusing to let them go out in the first place.[52]

To be able to put all this advice into practice, a homogeneous environment is indispensable. There lies the importance of Christian communities and Church schools or home-schooling, which will help keep the environment of children under control to an extent that could not be attainable if they go to a public school and live in mixed suburbs. As Linda Kintz explains:

> [...] as the upper classes now send their children to elite private schools and determine their neighborliness according to property values, evangelical Christians retreat to communities of other born-again Christians, where they open private religious schools or school their children at home.[53]

Surrounded by people who share the same values and will have the same dating guidelines, it should be reasonably easy to apply the LaHayes' advice.

But for Christians who do not benefit from such an environment, it seems to be much more difficult, as their parental authority will run the risk of being questioned by their children's confrontation with different educational rules.

Chapters X and XI deal with what the LaHayes consider as the differences between male and female sexuality and response to sexual stimulation. They insist on warning girls of boys' stronger sexual drives and of the fact that, contrary to girls, they are very likely to be more attracted to sex than to romance. Girls are to be taught that they should date respectable boys, and avoid promiscuity or public displays of affection to protect their reputation. The chapter closes by the following cautionary note:

> Girls need to know that they have the most to lose. Therefore, they must be taught that they are the moral cop in their relationship. She must know when to say *no!* and to insist he take(sic.) her home *right now!* Until the day she marries, she must always remember that she has the most to lose.[54]

Boys do not have as much to lose, as they cannot get pregnant. Still, they must be told that they should be the "moral cop" in the relationship as well. Though men are "high-octane sexual creatures," this can be no excuse, as they can be seduced only if they put themselves in the situation to be seduced. All the more so that "God holds men accountable to be the spiritual leader in all couple relationships, both before and after marriage."[55] The LaHayes also insist that dating should hinder neither their spiritual growth nor their education as they will one day have the responsibility to lead and provide for a family.

To give their advice a legitimacy coming from teens themselves, Chapter XII, "What Christian teens say about sex that their parents need to hear," synthesizes group discussions that the LaHayes had with Christian school pupils in Virginia, Maryland, California and Oregon. The main conclusions they draw from those discussions are very much in agreement with their own recommendations. They explain, for example, that a majority of teens wished that their parents would insist more on sexual education and abstinence at an earlier age, and that the people by whom they would like best to be taught about sex are their parents. They also "complain[ed] that their [sex education] classes were too explicit"[56] in particular in the case of teens attending public schools. They agreed with most of the dating rules suggested by the LaHayes and regretted that most of their parents did not set any and thought that a "commitment to virtue" was a very good idea and was very much needed given the sexual pressures they are exposed to in contemporary society.

The final and fourth part of the book brings together several other themes related to children and sexuality. Starting with sexual abuse and what the LaHayes call "the myth of safe sex," moving on to questions like "what to do if your daughter becomes pregnant?" or the special concerns that single parents might have regarding their children's sexual education. Those chapters are followed by a glossary explaining terms ranging from "adolescence" to "Y chromosome," as well as an indictment of the "abstinence" teaching of SIECUS and a few useful "Biblical Passages Forbidding Adultery and Fornication."

The LaHayes' book is centered on the idea that children should remain abstinent on religious grounds, adding that STDs only point to the fact that God did not intend for Christians to have sex with anyone else than their spouse. Pediatrician Meg Meeker, on the contrary, centers her defense of abstinence on the threat of STDs. Similar to the LaHayes, she deals with themes like the necessity of love and family connectedness to "protect" children, but focuses her argumentation primarily on medical concerns. It is this different approach that is presented in the next chapter.

Notes

[1] N T Ammerman, 'North American Protestant Fundamentalism,' in L Kintz and J Lesage (eds), *Media, Culture and the Religious Right*, University of Minnesota Press, Minneapolis, 1998, p.57.

[2] ibid., p.59.

[3] ibid., p.59.

[4] ibid., p.59.

[5] W A Elwell (ed), *Evangelical Dictionary of Theology*, Baker Academic, Grand Rapids, 2001.

[6] Ammerman, op. cit., p.60.

[7] ibid., p.61.

[8] ibid., p.63.

[9] Timlahaye.com, 'Tim LaHaye Biography,' 2004, viewed on 13 march 2007, <http://www.timlahaye.com/about_ministry/index.php3?p=bio&section=Bio graphy>

[10] ibid..

[11] Timlahaye.com, 'Pre-Trib Research Center,' 2004, viewed on 13 March 2007, <http://www.timlahaye.com/about_ministry/index.php3?p=pretrib&section= PreTrib%20Research%20Center>

[12] S D O'Leary, *Arguing the Apocalypse: A Theory of Millennial Rhetoric*, Oxford University Press, New York, 1994.

[13] E Pagels, *The Origin of Satan*, Random House, New York, 1995, p.181.
[14] Kintz, op. cit., pp.8-9.
[15] Diamond, op. cit., p.72.
[16] W Martin, *With God on Our Side*, Broadway Books, New York, 1996, p.270.
[17] Leftbehind.com, 'Dr. Tim LaHaye Bio,' 2007, viewed on 13 March 2007, <http://www.leftbehind.com/channelbooks.asp?pageid=1267&channelID=225>
[18] D Gates, 'Religion: The Pop Prophets,' *Newsweek Online*, 24 May 2005, viewed on 19 June 2007, <http://www.msnbc.msn.com/id/4988269/site/newsweek/>
[19] ibid..
[20] T and B LaHaye, *The Act of Marriage: The Beauty of Sexual Love*, Zondervan, Grand Rapids, 1998, p. 34.
[21] Concerned Women for America, 'Our Core Issues,' January 2007, viewed on 13 March 2007, <http://www.cwfa.org/coreissues.asp>
[22] S Faludi, *Backlash: the Undeclared War Against American Women*, Anchor Books Doubleday, New York, 1991, p.248.
[23] ibid., p.248.
[24] B Friedan, *The Feminine Mystique*, W W Norton, New York, 1963.
[25] Kintz, op. cit. 1997, p. 36.
[26] See L Kintz, 'Clarity, Mothers and Mass-Mediated Soul: A Defense of Ambiguity,' in L Kintz and J Lesage (eds), *Media, Culture and the Religious Right*, University of Minnesota Press, Minneapolis, 1998.
[27] For a more extensive analysis of *The Act of Marriage*, see Kintz, 1997.
[28] J M Irvine, *Talk About Sex: The Battles Over Sex Education in the United States*, University of California Press, Berkeley and Los Angeles, 2002, p.81.
[29] ibid., p.82.
[30] LaHaye, op. cit., p.11.
[31] ibid., p.24.
[32] Kintz, op. cit. p.67.
[33] LaHaye, op. cit., p.32.
[34] Irvine, op. cit., p.87.
[35] ibid., p.87.
[36] T and B LaHaye, *Raising Sexually Pure Kids: How to Prepare Your Children for the Act of Marriage*, Mutnomah Publishers, Sisters, 1998a, p.29.
[37] ibid., p.10.
[38] The end of *Raising Sexually Pure Kids* features a "Glossary of Sex Information Parents Need So They Know More Than Their Children."
[39] LaHaye, op. cit. pp.15-59.
[40] ibid., pp.63-111.

[41] ibid., p.65.
[42] ibid., p.65.
[43] ibid., pp.115-190.
[44] ibid., p.117.
[45] ibid., p.117.
[46] ibid., p.135.
[47] Kintz, op. cit., pp.8-9.
[48] R Durfield, 'A Promise with a Ring to It,' *Focus on the Family Magazine*, 1990, quoted in T and B LaHaye, *Raising Sexually Pure Kids: How to Prepare Your Children for the Act of Marriage*, Mutnomah Publishers, Sisters, 1998, p. 144.
[49] LaHaye, op. cit., p.24.
[50] ibid., p.151.
[51] ibid., p.156.
[52] ibid., p.151.
[53] Kintz, op. cit., p.108.
[54] LaHaye, op. cit., p.168, emphasis in the original.
[55] ibid., p.175.
[56] ibid., p.185.

Chapter 3
"Medical" Pro-Abstinence Discourses: Meg Meeker

Contrary to the LaHayes, Meg Meeker is neither nationally famous nor written about by academics. She is not a political leader but a single-issue activist and is probably barely read outside of the conservative community. Her books are not bestsellers. *Epidemics: How Teen Sex is Killing Our Kids* (2002), for which she is best known, had sold only 6,471 copies by July 2005 according to its publisher, yet her books are often used and referred to by pro-abstinence organizations and leaders.

I have chosen to include her writings in my analysis as they are very much respected in the conservative circuit and as they present a significant trend in pro-abstinence discourses. This trend is based on a medical argumentation which advocates abstinence as the only 100% safe way to prevent youths from being infected with STDs or becoming pregnant. Underlining the failure rates of condoms and their inefficiency in protecting from STDs like herpes, some doctors like Meeker argue that promoting any other protection than abstinence is criminal and represents a risk that cannot be taken regarding children's lives and health.

The effectiveness of this discourse in general and of Meeker's in particular, lies in its grounding in apparently scientific facts. Meeker's legitimacy is also established by her position as a pediatrician and mother. Moreover, she does not appear to be affiliated with any political organization, which gives her an appearance of neutrality and reliability. As argued by a researcher of Concerned Women for America:

> Meeker has not been tapped by the Bush Administration to push abstinence-only education in America's public schools. She is not a conservative spokesperson for pro-family organisations paid to decry the ills of risky sexual behavior and condom distribution. She is a physician, who stares into the eyes of scared teenagers every day, telling them they have STDs that are incurable and helping them cope with the depression that ensues.[1]

Still, this alleged neutrality can be questioned by a number of significant facts. Though Meeker is not affiliated to any conservative organisation, her books are published by conservative publishing houses such as Regnery, which claims to be "the nation's leading conservative publisher."[2] Moreover, her third book, *Strong Fathers, Strong Daughters, 10 Secrets Every Father Should Know* (2006), published by Regnery, features a markedly conservative agenda of reasserting traditional fatherhood, and is much less medically oriented. Meeker also contributed to *The Focus on the Family*

Complete Book of Baby and Child Care published by Christian publisher Tyndale (publisher of numerous books by the LaHayes, including the *Left Behind* series) and edited by James Dobson's prominent conservative Christian organization, Focus on the Family. She also appeared on conservative TV shows and radio programs like *Concerned Women Today,* the radio program of Beverly LaHaye's CWA; the *700 club,* the TV show of Pat Robertson, founder and former president of the prominent conservative Christian Coalition; as well as on *Dr. Laura,* the radio show of the conservative Jewish host Laura Schlessinger. In 2003 Meeker gave a talk at the Conservative Political Action Conference, which celebrated the twentieth anniversary of the defeat of the ERA (Equal Rights Amendment). She also participates in conferences given by the Christian pro-abstinence organisation the Silver Ring Thing, which in 2005 lost its federal funding as it was proven to promote specific religious values in its abstinence promotion programmes. Moreover, her book *Restoring the Teenage Soul* is prefaced by Elayne Bennett, founder of the pro-abstinence organization Best Friends and wife of former secretary of education and prominent Heritage Foundation member, William J. Bennett. Given this significant involvement of Meeker with conservative and religious leaders and organisations, the ideological neutrality of her discourses can legitimately be questioned.

The image presented by Meeker is a very reassuring one. Her pictures, on the cover of her books or on websites, show a smiling blond woman in her forties. She looks both motherly and professional. Her curriculum vitae and family life also confirm this comforting image. Meeker has been a medical doctor for pediatric and adolescent medicine for more than twenty years and she has a medical practice in Traverse City, Michigan, with her husband. She is a fellow of the American Academy of Pediatrics and of the National Advisory Board of the Medical Institute, a pro-abstinence medical organization founded in 1992 "to confront the global epidemics of nonmarital pregnancy and sexually transmitted disease with incisive health care data".[3]

Another aspect which reinforces her credibility is that, as she claims, she used to advocate birth control. But she explains,

> [t]wenty years ago, I wouldn't have hesitated to prescribe oral contraceptives to teenage girls. In fact, *any* form of birth control was fine with me, as long as my patient used it consistently. As a young doctor swept away by the message of 'safe' sex, I didn't know any better. To me, "safe" meant not getting pregnant. I was so focused on the pregnancy epidemic that I wrote hundreds of prescriptions for birth control pills and gave more injections of Depo-Provera than I care to remember. But today, I think long and hard

about prescribing birth-control pills or Depo-Provera to kids because this puts them in such grave danger of contracting an STD. In giving a girl birth control that I know will protect her from pregnancy, am I inadvertently encouraging her to pick up a sexually transmitted disease? And if you might ask, 'What about condoms?' read on. [...] In most cases, the chances of condoms preventing STDs is almost as thin as the condoms themselves. Hence, I think carefully about advising teens to use condoms, as well as other forms of birth control. The risks are just too high.[4]

Meeker argues that prescribing birth-control or condoms to teenagers gives them the impression that sex is "safe" as long as they use these adequately. But for her, like for the LaHayes, "safe" sex is a myth. The only means providing complete protection from STDs and teen pregnancy is abstinence. Therefore, they argue, parents have to teach their children to remain abstinent in order to protect them.

The strategy used by Meeker to convince parents and teens can be qualified of being a "scare tactic." As will be shown further on, she uses statistics and gruesome stories of STD-infected patients to scare parents into demanding that their kids remain abstinent. However, this strategy has been questioned even by parents who support abstinence education. In January 2005, SIECUS reported that a School District's Board of Trustees in Nevada rejected a video created, among others, by Meeker[5] on the grounds that:

"The over-hyped, fear-based tone was felt to be a turnoff for many teens who most needed to hear the abstinence message," [...] "Examples of the alarmist format included blood dripping into a sink when a link was drawn between teen suicide rates and teen sexuality."[...] "In several instances throughout the film, [...] kids could be led to believe that if you're sexually active, depression can follow and also suicide."[6]

Indeed, in *Epidemic*, the vision of teenage sexuality as "fundamentally and essentially risky for youth"[7] is constantly reinforced through gruesome examples and endless catalogues of the potentially tragic medical consequences of sexual activity. As early as page five, Meeker recounts the comments of a surgeon who had just operated one of her young patients:

"When I opened her, she had an abdomen full of pus. She had a tubo-ovarian abscess which had ruptured. I had to

> take her right ovary and her left one [didn't] look so hot.
> Frankly, she'll be lucky if she pulls through," he told me.
> What [the surgeon's] findings told me was that Lori had
> pelvic inflammatory disease, caused by either chlamydia or
> gonorrhea. ... This type of infection is always life-
> threatening. How had she gotten the infection in the first
> place? Whether she had had sex once, twice, five times - it
> didn't matter.[8]

The sense of threat conveyed by this quote is representative of the tone of the whole book the main achievement of which is to emphasise that sex outside of a committed life-long relationship, which is particularly the case of teen sex, always carries at the most the threat of death and at the least the possibility of life-long disabilities be they mental or physical. The discursive strategies developed by Meeker in her pro-abstinence writings will now be highlighted in further detail through an overview of her first two books: *Restoring the Teenage Soul: Nurturing Sound hearts and Minds in a Confused Culture* (1999) and *Epidemic: How Teen Sex is Killing Our Kids* (2002).

Meg Meeker is the author of four books dealing with children's and teenagers' physical and mental well being, two of which are analysed in the book: *Restoring the Teenage Soul: Nurturing Sound hearts and Minds in a Confused Culture* (1999), which mainly deals with teen depression and thus also targets premarital sex and abstinence, and *Epidemic: How Teen Sex is Killing Our Kids* (2002), focused on premarital sex and STDs.

A good summary of the themes and aims of *Restoring the Teenage Soul* is provided by Elayne Bennett in her preface to the book:

> Adolescence is a time of conflict and confusion for most
> young people. Teen friendships and love relationships are
> transitory; there is pressure to achieve, to 'fit in,' to be
> popular and attractive. Many adolescents do not hold
> themselves in high regard, and the absence of self-worth
> can be a serious handicap which makes them more
> vulnerable to negative peer pressure, early sexual activity,
> drug and alcohol abuse, and violent and aggressive
> behavior. [...] Dr. Meeker, a physician practicing child and
> adolescent medicine in Michigan, believes that parents
> need to see what she sees in her examination rooms:
> confused adolescents with emotional and health problems
> caused by lack of self-respect, depression, illegal drug and
> alcohol use, and sexual activity. [...] Meg Meeker
> eloquently makes the case that adults must roll up their

sleeves and get involved with their teens. She reminds us
that while teens may want adult privileges, their reasoning
ability and emotional stability are often still those of a
child. In spite of their protest to the contrary, they need an
abundance of parental involvement in their lives.[9]

The reasons presented by Meeker for the state of teenagers' emotional and
physical health are: a lack of parental presence in the home due to long work
days and working mothers; the "culture," especially the media like movies,
TV series, MTV, music or fashion; the sexual revolution; permissiveness as
well as the lack of moral values and spirituality. Those elements are similar
to the ones presented by the LaHayes' and, as will be shown later, to those
evoked by the Heritage Foundation and the Bush administration.

They are also at the core of her book, *Epidemic*, which is organised
along the following structure. Meeker begins by explaining that STDs are an
"epidemic" menacing the nation and causing many more casualties than
citizens are aware of. She then presents a catalogue of statistics and describes
numerous STDs, classifying them in three categories: lethal; "curable but
dangerous", and "emotional STD." According to Meeker, "one of the major
causes of depression is sex",[10] which is why in most cases she considers
depression as a sexually transmitted disease, an "emotional STD." Meeker
explains that

> [t]eenage sexual activity routinely leads to emotional
> turmoil and psychological distress. Beginning in the 1970s,
> when the sexual revolution unleashed previously unheard-
> of sexual freedoms on college campuses across the country,
> physicians began seeing the results of this 'freedom'. This
> new permissiveness, they said, often led to empty
> relationships, to feelings of self-contempt and
> worthlessness. All, of course, precursor to depression.[11]

This idea of "self-contempt and worthlessness" pervades pro-abstinence
discourses. It can be related to premarital sex, as in Meeker's text, but can
also be more widely connected to a lack of "moral values" and religious
beliefs. For conservative Christians an absence of faith in God inevitably
entails a lack of self-esteem, as the individual is not related to something
larger than himself through a loving creator.

In the second part of her book, "The Forces at Work," Meeker goes
on to explain that protecting children from pregnancy is not equivalent to
protecting them from STDs. She claims that condoms, especially used
irregularly and imperfectly by careless teenagers, are not "safe", and fail to
protect from numerous STDs like those transmitted by skin contact. Further

on she underlines the negative effects of the media, MTV, fashion and advertisement. She concludes this section of her book with a chapter entitled "High Risk Sex" where she points to the risks of oral sex (a practice she believes widespread among ever-younger teens); homosexual activity; multiple partners, simultaneous or not; voyeurism between teens; the connection between drug and alcohol use and sex; or the dangers of the internet. In this last chapter she draws the picture, often supported by the media, of a teenage sexuality reminiscent of "pornography." Though she provides statistics concerning the rise of oral sex among teens, her reports of group sex and voyeurism are only based on rumors, isolated cases, or shocking examples from the media.

Though Meeker might be right in presenting these tendencies as widespread, it is to be noted that she nowhere nuances her assertions by acknowledging the lack of conclusive statistical data on these phenomenon. On the contrary, she accumulates examples in order to imply that teen sex can only be "risky" and "inappropriate." The ambiguity she thus entertains by blurring the boundaries between empirical facts and personal opinion or "gut feelings" is one of the central mechanisms of her rhetoric.

Meeker constantly fuels this ambiguity by leading the reader into considering her writings as scientific and objective when they are in fact very much tainted by her own moral values and beliefs. An example of this "moral" positioning can be found in her advice to parents watching TV with their children:

> During scenes where unmarried people are having sex, ask your kids how much they believe those people value their bodies, their sexuality. Then let them know that you want better for your children, that their sexuality, their bodies, are too important to be shared randomly, even with people they think they love.[12]

While her defense of abstinence is grounded in a medical rationale, making marriage, and not for example committed cohabitation, a prerequisite for sexual activity is not a medical but a moral positioning. In making marriage a prerequisite for sex, Meeker reveals her conservative orientations in a clearer way than anywhere else in her text. For her, as for the Heritage Foundation, and as stated in the *Personal Responsibility and Work Opportunity Reconciliation Act of 1996* "a mutually faithful monogamous relationship in the context of marriage is the expected standard of human sexual activity."

Meeker's publisher presents her as a medical doctor, a scientific authority. The back cover of *Epidemic* features a short review by Dr. David Hagar, "Head of Infectious Diseases/University of Kentucky" who writes that

[i]n this shocking book, Dr. Meeker describes the epidemic proportions of the STD explosion that has erupted in America. The statistics are startling, the data medically sound, the consequences alarming and the personal stories will move you to tears.[13]

In this comment the personal dimension of the book is acknowledged but the emphasis, laid both by the text itself and the position of authority of the writer, is clearly on the scientific reliability of the book. While throughout her writings Meeker quotes numerous statistics and apparently scientific works, she often does not reference them, thus preventing the reader from checking for him/herself. Meeker establishes herself as a scientific authority, but her discourse is devoid of epistemological nuance. She presents teenage sexuality only in negative terms, entirely overlooking its potentially positive aspects. Besides, her theories are very much grounded in her personal experience. This would not constitute any ambiguity if her books were presented as an account of her personal practice as a pediatrician, but her opinions are often implicitly described as being shared by the medical community at large. This is the case, for example, in sentences like: "Just ask any doctor, therapist, or teacher who works closely with teenagers and they'll tell you."[14]

Under the guise of "simplifying" psychological theory "into a workable, understandable fashion for adults who are intent on helping teens",[15] Meeker also deliberately blurs the boundaries between science and "morals." She integrates in this discourse moral and religious comments that have more to do with personal beliefs and "common sense" than with the scientific discipline that psychology is. For example, she explains that most teens in depression lack what she calls "spiritual intimacy" that she defines as "[…] an exchange of feelings and experiences with God. It includes the giving of feelings and thoughts to an invisible deity, believing that God receives them and responds back."[16] In so doing, Meeker entertains, consciously or not, an ambiguity between personal beliefs and empirical facts that can be considered as an abuse of the readers' trust. The impression made by her discourse on the reader is that she is very much convinced of the threat constituted by teenage sex, thus she might not be aware of the ambiguity of mixing scientific and personal discourses in the way she does. Yet this ambiguity, as well as her extensive use of a vocabulary of emotions and fear, are major assets to reach a conservative audience and are widely used by conservative authors. Hence the possibility that this discursive strategy might be consciously elaborated cannot be discarded.

The use Meeker makes of emotions and in particular fear, are well illustrated by the two following examples:

> Chances are you don't realize it, but right now, at this very
> minute, there is an epidemic racing through the lives of our
> teenagers. This epidemic literally threatens their very lives.
> I am a pediatrician. I see and treat these youngsters every
> day. I'd like you to meet some of my patients.[17]

Or,

> [a]s I swept the gray drapery surrounding Lori's emergency
> room bed behind me, I was startled by the intensity of pain
> I saw on her young face. Her mother said she was having
> abdominal discomfort, but clearly she understated the
> situation or something had happened on the car ride over.
> This was one sick kid.[18]

In both of these examples, Meeker deals with medical events in a very
emotional and subjective way. This constant wavering between "neutral"
scientific discourse and an emotional and personal one is a recurring feature
of religious conservative discourses. As Linda Kintz explains,

> [t]he intensity of mattering [or commitment], while
> ideologically constructed, is nevertheless 'always beyond
> ideological challenge because it is called into existence
> affectively.'[19]   And   in   postmodern   America,   where
> pessimism and a very strategic depoliticisation had become
> the norm, affective investments increasingly became the
> most valuable political prize: 'the condition of possibility
> for the optimism, invigoration and passions which are
> necessary for any struggle to change the world.'[20] Thus the
> conditions of postmodernity described by postmodern
> theory - fragmentation, lack of a center, unease, fear - have
> proved to be precisely the resources drawn on to construct
> popular conservatism's conditions of possibility.[21]

By touching on one of the reader's deepest fear, the fear for his/her children,
and relating to him/her at an emotional level, Meeker, like the LaHayes, uses
the rhetorical strategy which makes for the success of the Religious Right,
and to which Christian conservatives respond best.

Though Meeker is presented as a medical and consequently
"neutral" source, her discourse revolves around a conservative rhetoric and
supports a conservative ideology actually very close to the LaHayes' own.
Like them she targets fears that are shared by conservatives and liberals alike,
in particular, the fear of physical or psychological pain associated with sexual
activity, from which most parents would like to shield their children. Her
concerns, like the LaHayes', are often legitimate, and should not only be

dismissed as conservative "paranoia" but should also question the society at large. Yet they are framed in a conservative discourse, which in the case of Meeker attempts to be legitimated by her medical position of authority. The LaHayes are conservative political and religious leaders and their writings reflect this status. On the contrary, Meeker is not presented in *Restoring the Teenage Soul* and *Epidemic* as being openly associated with conservative groups. Her strongest affiliation is to the medical profession. Therefore the expectations of Meeker's readers are different from those of the LaHayes'. By playing with the boundaries between medicine and ideology, Meeker's discourse is more ambiguous and thus probably more apt at rallying a wider audience than the LaHayes'. Though liberal readers could be tempted to dismiss her books as barely scientific propaganda, the power of the ambiguity she entertains should not be overlooked as it is one of the major strength of conservative rhetoric.

One of the most successful examples of this strategy of ambiguity can be found in the discourse of the Heritage Foundation, which like Meeker's, constantly uses apparently scientific research to support the organisation's conservative positions, while grounding its core beliefs in religion and "moral" values. We shall turn to an exploration of this foundation in the next chapter.

Notes

[1] A Vineyard, 'Protection Teens Are Still Not Getting,' 19 December 2002, viewed on 19 June 2007, <http://www.beverlylahayeinstitute.org/articledisplay.asp?id=2944&department=BLI&categoryid=femfacts&subcategoryid=blicul>
[2] See www.regnery.com.
[3] Medinstitute.org, 'Employment or Internship Opportunities,' 2007, viewed on 13 March 2007, <http://www.medinstitute.org/content.php?name=employment>
[4] M Meeker, *Epidemic: How Teen Sex is Killing Our Kids*, LifeLine Press, Washington, D. C., 2002, p.98, emphasis in the original.
[5] M Meeker, P J Warren and M Maxwell Billingsly (narrators), *The Rules Have Changed the Teen STD Epidemic*, 2004.
[6] SIECUS, 'State Profile 2005: Nevada,' 2006a, viewed on 13 March 2007, <http://www.siecus.org/policy/states/2005/mandates/NV.html>
[7] Fields and Tolman, op. cit., p.67.
[8] Meeker, op. cit., p.5.
[9] M Meeker, *Restoring the Teenage Soul: Nurturing Sound Hearts and Minds in a Confused Culture*, McKinley and Mann, Traverse City, 1999, pp.IX-X.
[10] Meeker, op. cit., p.63.
[11] ibid., pp.63-64.

[12] ibid., p.216.
[13] ibid., back cover.
[14] ibid., p.63.
[15] Meeker, op. cit., p.20.
[16] ibid., p.27.
[17] Meeker, op. cit., p.3.
[18] ibid., p.3.
[19] L Grossberg, *We Gotta Get Out of This Place: Popular Conservatism and Postmodern Culture*, Routledge, New York, 1992, p.86.
[20] ibid., p.86.
[21] Kintz, op. cit., p.61.

Chapter 4
"Political" Pro-Abstinence Discourses:
The Heritage Foundation and Rebecca Hagelin

The Heritage Foundation was created in 1973, by a team of young conservatives, led by Paul Weyrich and Ed Feulner. It was the financial support of Joseph Coors, president of Coors Beers, that enabled them to realise the project they had had in mind for several years. Later financial supporters would also include prominent firms like "Amway, Chase Manhattan, Dow Chemical, General Motors, Loctite, Milliken, Mobil, Pfizer, Sears Roebuck, and SmithKline."[1] The aim of this new political research organization, or "think-tank"[2] was, according to Weyrich, to

> provide some intellectual underpinnings for some members of Congress who wanted to articulate a different approach from the Nixon administration. We did not regard the Nixon administration as conservative on many issues and we wanted to provide an alternative course. There were any number of members of Congress who were interested in taking that alternative course; they just didn't have the staff and the intellectual back-up to make that happen.[3]

It was this staff and "intellectual back-up" that the Heritage Foundation wanted to provide. Producing research and policy recommendations in a format that could be easily digested by congressmen and the media was to be the main function of the foundation. In 1979, Heritage, close to Jerry Falwell's Moral Majority, supported Ronald Reagan's presidential campaign. During Reagan's two consecutive terms in office the think-tank had its heyday. Its budget consistently increased as well as the number of its employees, and nine years after its founding it could boast an annual budget of $7 million.

Today, the Heritage Foundation is one of the most prominent right wing think-tanks in Washington. Its permanent research team writes on a very wide array of topics like agriculture, crime, economy, education, energy and environment, family and marriage, welfare, internet and technology, political philosophy, religion and civil society, NATO, foreign policy, and the study of the economies of the various continents. To promote its ideas, the Heritage Foundation organises conferences, often featuring members of Congress or of the government. It also uses its extensive mailing list and internet website to reach its donors and supporters. One of the foundation's major projects was, and still is the *Mandate for Leadership*. This series of books of more than 3,000 pages, first published in 1980, then in 1984, 2000 and 2005, gathers the political recommendations of the researchers of the Heritage Foundation to the Republican governments taking office. According to the foundation's website, President Reagan

> gave copies [of *Mandate for Leadership*] to every member of his Cabinet. The result: Nearly two-thirds of 'Mandate's' 2,000 recommendations were adopted or attempted by the Reagan administration.[4]

Though the Heritage Foundation now presents its relationship to the Reagan administration in very positive terms, the impact of his presidency was questioned by numerous conservatives. Many of them felt that the president had only paid lip service to issues like school prayer, abortion and family values. They also noticed that Ronald Reagan had actually appointed very few social conservatives to his administration. Yet, one of the important impact of the Reagan presidency for the Heritage Foundation in particular and the Religious Right in general was not what he actually accomplished, but rather the way he brought conservative Christian agendas in the national political discourse. In the case of the Heritage Foundation those agendas are articulated as follows:

> To promote conservative public policies based on the principles of free enterprise, limited government, individual freedom, traditional American values, and a strong national defense. Heritage analysts believe that:
> The private sector can be depended upon to make better economic decisions than the public sector in ninety-nine out of one hundred cases.
> Government serves the governed best when it is limited.
> Individuals need freedom to exercise responsibility.
> Good men and women produce a good society rather than the reverse.
> Peace is best protected through military strength.
> America should not hesitate to use its power and influence to shape a world friendly to American interests and values.[5]

As explained by Lee Edwards, adjunct professor of politics at the Catholic University of America in Washington, D.C., and Heritage Distinguished Fellow, in his book *The Power of Ideas: The Heritage at 25 Years*,

> the phrase "traditional American values" was not formally added to Heritage's mission statement until 1993. As a matter of policy, the foundation decided in the late 1970s to

concentrate on economic and foreign policy/national security questions, leaving social issues like abortion, gay rights, and prayer in the schools in the main to other public-policy organizations. But by the early 1990s, the decline of American culture had become so pronounced that Heritage felt compelled to start a cultural policy studies program.[6]

From then on, issues like abortion, gay rights, school prayer and vouchers, marriage, and sexual abstinence became privileged fights of the Foundation. All these issues are connected together under a larger one, the defense of the traditional family. Under the Bush administration, the Heritage Foundation remained one of the most prominent think-tanks in Washington. Overall it markedly supported the president and consistently approved his stance on such important issues as Iraq or federal spending.

A recurring criticism against the Heritage Foundation has been its lack of scientific reliability. Researching and publishing articles on the major issues it seeks to promote is the major activity of the foundation; however, various scholars have questioned the scientific reliability of its researchers' methods. First of all, the work of the Heritage Foundation specialists is not peer-reviewed by any exterior observer and their writings often refer as their major sources to other articles by the foundation's researchers. Various scholars and journalists have underlined the weaknesses of the research on abstinence education produced by the Heritage Foundation. For example, in several of their articles, Heritage researchers did not mention reliable scientific objections to abstinence-only programs, manipulated statistics and distorted other researchers' claims to support their views.[7] They also used solipsistic logic instead of science, for example when they derive from the observation that "sexually active boys are eight times more likely to attempt suicide than boys who are not sexually active"[8] that there is a direct correlation between sexual activity and depression.[9] Similarly scholars like Stephanie Coontz and Nancy Folbre of the Council on Contemporary Families question the assertion of Heritage's senior research fellow on domestic policy, Robert Rector, that "the sole reason that welfare exists is the collapse of marriage."[10] They argue that:

> The current pro-marriage agenda in anti-poverty policy is misguided for at least four reasons:
> Non-marriage is often a result of poverty and economic insecurity rather than the other way around.
> The quality and stability of marriages matters. Prodding couples into matrimony without helping them solve problems that make relationships precarious could leave them worse off.

> Two-parent families are not immune from the economic
> stresses that put children at risk. More than one third of all
> impoverished young children in the U.S. today live with two
> parents.
> Single parenthood does not inevitably lead to poverty. In
> countries with a more adequate social safety net than the
> United States, single parent families are much less likely to live
> in poverty. Even within the United States, single mothers with
> high levels of education fare relatively well.[11]

This view is supported by Scott Coltrane, former president of the Pacific
Sociological Association, who argues that many "political-religious"
organizations "are guilty of oversimplifying and often misrepresenting
research on marriage, divorce and parenting" while the "social evidence on
these topics is much more mixed."[12] Consequently, the research produced in
abstinence education by the Heritage Foundation needs to be approached
with caution and can be considered to reflect a clear ideological bias.

Abstinence is one of the main domestic issues featured on the
Heritage Foundation's website. While the site features one article on
abstinence as a solution to out-of-wedlock births from 1995,[13] the rest of the
articles are dated back from 2002 at the earliest, with a steady increase in
their number up to 2005, when the foundation's involvement in the issue
appears to have waned. This heightened interest at the beginning of the Bush
presidency can be accounted for by the strong investment of the foundation in
the support to the pro-marriage, pro-life and pro-abstinence policies of the
Bush administration. The later decrease in the production of research and
articles on the issue might be explained either by the numerous studies
underlining abstinence education's inefficiency, which started being
published around 2004-2005, dates at which enough time had passed to
assess these programs; or by the fact that the foundation might have
considered that its objectives regarding this particular issue had been
achieved. However, the Heritage Foundation still features extensive pro-
abstinence data on its main website as well as on a more recent one,
familyfacts.org.

According to Heritage, "abstinence education programs can
substantially reduce teen sexual activity" and are widely popular among
Americans.[14] In the view of its researchers,

> [t]eens who are sexually active are more likely to be
> depressed and are more likely to attempt suicide. [...]Early
> sexual activity seriously undermines the ability of girls to
> form stable marriages as adults. [...] Beginning sexual

activity at an older age, however, is linked to higher levels of personal happiness in adult years.[15]

Moreover, the Heritage Foundation explains that the younger a teen starts being sexually active, the more s/he is at risk of being infected by a STD since s/he is likely to have a higher number of sexual partners than people who start being sexually active at a later age. They also maintain that girls who start being sexually active younger run a higher risk of undergoing abortions and of having children out of wedlock. They are also more likely to become single mothers, and "since single mothers are far more likely to be poor, early sexual activity is linked to higher levels of child and maternal poverty."[16]

What is significant here is the link made by Heritage, and already evoked in Coontz and Folbre's quote, between early sexual activity, single motherhood and out-of-wedlock births and poverty. For the Heritage Foundation, abstinence is a tool in the defense of marriage and of the traditional family cell that its researchers define as "the basic unit of society."[17] The role that abstinence can play in promoting marriage follows from the Foundation's vision of poverty and welfare. The think-tank defends a vision of welfare inspired by "social Darwinism" which sees poverty mainly in terms of personal failings. In the view of its researchers there is little "real" poverty in the United States and the majority of the poor are in this situation mainly because they lack proper moral values and self-discipline. The main problem caused by this lack of values is out-of-wedlock births, which cause fatherless children to be raised without proper moral leadership and thus contribute to a vicious circle of crime, drug addiction, promiscuity and welfare dependency. Consequently, the Foundation advocates abstinence as a privileged solution in solving these problems as it prevents teen-pregnancy, develops self-discipline and encourages marriage.

The present work analyses the pro-abstinence discourses of the Heritage Foundation through texts from its websites. The two authors most often referred to throughout the text are Robert Rector, a senior research fellow on domestic policy at the Foundation, who drafted the definition of abstinence included in the welfare reform law of 1996, the *Personal Responsibility and Work Opportunity Reconciliation Act (PRWORA)*[18] and Heritage Vice-president Rebecca Hagelin. While Rector's articles are mostly "research" pieces, Hagelin's are more personal columns on family issues. Extracts from her book *Home Invasion*, which in most cases are featured as articles on the Heritage website, are also used as representative of the Foundation's position. Since her writings are extensively used in this book and are of a much more personal nature than Rector's, Hagelin herself and her book are characterised here in greater detail.

Hagelin is the daughter of pediatrician Dr. Henry Redd and his wife Alice Faye Redd. She was raised in Florida and attended Troy State University in Alabama.[19] Hagelin's mother gave her a strong example of leadership. She was

> president of the P.T.A., the Junior League and the Garden Club. She was honored as one of 10 outstanding young women of America at Richard M. Nixon's White House and even had her own program on the local Christian radio station, "The Happy Homemaker."[20]

However, her family discovered in the mid-1990s that Alice Faye Redd had organised a pyramid scheme that ruined a hundred people of her community and for which she was sent to jail. The payment of the damages ruined her formerly wealthy husband. Her family and her defense argued that a mental disorder was the cause for her behaviour and that she should be sent to a mental institution rather than to jail. This explanation helped Hagelin cope with the actions of her mother, who recently died. In spite of this later problematic family history, Hagelin's accounts of her childhood provide the image of the ideal traditional white middle-class family that her writings defend so staunchly. Today, Hagelin is herself married and the mother of three teenagers.

Hagelin has had a productive career. She became the director of public relations for the Center for Judicial Studies in 1983[21] and "helped develop communication strategies for Pat Robertson and the Christian Coalition."[22] In 1986, she took a position as director of communications for Concerned Women for America. Hagelin devoted several pages of her book *Home Invasion* to a eulogy of Beverly LaHaye, who has been an important mentor for her and who, as early as 1987, gave her "the incredible opportunity to have a home office"[23] and thus be closer to her children. In 2005, CWA elected Hagelin one of the prominent Evangelical Women of the Year. The conservative Clare Boothe Luce Policy Institute awarded her a similar honor by naming her one of the twelve Great American Conservative Women in 2007.

No longer working for CWA, Hagelin is currently vice president for Communications and Marketing at the Heritage Foundation. The Foundation's website publishes her columns along with several conservative news websites like WorldNetDaily.com, Townhall.com and PatriotPost.us. According to her own website, Hagelin also worked as a "commentator for Salem radio," "a guest co-host of Point of View as well as guest host for ABC Radio's WMAL."[24] She also made numerous appearances on CNN, FOX news or on CBN's *700 Club*. In 2005 Hagelin's first book, *Home*

Invasion: Protecting Your Family in a Culture That's Gone Stark Raving Mad, was published.

In her book *Between Jesus and the Market: The Emotions that Matter in Right-Wing America* (1997), Linda Kintz insightfully analyses the communication strategies used by Hagelin. She argues that her main asset lies in her southern familiarity and ordinariness. She describes Hagelin' appearance on a tape of the Christian Coalition's Leadership School Series:

> Hagelin presents a powerful image for this lesson in press relations. Dressed in a red dress with white polka dots and sporting a hairdo that is almost, but not quite, Big Hair, she looks and sincerely acts out the almost perfectly illustrative intelligent, decent, white southern woman who does not at all come across as puritanical or mean or even bigoted; she could be either from the suburbs or from a small town, and she is, of course, very nice. Small-town white girls like me know her well; in fact many of us probably were her at one time or another. But one could not imagine a more powerful construction, for she and her message are anything but naïve. And while a progressive audience simply ignores the message by laughing at her appearance, a radical conservative audience with fundamentalist or evangelical beliefs hears every word of her message about how to translate biblical principles into an effective media strategy that takes into account the blindnesses (sic.) and interests of its secular audience and reporters.[25]

She offers a similar image in her writings as well as on the cover of her book *Home Invasion*: the image of a white suburban mother.

Issued by the Christian publisher Nelson Current, *Home Invasion* features on its back cover recommendations from Tim and Beverly LaHaye and Laura Schlessinger, who also recommended Meeker's three books. A great percentage of *Home Invasion* is made of columns that Hagelin wrote for the Heritage Foundation and conservative news websites. It is therefore quite representative of the whole of her articles since 2002 when she appears to have started writing for Heritage. Besides, throughout the book she extensively quotes and refers readers to the research of the Foundation. Abstinence promotion is only one of the agendas featured in *Home Invasion*; however the other issues she deals with in her book, like "parental rights," marriage or the "culture war," are closely connected to abstinence and pervade pro-abstinence discourses as is explained throughout this book.

The content of Hagelin's book is well summed up by its title and by the four small paragraphs featured on its front cover to explain in what it can help the reader. *Home Invasion* offers to assist you in:

- Finding allies in the fight for your child's innocence.
- Safeguarding your family from cultural terrorism.
- How moms can set a better tone for their homes.
- Surefire tips to becoming a better father.[26]

Similar to the LaHayes' and Meeker's, Hagelin's book stimulates the sense of being under constant threat and evokes the nostalgic memories of an ideal past when America was a place where parents could raise their children in a "moral" environment "free from exposure to 'adult issues.'"[27] Today, she argues, "cultural terrorists" are menacing American families and homes and their children's innocence. Even the suburban middle-class neighborhoods are not a guarantee of safety anymore. Therefore, evoking the all-American image of the 19th-century frontier men and women who organized their wagons in circle at night for protection, she lyrically calls out to American families:

> Moms, dads, grandparents, pastors community leaders, teachers, this book is for you, it's for me - it's for all of us. It's to encourage us to draw that proverbial line in the sand, to reflect on the protective image of the wagons protectively encircling the fire to create a true safe haven for our children, and to do that in a real sense, in the modern culture. It's to protect our families, our children, and their futures. Why would we engage in this battle? Why would we take these bold steps? Because we love our kids. Because our children are depending on us to protect them. Because it's the right thing to do. And because we can win.[28]

The "cultural terrorists" against which families must wage war are, according to Hagelin and echoing the LaHayes and Meeker, the media, pornography, sex education, the fashion industry or the lack of religious values. She argues that these terrorists creep into American homes through MTV, the internet, movies, advertisement, and fashion, and are guilty for the current state of "moral" decay of the nation which leads to tragic consequences like the Abu Ghraib scandal among others.[29] What are the goals pursued by these terrorists? Make money in most cases, in others to exploit children sexually by abducting them or using their image for pornographic ends and to promote the secular value of "diversity." For Hagelin, in the name of "free speech" and

> "diversity," the cultural elite in Hollywood, in education, even some religious leaders, want us to believe that everything is okay, that no dangers exist, that there is no such thing as depravity, and to say otherwise is to be judgmental. They believe that choice is everything - but that the range of choice must include everything imagination can create. [...] those of us who choose to provide a protective space of innocence for our children; who dare to define right and wrong; who seek to preserve traditional values of decency - well, we're just bigots who must be silenced.[30]

To counteract the absence of moral values and decency promoted by this "cultural elite," Hagelin provides advice and resources to parents throughout her book.

First of all, parents should be cautious not to literally buy into the "culture" even if they feel that their children might feel rejected by the mainstream. She argues that if little girls are dressed provocatively and children watch indecent movies, it is because parents buy the clothing and let them watch the movies. For her, parents need to react, be committed parents, take back the control over their children's education and not relinquish it to public schools or the media. This can be achieved in a number of ways, *Home Invasion* explains. First of all parents should be really committed to their faith in God and establish it in their family. They should also get married and stay married. In this Hagelin follows the pro-marriage agenda of the Heritage Foundation, the research of which she quotes extensively in her book to back her points. She explains that children of unmarried parents fare worse than others. Consequently, she opposes cohabitation and condemns premarital sex as going against God's commands. She argues that

> America must promote and encourage the inherent value in strong marriages and families if we are to survive as a nation. If we as a society continue to promote and casually accept cohabitation, rampant divorce, sex outside of marriage, and homosexual partnerships as alternative to traditional marriage, we can expect more poverty, more crime, more emotional problems, and more social chaos.[31]

Spouses should also, against feminist teachings, maintain traditional gender roles in their couple relationships as well as in their parenting. For

Hagelin men and women are different and their roles as mothers and fathers are not interchangeable. She advises wives to make their husband feel appreciated and valued as "heroes" for their job as breadwinner[32] and not to succumb to the feminist "me, myself and I" mindset.[33] As for men they should not behave like "wimps," but be "real men" and show their love for their wives. Rephrasing the opinion of Laura Schlessinger, Hagelin argues that when "women reject the 'me first' mantra of radical feminism and become more selfless something magic happens: decent men respond in kind."[34] Thus, most men are not responsible for being wimps since they are being inhibited by a wife "acting like Medusa."[35] Likewise in parenting, fathers and mothers should preserve their own role as respectively "servant" and "nurturer"[36] and as moral leader and role model.[37] Yet similar to Beverly LaHaye, Hagelin's personal life seems to be in opposition to the conservative vision of the family she promotes. Indeed, her readers wonder at how she can humanly manage to be a "traditional" mother and wife with her apparently busy schedule. Susan Faludi here again provides an interesting insight on the question in her account of her meeting with Hagelin more than fifteen years before, when she was working for CWA:

> [P]ublicity director Rebecca Hagelin is on the phone with her husband. "Now, let's see, the carpet needs to be vacuumed," she instructs. "And if you could straighten up the living room a bit." It's past six P.M., and Hagelin is still at the office. Her husband is at home making dinner, taking care of their baby and preparing the house for guests that evening. The Hagelins might have found the blueprint for their domestic arrangement in an early-'70s manual for liberated couples: they split the chores and trade off child care. "See, I really wanted to have a baby, but I really wanted to work," Hagelin says. "I love to work." She likes the fifty-fifty arrangement. "That's the way it is in the '80s, it's not an either-or situation. It really is possible to have it all."[38]

For Hagelin it seems to be possible to "have it all" but again only on the condition of encouraging other women not to attempt it and denouncing the feminist gains from which she benefits fully herself.

Another crucial piece of advice Hagelin gives to parents is to take back charge of their children's education. She explains that this is particularly important regarding sex-education and school in general. She warns parents of the "immoral" and "oversexualised" content of comprehensive sex education and so-called "abstinence-plus" programs and recommends that they be kept under close scrutiny. Parents should review their children's sex-education curriculum and if necessary opt their children out of the course, even if this decision is unpopular with the child or the teachers. If the entire curriculum of the school reveals itself to be in disagreement with the parents' moral and religious beliefs, which can particularly be the case in public schools, Hagelin recommends private schools. If none is available, parents should resort to homeschooling. The defense of children's access to "a competitive market of public, private, charter, and home schools"[39] regardless of their parent's income is also one of the issues defended by the Heritage Foundation.

Parents should also, as recommended by Meeker, control what their children watch, read, listen to or wear. In order to do so, Hagelin recommends throughout her book a number of resources available to parents like internet filters, DVD filters, and "family friendly" publishing houses and magazines as well as retailers of appropriate clothing. *Home Invasion* closes with an almost forty-page-long catalogue indexing resources like organisations, books or websites dealing with issues like homeschooling, entertainment, marriage, parenting, prayer or sex. Some of the organizations she lists are: the Home School Legal Defense Association; the American Decency Association; Boy Scouts of America; CWA; James Dobson's Focus on the Family; the all-male religious organization, Promise Keepers; Shirley Dobson's National Day of Prayer Taskforce; the Abstinence Clearinghouse; and of course, the Heritage Foundation.

In *Home Invasion* Rebecca Hagelin takes on, in a more personal manner, the "traditional American values" issues defended by the Heritage Foundation, many of which were also at the heart of the pro-abstinence discourse of the Bush administration, as will now be explained.

Notes

[1] L Edwards, *The Power of Ideas: The Heritage Foundation at 25 Years*, Illinois: Jameson Books, Inc., Ottawa, 1997, p.27.
[2] As characterised by British civilization professor Keith Dixon, think-tanks are organisations "which present themselves as reflection forums, but which should rather be considered as privileged lobbies for the political activism of some intellectuals, and as key foundations to influence the economic and political fields," K Dixon, *Les évangélistes du marché*, Raisons d'Agir Éditions, Paris, 1998, pp.5-6, my translation.
[3] Quoted in Martin, op. cit., p.171.
[4] A Blasko, 'Reagan and Heritage: A Unique Partnership,' June 7, 2004, viewed on 18 June 2007,
<http://www.heritage.org/Press/Commentary/ed060704e.cfm>
[5] Edwards, op. cit., p.128.

[6] ibid., p.18.

[7] M Ginsberg, 'The Politics of Sex Education,' *Educational Law and Policy Forum*, 2005, 1, pp. 1-25, pp.10-11; J Ellenberg, 'Sex and Significance: How the Heritage Foundation cooked the books on virginity,' *Slate.com*. 7 July 2005, viewed on 21 August 2007, <http://slate.com/id/2122093/>; Kirby, 2002.

[8] M G Pardue, 'Waxman Report Is Riddled with Errors and Inaccuracies,' 2 December 2004, viewed on 15 March 2007, <http://www.heritage.org/Research/Abstinence/wm615.cfm>

[9] Ginsberg, 2005, p.14.

[10] C Wetzstein, 'Unwed Mothers Set a Record for Births,' *The Washington Times*, April 18, 2001.

[11] S Coontz, and N Folbre, 'Marriage, Poverty, and Public Policy: A Discussion Paper from the Council on Contemporary Families,' 28 April 2002, viewed on 10 November 2006, <http://www.contemporaryfamilies.org/subtemplate.php?t=briefingPapers&ext=marriagepovertypublicpoli>

[12] S Coltrane, 'Marketing the Marriage 'Solution': Misplaced Simplicity in the Politics of Fatherhood,' *Sociological Perspectives*, Winter 2001, 44 (4), pp.347-418, p.405.

[13] J J Piccione and R A Scholle, 'Combatting Illegitimacy and Counseling Teen Abstinence: A Key Component of Welfare Reform,' 31 August 1995, viewed on 19 June 2007, <http://www.heritage.org/Research/Abstinence/BG1051.cfm>

[14] M G Pardue, R Rector and S Martin, 'Executive Summary: Government Spends $12 on Safe Sex and Contraceptives for Every $1 Spent on Abstinence,' 14 January 2004, viewed on 17 June 2007, <http://www.heritage.org/Research/Family/bg1718es.cfm>

[15] ibid.

[16] ibid.

[17] P F Fagan, 'Marriage and the Family,' in HERITAGE FOUNDATION, *Issues 2006: The Candidate's Briefing Book*, 2006, viewed on 18 June 2007, <http://www.heritage.org/research/features/issues/pdfs/BriefingBook2006.pdf>

[18] J Wildermuth, 'Welfare reform heading back to Congress next year,' *San Francisco Chronicle*, 4 November 2001, p. A11; L Beil, 'Abstinence Education Faces an Uncertain Future,' *The New York Times*, 18 July 2007, viewed on 20 August 2007, <http://www.nytimes.com/2007/07/18/education/18abstain.html?ex=1187841600&en=a6f6061787e7cf9c&ei=5070>

[19] Kintz, op. cit., p.10.

[20] F Butterfield, 'This Way Madness Lies: A Fall From Grace to Prison,' *The New York Times*, 21 April 1996, viewed on 15 March 2007, <http://query.nytimes.com/gst/fullpage.html?res=9F02E5D61E39F932A1575 7C0A960958260&sec=health&spon=&pagewanted=all>

[21] Rwnetwork.net, 'Rebecca Hagelin,' 2007, viewed 15 March, 2007, <http://www.rwnetwork.net/Rebecca_Hagelin>

[22] Kintz, op. cit.,p.100.

[23] R Hagelin, *Home Invasion: Protecting Your Family In a Culture That's Gone Stark Raving Mad*, Nelson Current, Nashville, 2005b, p.150.

[24] Homeinvasion.org, 'About Rebecca Hagelin,' 2007, viewed on 15 March 2007, <http://www.homeinvasion.org/AboutTheAuthor.cfm>

[25] Kintz, op. cit., p.101.

[26] Hagelin, op. cit., front cover.

[27] ibid., p.xi.

[28] ibid., p. xxi.

[29] ibid., p. 4.

[30] ibid., p. 18.

[31] ibid., p. 81.

[32] ibid., p. 89.

[33] ibid., p. 91.

[34] ibid., p. 92.

[35] ibid., p. 92.

[36] ibid., p. 151.

[37] ibid., pp.173-180.

[38] Faludi, op. cit., pp.255-56.

[39] Heritage Foundation, 'Issues: Education,' 2007, viewed on 16 March 2007, <http://www.heritage.org/research/education/>

Chapter 5
"Governmental" Pro-Abstinence Discourses:
The G. W. Bush Administration

In order to study the pro-abstinence discourses of the G.W. Bush administration, different types of texts issued by the White House will be used: extracts of speeches, summaries of policies, legal texts as well as the content of a governmental website devoted to abstinence, 4Parents.gov. Before presenting these different texts, this section will take a closer look at the role of religion in shaping G.W. Bush's personal life and political views and at the history of government funding of abstinence programs.

1. A Vision Shaped by Religion?

Numerous journalists and academics have written about G.W. Bush, and about his religious beliefs in particular. Some have at times questioned his religious commitment as a mere façade designed to win over the evangelical electorate. It appears clear that many of the Bush administration's policies were crafted to attract conservative Christian voters. While G.W. Bush's Christian faith appeared genuine, the debate over the nature of the religious convictions of the president and their impact on his policies is still open. While he certainly displayed a strong religiosity while in office, G.W. never took a clear "conservative Christian" stand on issues like abortion, gay marriage or creationism but rather entertained an ambiguity which served his political aims. Some observers have underlined that he also did not identify himself openly as a "born-again" Christian or an evangelical, in spite of a religious discourse and a personal religious narrative that appeared to clearly affiliate him with these religious tendencies.[1] A *Washington Post* article summing up the work of various authors on the question explained that David Aikman,

> who was given wide access to Bush's friends and senior officials to write "A Man of Faith," [...] concluded that Bush is "a mainstream evangelical with a higher-than-normal tolerance of dissent."
>
> Stephen Mansfield wrote in "The Faith of George W. Bush" that Bush is "a conservative Christian," but added: "On many issues, Bush is less doctrinaire than his faith would make him appear, and this too is part of the mystery of George W. Bush." [...]
>
> Tim Goeglein, who directs the White House Office of Public Liaison and is the president's official intermediary with Christian groups, said Bush is an evangelical but also fits the English theologian C.S.

> Lewis's definition of a "mere Christian" - someone who
> looks beyond denominational lines to the central, common
> teachings of the universal church.[2]

While C.S. Lewis insisted on the ecumenical nature of his religious views, it is important to note that his definition of "mere Christianity" as following a set of absolute doctrines[3] - such as the belief that unbelievers will go to hell and believers will know eternal life - is today extremely popular within the fundamentalist Christian community and has been defined by some commentators as an expression of Lewis' "proto-fundamentalism."[4]

What the ambiguity of Bush's religious views was hiding is unclear. Some argued that he maintained it in order to please conservative Christian voters without alienating more moderate ones. In this case, it would mean that his faith had relatively little influence over his policy decisions.[5] However, many observers differed with this opinion. In the same *Washington Post* article Rev. Shaun Casey, an assistant professor of Christian ethics at the Methodist Church's Wesley Theological Seminary in Washington, was asked

> if Bush's beliefs are so ecumenical and his prayers so
> generic, […] do the president's positions on such matters as
> abortion and same-sex marriage really derive from his
> faith? And what influence do his religious beliefs have on
> his budget priorities or tax policies?
> Casey, who went to college in West Texas, said he
> recognizes in Bush an "indigenous West Texas evangelical
> piety" and thinks "the critics who dismiss him as purely
> manipulating religion" are wrong.[6]

Similarly, sociologist Barbara Finlay argued, taking the example of the president's conservative appointments, that

> while many have believed that Bush was making such
> extremist appointments to consolidate his conservative
> religious base, the fact that in his second term he appointed
> such people to more central positions indicates that he
> himself wants to promote these views and enact them into
> policy and law.[7]

The impact of his faith, especially on his foreign policy has been underlined by the evangelical Christian writer and activist Jim Wallis

America's foreign policy is more than pre-emptive, it is theologically presumptuous; not only unilateral, but dangerously messianic; not just arrogant, but bordering on the idolatrous and blasphemous. George Bush's personal faith has prompted a profound self-confidence in his "mission" to fight the "axis of evil," his "call" to be commander-in-chief in the war against terrorism, and his definition of America's "responsibility" to "defend the ... hopes of all mankind."[8]

Likewise former *Wall Street Journal* reporter and Pulitzer Prize winner Ron Suskind wrote in the *New York Times* that after 9/11

the faith-based presidency truly takes shape. Faith, which for months had been coloring the decision-making process and a host of political tactics - think of his address to the nation on stem-cell research - now began to guide events.[9]

The narrative of G.W. Bush's religious "conversion" is a famous one and was retold by Suskind in the same article:

It was in 1985, around the time of his 39th birthday, George W. Bush says, that his life took a sharp turn toward salvation. At that point he was drinking, his marriage was on the rocks, his career was listless. Several accounts have emerged from those close to Bush about a faith "intervention" of sorts at the Kennebunkport family compound that year. Details vary, but here's the gist of what I understand took place. George W., drunk at a party, crudely insulted a friend of his mother's. George senior and Barbara blew up. Words were exchanged along the lines of something having to be done. George senior, then the vice president, dialed up his friend, Billy Graham, who came to the compound and spent several days with George W. in probing exchanges and walks on the beach. George W. was soon born again. He stopped drinking, attended Bible study and wrestled with issues of fervent faith.[10]

It can be argued that this "fervent" faith significantly affected his vision of the family with which we are here concerned. However, the extent to which his support of certain conservative Christian issues was focused on preserving the backing of the conservative Christian that his father had difficulties maintaining, cannot be underestimated.

Although Edward Ashbee emphasised that the attitude of President Bush regarding abortion was ambiguous, and that he chose to defend the concept of a "right to life" rather than explicitly condemn abortion, the successes of the pro-life camp under his presidency are undeniable.[11] Ahsbee's assertion that the phrase "culture of life" was a way to avoid directly referring to abortion needs to be nuanced, since this phrase was previously used by Pope John Paul II in explicit reference to abortion.[12]

At the discursive level, the position of the president appeared definitely attune to that of conservative Christians and Catholics. In many speeches, G.W. Bush claimed that the "right to life" conferred by God and guaranteed by the Constitution is sacred and is neither the resort of the Courts nor the government's. In one of his speeches, he underlined that for him abortion was akin to terrorism:

> Consistent with the core principles about which Thomas Jefferson wrote, and to which the Founders subscribed, we should peacefully commit ourselves to seeking a society that values life - from its very beginnings to its natural end. Unborn children should be welcomed in life and protected in law. On September 11, we saw clearly that evil exists in this world, and that it does not value life. The terrible events of that fateful day have given us, as a Nation, a greater understanding about the value and wonder of life. Every innocent life taken that day was the most important person on earth to somebody; and every death extinguished a world. Now we are engaged in a fight against evil and tyranny to preserve and protect life. In so doing, we are standing again for those core principles upon which our Nation was founded.[13]

In this passage George Bush defines terrorism and abortion as both going against what he calls the "American culture of life." As such, he sees them as being "un-American" activities, just as communism was under McCarthy. Consistent with this argument, during his time in office, the President delivered speeches, live or recorded, at each of the anti-abortion Marches for Life that takes place on the Washington Mall each year on the anniversary of *Roe v. Wade*, the Supreme Court decision which legalized abortion. An example of Bush's pro-life stance can be found in his vigorous support of the *Unborn Victims of Violence Act of 2004*, which became federal law that same year. This act allows to sue and condemn a person who "causes the death of, or bodily injury [...] to, a child, who is *in utero* at the time," a provision which legally separates the entity of the unborn child from that of the mother. By recognising the status of the unborn child, "a member of the species homo sapiens, at any stage of development, who is carried in the womb," as that of a full legal person, this law by extension could impose significant restrictions on abortion, though it is mentioned in the bill that it does not concern voluntary abortion. By further amendment, this law could lead to the prohibition of abortion as murder.

Condemning abortion is not only an ethical issue, it is also a means for conservatives to question the legitimacy of an out-of-wedlock sexuality that is not concerned with reproduction. The Bush administration answered this concern in several ways. Among others, it supported the *Child Interstate Abortion Notification Act* (which was eventually defeated), which would have prevented any adult from helping a minor cross state borders in order to obtain an abortion in a state where parental notification was not required.[14] The president also strongly encouraged the use of abstinence-only funding to support "pregnancy resource centers" to which teens and women can turn for advice in case of an unintended pregnancy. In most cases these are religious organisations with a strong pro-life agenda.[15] In 2006, a report of the Committee on Government Reform of the House of Representative found out that 87% of the centers it surveyed provided "false and misleading information about a link between abortion and breast cancer [;…] about the effect of abortion on future fertility [… and] about the mental health effects of abortion."[16] Thus "pregnancy resource centers" attempt to dissuade teens from seeking an abortion and encourage them to keep their child or put it up for adoption.

The position of G.W. Bush on contraception also appeared far from supportive. In addition to promoting abstinence-only programmes and underlining the failure rates of contraception methods, the Bush administration restricted the access to contraception for many women. In her book *George W. Bush and the War on Women*, Barbara Finlay notes that at the beginning of his first term in office, G.W. Bush proposed to cut health insurance coverage of contraceptives for federal employees.[17] Later in 2001, the Bush administration refused a request by the state of New York to raise the income limit for eligibility for contraception coverage for Medicaid recipients.[18] Finally, the White House press secretary refused several times to provide any clear answer to the question of Bush's position on contraception. In spite of letters from members of Congress, the only answer he provided was that the president supported "building a culture of life,"[19] an expression openly associated with Bush's anti-abortion stance.[20] Ashbee explains that the argument provided by the administration for this limitation of the availability of contraceptives is that it is a private matter that should not be promoted by the government.[21] While many conservative Christians do not oppose contraception for married couples, the case of emergency contraception is distinguished, since some see it as a form of abortion. Contraception is also seen by conservatives as encouraging promiscuity among unmarried people. This can account for the opposition of the Bush administration.

During his presidency, G.W. Bush also defended a traditional heterosexual vision of marriage, as witnessed by his promotion of the *Marriage Protection Act of 2003*, which was defeated in the 108th Congress and the *Marriage Protection Amendment* which also did not pass the 109th Congress. The *Defense of Marriage Act of 1996* already stated that

> the word 'marriage' means only a legal union between one man and one woman as husband and wife, and the word 'spouse' refers only to a person of the opposite sex who is a husband or a wife.[22]

and reasserted the rights of states to deny recognition of same-sex marriages pronounced in other states.

On February 24, 2004, George Bush endorsed the *Marriage Protection Act of 2003*. If it had passed both houses, it would have added to the provisions of the 1996 Act that "neither the Supreme Court nor any court created by Act of Congress shall have any appellate jurisdiction to hear or determine any question pertaining to the interpretation of section 7 of title 1[23]" which defines the meaning of "'marriage' and 'spouse.'" This act would thus have made same-sex marriage illegal in the USA. Yet, it was very unlikely that such an act would pass as it undermined the check and balances of power and can be considered unconstitutional. In an even clearer way the "Marriage Protection Amendment," which was also defeated and has not been reintroduced, would have added to the constitution an article stating that

> [m]arriage in the United States shall consist only of the union of a man and a woman. Neither this Constitution, nor the constitution of any State, shall be construed to require that marriage or the legal incidents thereof be conferred upon any union other than the union of a man and a woman.[24]

Even if these acts did not pass, this did not weaken their political impact and the statement they make that the courts have no right to alter the traditional definition of marriage.

The Bush administration, like the Heritage Foundation, also advocated programmes of "Promotion of family formation and healthy marriage" as part of the *Personal Responsibility, Work, and Family Promotion Act of 2003* which it strongly supported. This strengthening of the traditional family is also at the heart of the administration's conservative vision of welfare which, similar to the vision of the Heritage Foundation, sees moral and religious education, discipline and sexual self-control as the best remedies to poverty.

The nature of the faith of G.W. Bush and its impact over his policy decisions still remain unclear. However, there is a high likelihood that his support of conservative Christian issues was not only a political strategy but was also motivated by personal ideological views in keeping with his religious convictions. Through his religious personal narrative and his speeches and declarations, the president constructed an image that strongly appealed to conservative Christian audiences who described him as "one of their own."

2. Overview of Government Funding of Abstinence Programs

The history of government funding of pro-abstinence programs started in 1981 with the *Adolescent Family Life Act* (AFLA), which passed discreetly with the support of conservative Christians. The aim of this act was to decrease teen pregnancies through the promotion of abstinence. At its beginning, the budget appropriated under this act was around $11 million in federal funds, by the year 2000 it had almost doubled.

In 1983, the AFLA programs were the objects of a suit for unconstitutionality filed by the American Civil Liberties Union (ACLU). The suit went through various courts, and in 1985 a U.S. district judge found the AFLA (which was promoting specific religious values and promoting abstinence as the only choice for teens) unconstitutional, as violating the separation between church and state clause of the Constitution. In 1988, after an appeal to the U.S. Supreme Court, the decision was reversed and sent back to a lower court.

In 1993 an out-of-court settlement restricted the AFLA by stating that the sexual education programs it funded must

- Not include religious references.
- Be medically accurate.
- Respect the "principle of self-determination" regarding contraceptive referral for teenagers.
- Not allow grantees to use church sanctuaries for their programs or to give presentations in parochial schools during school hours.[25]

Yet, this issue remained very present in the abstinence debate. In August 2005, the federal government decided to suspend the funding to the pro-abstinence organization the Silver Ring Thing, after the ACLU filed a lawsuit in May 2005. It accused the organization of "us[ing] abstinence-only-until-marriage sex education as a means to bring 'unchurched' students to Jesus Christ."[26]

In 1994, an attempt was made by Congress to impose abstinence-only-before-marriage[27] education in state schools through an amendment, proposed by the Republican Representative John Doolittle, to the *Elementary and Secondary Education Act*. However, this amendment was significantly weakened by four federal statutes that "prohibited the federal government from prescribing state and local school curriculum standards."[28]

1996 marked a new victory for conservative Christians with the addition to the *Federal Welfare Act* of a provision to fund abstinence-only-until-marriage programs. The provision included eight rules that the states had to apply to get federal funding. They were also required "to match every four federal dollars with three state-raised dollars."[29] The eight rules that states have to implement in order for their programs to be funded, and commonly referred to as "A-H", were that such a program

> A – has as its exclusive purpose teaching the social, psychological, and health gains to be realized by abstaining from sexual activity;
> B - teaches abstinence from sexual activity outside marriage as the expected standard for all school-age children;
> C - teaches that abstinence from sexual activity is the only certain way to avoid out-of-wedlock pregnancy, sexually transmitted diseases, and other associated health problems;
> D - teaches that a mutually faithful monogamous relationship in the context of marriage is the expected standard of sexual activity;
> E - teaches that sexual activity outside of the context of marriage is likely to have harmful psychological and physical effects;
> F - teaches that bearing children out-of-wedlock is likely to have harmful consequences for the child, the child's parents, and society;
> G - teaches young people how to reject sexual advances and how alcohol and drug use increase vulnerability to sexual advances, and
> H - teaches the importance of attaining self-sufficiency before engaging in sexual activity.[30]

Starting in fiscal year 1997, funds allocated through the AFLA were also tied to this eight-point definition and therefore to "a stricter interpretation of what must be taught."[31]

In late 2000, the federal government created another source of funding for abstinence-only programs in addition to the AFLA and Title V of the *Social Security Act*. Originally designed as the Special Projects of Regional and National Significance - Community-Based Abstinence Education (SPRANS-CBAE), this third source of funding enabled the federal government to directly award grants to national and local pro-abstinence organizations. At beginning of fiscal year 2005 SPRAN-CBAE, which was originally administered by the Maternal and Child Health Bureau of the U.S. Department of Health and Human Services (HHS) was placed under the responsibility of the HHS' Administration for Children and Families (ACF) and started being "referred to simply as Community-Based Abstinence Education (CBAE)."[32] As underlined by the website www.nonewmoney.org, created by SIECUS and supported by organizations like Planned Parenthood, Advocates for Youth, or the YWCA, and which opposes government funding of abstinence-only programs, ACF is a particularly conservative division of HHS. Until his resignation in April 2007 - after the shift to a Democratic majority in Congress - it was headed by Wade Horn, a prominent conservative and co-creator of the National Fatherhood Institute. This organization promotes the view that "widespread fatherlessness is the most socially consequential problem of our time"[33] a claim from which its leaders derive their opposition to single and homosexual parenthood and their strong support of marriage and premarital chastity.

While the decision to provide funding for programs was, under Title V, ultimately the state's resort. CBAE enabled the government to fund individual organizations without having to involve the states in its decision. Like programs funded under Title V, CBAE programs had to respect "A-H." In 2006, ACF made these requirements even stricter by detailing and expanding the eight-point definition. For example, programs were required to reinforce point B by being consistent with the statements that: "pursuing the expected standard of abstinence serves to establish an understanding of and respect for others"; "abstinence reflects qualities of personal integrity and is honorable."[34] Likewise point C, D and E had to be reinforced by, among others, the following or similar statements:

> (C) Teaches that contraception may fail to prevent teen pregnancy and that sexually active teens using contraception may become pregnant
> Does not promote or encourage the use or combining of any contraceptives in order to make sex "safer."
> (D) Teaches that non-marital sex in teen years may reduce the probability of a stable, happy marriage as an adult.
> Teaches that the lack of commitment associated with non-marital sex may increase the potential for emotional harm.

(E) Teaches the potential psychological effects (e.g., depression and suicide) associated with adolescent sexual activity.

Teaches that teen sexual activity is associated with decreased school completion, decreased educational attainment, and decreased income potential.

(F) Teaches the importance of marriage to economic well-being and prosperity and the importance of abstinence in the teen years to long-term healthy and happy marriages.

Teaches the association between healthy marriage and adult happiness.

Teaches the relationship of abstinence before marriage and fidelity in marriage to responsible parenthood.[35]

In keeping with the conservative vision of welfare promoted by the Bush administration and the Heritage Foundation, these statements promoted a vision of abstinence as morally superior and as the only path to achieve happiness, a stable marriage, economic prosperity and good parenthood.

Conversely, premarital sexual activity was presented as necessarily entailing negative emotional and psychological consequences and was related to low achievements in all areas of life - even though no study backs these points.[36] In addition, the use of contraceptives as a potential method to prevent these negative consequences was discouraged. A report by SIECUS interestingly underlined that

ACF's contention that "teen sexual abstinence improves preparation for stable marriage" appears to have come solely from two papers issued by The Heritage Foundation. Both papers were co-authored by Heritage's resident abstinence-only guru, Robert Rector, also the chief architect of the expansion of abstinence-only-until-marriage programs in 1996. Neither of the papers has been published in reputable, peer-reviewed journals and one, "Teenage Sexual Abstinence and Academic Achievement," is based simply on an inaccurate analysis of data from the National Longitudinal Survey of Adolescent Health [...].[37]

The potential impact of the Heritage Foundation's research on government policy appears here in a particularly problematic light. This report from SIECUS pointed to further questionable points in these extended requirements. Their major arguments were that they

- Use scare tactics
- Rely on messages of shame
- Discourage contraceptive use
- Suggest premarital abstinence is a cure-all
- Promote marriage as the only acceptable family structure
- Violates the dignity of LGBTQ young people
- Retraumatizes survivors of sexual abuse, rape, and/or molestation[38]

The last two remarks were based on the promotion by the federal document of monogamous heterosexual marriage as the only legitimate frame for sexuality; and on the assertions that "sexual desires are natural and controllable and [...] individuals are capable of making choices to abstain from sexual activity" and that "personal character and self-discipline [are important] in deciding to remain sexually abstinent."[39] Another criticism raised by SIECUS regarding the CBAE extensions of requirements was that the definition it provided of abstinence as

> voluntarily choosing not to engage in sexual activity until marriage. Sexual activity refers to any type of genital contact or sexual stimulation between two persons including, but not limited to, sexual intercourse.[40]

was both "unclear and unrealistic for today's teens" since under this definition "activities such as holding hands, looking into someone's eyes, or kissing - anything that might provoke a physiological response-could be construed as going against the tenets of premarital abstinence."[41]

SIECUS also pointed out that these new requirements did not adequately address the need for reliable scientific evaluations of the programs' efficiency, a need which in the more than two decades of funding of abstinence-only programs had never been properly addressed by the Department of Health and Human Services and raised recurring criticism from scientists and advocates. The extension of 2006, for example, only provided for a superficial documentation of

> "the number of youth served; the hours of service provided to each youth; and the number of youth that complete the program." While there is some discussion of grantees having the option to evaluate program participants' behaviors and attitudes, the ideal outputs are described to "calculate program efficiency and answer such questions as, 'What is the overall cost of providing services per

program graduate?' or 'What is the overall cost per student per hour of abstinence education?'"[42]

The question of the lack of efficiency of abstinence-only programs in reducing STD, teen pregnancy and abortion rates, as well as of the scientific reliability of the data released by the government on the issue, are central to this debate. The inefficiency of abstinence programs in postponing the initiation of sexual activity was confirmed by a report ordered by Congress and published in April 2007. The study led by Mathematic Policy Research, Inc. examined the impact of four federally funded abstinence-only programs over the course of nine years and concluded that they had no effect in delaying the initiation of first sexual intercourse.[43] Earlier studies had underlined that overall, abstinence education had little impact on student's sexual behavior. Some results had been noted with younger students who were not yet sexually experienced, but any intent to remain abstinent consistently decreased over time. Overall, in most programs the degree of sexual activity increased with the age of the participants.[44]

A review of federal abstinence policies and programs led by several researchers from institutions like Columbia University, the Indiana School of Medicine or the American College of Preventive Medicine, also severely criticized the pro-abstinence policy of the Bush administration and recommended abandoning abstinence-only "as a basis for health policy and programs"[45] on the grounds that

> policies or programs offering "abstinence only" or "abstinence until marriage" as a single option for adolescents are scientifically and ethically flawed. Although abstinence from vaginal and anal intercourse is theoretically fully protective against pregnancy and disease, in actual practice, abstinence-only programs often fail to prevent these outcomes. Although federal support of abstinence-only programs has grown rapidly since 1996, existing evaluations of such programs either do not meet standards for scientific evaluation or lack evidence in delaying initiation of sexual intercourse. Although health care is founded on ethical notions of informed consent and free choice, federal abstinence-only programs are inherently coercive, withholding information needed to make informed choices and promoting questionable and inaccurate opinions. Federal funding language promotes a specific moral viewpoint, not a public health approach. Abstinence-only programs are inconsistent with commonly accepted notions of human rights.[46]

Similarly in 2004 a report prepared for Congressman Henry A. Waxman, and commonly referred to as the "Waxman report" found that

> over 80% of the abstinence-only curricula, used by over two thirds of SPRANS grantees in 2003, contain false, misleading, or distorted information about reproductive health. Specifically, the report finds that

> - Abstinence-only curricula contain false information about the effectiveness of contraceptives. [...]
> - Abstinence-only curricula contain false information about the risks of abortion. [...]
> - Abstinence-only curricula blur religion and science. [...]
> - Abstinence-only curricula treat stereotypes about girls and boys as scientific fact.
> - Abstinence-only curricula contain scientific errors.[47]

That same year, the Union of Concerned Scientists released a study entitled *Scientific Integrity in Policymaking: An Investigation into the Bush Administration's Misuse of Science*, which accused the Bush administration of "distorting science-based performance measures to test whether abstinence-only programs were proving effective" and suppressing "information at odds with its preferred policies."[48] It also quoted a scientist formerly occupying a high-ranking position at the Center for Disease Control and Prevention (CDC) who explained that "despite the absence of supporting data, this source and others contend, CDC scientists were regularly reminded to push the administration's abstinence-only stance."[49]

In spite of this mass of scientifically grounded objections, funding for CBAE increased from $20 million for Fiscal Year 2001, to $105 million for Federal Year 2005 and reached $113 million for Fiscal Year 2007, with an overall spending of $213.5 million in funding for abstinence-only program for that year.[50] Another set of recent requirements even extended the target of abstinence education up to adults aged 29 years old. This decision which caused a national uproar even from some conservatives[51] was justified by Wade Horn with the argument that more unmarried women within the 19-29 age range are having children. Therefore, he saw a need to remind abstinence program providers that their target was not only children and teens but also adults who needed to hear the message that "it's better to wait until you're married to bear or father children," and "the only 100% effective way of getting there is abstinence."[52] Stephanie Coontz and other commentators underlined that such strategy stigmatized unmarried people and made little sense both in practical and social terms since many single-mothers today deliberately chose to be so and while unmarried may not be raising their children without their fathers.[53] The sexist stigmatisation of unmarried women implied in this requirement was also highly problematic in a governmental discourse.

AFLA, Title V and CBAE were not the only sources of funding for abstinence-only education programs for example,

> in both Fiscal Years 2004 and 2005, Senator Arlen Specter (R-PA) earmarked over $3 million in federal funding for abstinence-only-until-marriage programs in his home state of Pennsylvania. Conservative organizations such as the Abstinence Clearinghouse and the Medical Institute [...], also receive funds specially earmarked by Congress. Increasingly, abstinence-only-until-marriage providers are also receiving funds through traditional HIV/AIDS and STD prevention accounts such as those administered by HHS and the [...] CDC.[54]

This approach of the Bush administration to teen pregnancy and STD prevention was particularly problematic especially given the high rates of STDs, teen pregnancy and abortion of the US. One of the most recent studies available so far on the issue and dated from 2001 noted that

> Adolescent childbearing is more common in the United States (22% of women reported having had a child before age 20) than in Great Britain (15%), Canada (11%), France (6%) and Sweden (4%); differences are even greater for births to younger teenagers. A lower proportion of teenage pregnancies are resolved through abortion in the United States than in the other countries; however, because of their high pregnancy rate, U.S. teenagers have the highest abortion rate. The age of sexual debut varies little across countries, yet American teenagers are the most likely to have multiple partners.[55]

The study added that American teenagers also had at that time a higher rate of STDs than teens from other developed countries.

The unwavering support of the Bush administration for abstinence-only education appears even more disturbing in light of various studies which since 2000 showed the overwhelming support for sex-education from parents of children of middle-school and high-school age.[56] One of the surveys reported that of the parents polled 90% "believed it was very or somewhat important that sex education be taught in school" whereas only 70% of parents disapproved of it, "only 15% wanted an abstinence-only form of sex education."[57]

Such a lack of public approval and of scientific backing for the government's support of abstinence-only education programs hints heavily at the ideological nature of this issue and consequently of the discourses surrounding it. It is some of these discourses, under the form of written texts issued by the government, which will be presented now.

The texts used in this book to represent the position of the Bush administration, and of previous administrations, on the question of abstinence education can be divided into four major groups: speeches by G.W. Bush himself, texts issued on the website of the White House, texts of laws supported by the Bush administration and previous governments, and internet resources provided by the government to inform citizens.

George W. Bush was not the first American president to use the theme of teenage sexuality in his speeches as an important issue. Before him Bill Clinton, for example, contributed to the construction of teen pregnancy as a national problem when he claimed in 1997 that there still were "some pretty big problems in our society" and that none stood "in our way of achieving our goals for America more than the epidemic of teen pregnancy."[58] However, G.W. Bush was the first president to promote abstinence as the best and unique means to target questions like teen pregnancy and STDs.

In almost all his speeches mentioning it, President Bush asserted that "abstinence work[ed] every single time" and was therefore an efficient solution to the public health and welfare problems constituted by STDs and teen pregnancies. In spite of this apparent pragmatism, this approach was not only motivated by public health concerns, but was closely intertwined with a discourse on public morality. The president proclaimed in his speeches that promoting abstinence also meant helping "our young children learn to make right choices in life,"[59] that is, helping them to chose "self-restraint" over "self-destruction" and thus to "counter the negative influence of the culture"[60] which sends "wrong messages" to American teenagers. In his view, it was underestimating teenagers to think that they could not "act responsibly"[61] and restrain from a premarital sexuality largely legitimated by "the culture" represented by Hollywood, the media and comprehensive sexual educators. Like the LaHayes, Meeker or Hagelin, Bush positioned himself and his values in opposition to a leftist and "amoral" environment. As he explained in 2002 in a speech delivered in North Carolina:

> We ought to try [abstinence]. We ought to work hard; we ought to shoot for the ideal in society and not get drug down by the cynics. And so part of making sure that welfare reauthorization is going to achieve objectives is to

promote family and to encourage right choices amongst American youth.[62]

The "ideal" to which he alludes here corresponds in his mind to what he defines as the traditional American values of which the traditional family unit, as defined by a conservative reading of the Bible, is a key component.

To preserve these values and this ideal of America, the G.W. Bush administration had to go further than its predecessors. Even if sexual abstinence can be seen as a private matter, the president explained that "when our children face a choice between self-restraint and self-destruction, government should not be neutral."[63] Here again, we find the same oppositions of permissiveness and morality, destruction and restraint, as in the LaHayes', Meeker's and the Heritage Foundation's discourses. In order to preserve restraint and morality the government, like ministers and doctors, had to get involved, even if this meant redefining the boundaries between the state and the church or between the public and private spheres - even more so as it was not only the morality of teenagers which was at stake but the ideal of the nation. The speeches by G.W. Bush oppose abstinence, family and marriage to a contemporary culture which defines new types of family cells and questions the definition of marriage as the union of one man and one woman. For the president, abstinence was not only a matter of public health, but first and foremost a tool in an ideological campaign to reassert the conservative vision of the traditional family cell against a postmodern culture which constantly redefines it.

A conservative vision of welfare consistent with these beliefs was reasserted in documents issued by the White House like *Working Toward Independence* (2002) a text explaining the projects of policies of the Bush administration regarding welfare. The text summed up the achievements of the *Personal Responsibility and Work Opportunity Reconciliation Act of 1996* of 1996 and explained "the Bush administration's detailed plan for [its] reauthorization"[64] which offered among other things to:

- Maximize Self Sufficiency Through Work
- Promote Child Well-Being and Healthy Marriages
- Encourage Abstinence and Prevent Teen Pregnancy
- Enhance Child Support Enforcement
- Reform Food Stamps to Promote Work[65]

Similarly, two of the nineteen chapters of the 2004 *Record of Achievement* of the Bush presidency were centered on the themes of child protection, the strengthening of the family and the promotion of a "culture of life."[66] The document listed the "achievements" of the Bush administration regarding these various issues. Here are some examples of what could be found under each heading:

> *Protecting Children:*
> A new abstinence initiative *will double the funding for abstinence-only education*; develop model abstinence-only education curricula; review all Federal programming for youth addressing teen pregnancy prevention, family planning, and STD and HIV/AIDS prevention, to ensure that the Federal government is sending consistent health messages to teens; and create a public education campaign designed to help parents communicate with their children about the risks associated with early sexual activity.[67]

> *Encouraging Safe and Stable Families:*
> [...] The President has proposed $240 million per year in Federal funds over five years to *support healthy marriages* through research, demonstration projects and technical assistance on family formation and healthy marriage activities.[68]

> *Building a Culture of Life:*
> [...] President Bush restored the Mexico City Policy, which states that *taxpayer funds should not be provided to organizations that pay for abortions or advocate or actively promote abortion, either in the United States or abroad.*[69]

Overall, the "achievements" referred to echo the conservative vision of the family, sexuality and welfare reflected in G.W. Bush's speeches. The initiatives concerning children's protection did not deal with the important questions of child health care and poverty but mostly with abstinence and the protection of children from sexual predators. Those concerning the strengthening of families did not address poverty, health care, parental leave or adaptable work schedules, but adoption - an alternative to abortion - and programs to strengthen marriages and to promote "responsible fatherhood." Finally, building a "culture of life" was understood as redefining the legal status of the foetus, limiting access to abortion at home and abroad, and developing alternatives to abortion like adoption and banning human cloning.

The exceptional nature of the Bush administration's support for abstinence education was visible in its choice to devote an entire governmental website to the promotion of abstinence. Launched in early

2005 by Department of Health and Human Services' (HHS) secretary Mike Leavitt as

> part of a new national public education campaign to provide parents with the information, tools and skills they need to help their teens make the healthiest choices. [As t]here is no substitute for caring parents who are involved in their children's lives.[70]

The website soon became the object of a controversy. In March 2005, 145 advocacy groups sent a letter to Leavitt "saying that the site provides biased and inaccurate information to parents and does not emphasize the need for contraception if a teenager becomes sexually active."[71]

In July of that year, California Representative Henry Waxman, Democratic author of the "Waxman Report", which had concluded that many federally funded abstinence programs were inaccurate and biased, gathered a panel of medical experts to review the website. The panel concluded that it

> contain[ed] inaccurate and misleading information about condoms, sexual orientation, dangers associated with oral sex and single-parent households and potentially could lead to riskier behavior among young people or alienation among families.[72]

Waxman himself questioned the scientific reliability of its creators, arguing that the website was based more on ideology than on facts.[73] But in spite of these oppositions it was only slightly altered and was still fully accessible until the late spring of 2007.

On June 21, 2007, the content and format of the website was changed. The new version of the website was part of a new public campaign of the government to encourage parents to talk to their children about abstinence.[74] 4parents.gov still emphasized the negative consequences of premarital sexuality as well as the failure rates of contraception methods, and kept promoting adoption over abortion. However its stance on the influence of religion on teen sexual behavior, among other things, was suppressed and new version started addressing directly the issue of homosexuality by encouraging respect, albeit emphasising the "difficulty" that this question represented. Before this change, most of the content of the website was also available in print in two booklets downloadable from 4parents.gov: *Parents Speak Up!* and *Teen Chat*.[75] These two texts as well as the site itself in its older version are extensively used throughout this book as representative of the position of the Bush administration regarding abstinence. Likewise, legal texts referred to previously, like the AFLA, Title V of the Welfare Act of

1996, or the extension of the requirements for CBAE funding, are frequently referred to.

Finally, the Waxman report is also used as a representative summary of the content of abstinence education programs funded and therefore supported, then and now, under CBAE. This report, published in 2004, was commissioned by Waxman in order to evaluate "the content of the most popular abstinence-only curricula used by grantees of the largest federal abstinence initiative, SPRANS."[76] As quoted earlier the investigators found most of these programs contained "false, misleading, or distorted information about reproductive health."[77]

Aimed at different audiences and fulfilling different functions, these various texts, taken together, provide a comprehensive overview of the type of pro-abstinence discourses produced by the White House during the G.W. Bush's presidency and of what the Bush administration comprised under the definition of abstinence.

This chapter has shown that contemporary abstinence advocacy, while being inscribed in a long tradition, also differs from it to a significant extent in its unique association of a relatively marginal but politically powerful religious community and a president who displayed an exceptional level of commitment to this issue. However, despite the clear ideological and discursive similarities between the conservative Christian community and the Bush administration, it is important to keep in mind that abstinence proponents do not constitute a homogenous group but stand on an ideological continuum which goes from the more "marginal" to the more "mainstream" type of abstinence advocacy. As will be shown in the next chapters, while they reached a high level of congruity in the past decade, these various pro-abstinence discourses do not necessarily emphasize the various issues connected to abstinence to the same degree and do not always seek to reach the same goals through their promotion of premarital chastity.

Notes

[1] A Cooperman, 'Bush Leaves Specifics of His Faith to Speculation,' *The WashingtonPost.com*, 16 September, 2004, viewed on 26 May 2007, <http://www.washingtonpost.com/wp-dyn/articles/A24634-2004Sep15.html>
[2] Cooperman, 2004; D Aikman, *A Man of Faith: The Spiritual Journey of George W. Bush*, Thomas Nelson, Nashville, 2004; S Mansfield, *The Faith Of George W. Bush*, Charisma House, New York, 2004.
[3] Professor of English Burton Hatlen explains that for Lewis: "anyone who calls him/herself a Christian must accept: the essential goodness of the world created by God, the Fall of human beings from an original state of perfection as a result of their willful disobedience of God's command, Christ as the true

and only Son of God, the redemption of humans from their state of sin through Christ's death on the cross, hell as the destiny of all unbelievers, eternal life in heaven as the reward of all who accept Christ as their Savior," B Hatlen, 'Pullman's *His Dark Materials*, a Challenge to the Fantasies of J.R.R. Tolkien and C.S. Lewis, with an Epilogue on Pullman's Neo-Romantic Reading of *Paradise Lost*,' in M Lenz and C Scott (eds), *His Dark Materials Illuminated: Critical Essays on Philip Pullman's Trilogy*, Wayne State University Press, Detroit, 2005, p.80.

[4] Hatlen, op. cit., p.80.

[5] See Ashbee, op. cit.

[6] Cooperman, op. cit.; Aikman, op. cit.; Mansfield, op. cit..

[7] Finlay, op. cit., p.80.

[8] J Wallis, 'Dangerous Religion,' *Sojourners Magazine*, September-October 2003, viewed on 26 May 2007, <http://www.sojo.net/index.cfm?action=magazine.article&issue=soj0309&article=030910>

[9] R Suskind, 'Without a Doubt,' *The New York Times*, October 17, 2004, viewed on 19 June 2007, <http://www.nytimes.com/2004/10/17/magazine/17BUSH.html?ex=1255665600en=890a96189e162076ei=5090>

[10] ibid.

[11] Ashbee, op. cit., pp. 193-225.

[12] John Paul II, *Evangelium Vitae*, 25 March 1995, viewed on 26 May 2007,<http://www.vatican.va/holy_father/john_paul_ii/encyclicals/documents/hf_jp-ii_enc_25031995_evangelium-vitae_en.html>

[13] G W Bush, 'National Sanctity of Human Life Day, 2002: A Proclamation by the President of the United States of America,' 18 January 2002a, viewed on 17 June 2007, <http://www.whitehouse.gov/news/releases/2002/01/20020118-10.html>

[14] A more detailed catalogue of the steps taken by G.W. Bush to "promote a culture of life" can be found in the fifteenth chapter of: White House, *President George W. Bush: A Remarkable Record of Achievement*, August 2004, viewed on 24 March 2007, <http://www.whitehouse.gov/infocus/achievement/Achievement.pdf>.

[15] H A Waxman (prepared for), *False and Misleading Information Provided by Federally Funded Pregnancy Resource Centers*, July 2006, viewed 26 May 2007, <http://oversight.house.gov/documents/20060717101140-30092.pdf>

[16] ibid., p.I.

[17] Finlay, op. cit., p.76.

[18] ibid., p.76.

[19] White House, 'Press Briefing by Scott McClellan,' 26 May 2005, viewed on 25 March 2007, <http://www.whitehouse.gov/news/releases/2005/05/20050526-1.html>

[20] Finlay, op. cit., pp.76-78.

[21] Ashbee, op. cit., p.114.

[22] *Defence of Marriage Act of 1996*, H.R. 3396, Public Law 104-199, 104th Congress.

[23] This refers to the amendment of Chapter 1 of title 1, of the United States Code with the section 7 of Public Law 104-199 of 1996 entitled: "Definition of 'marriage' and 'spouse.'"

[24] *Marriage Protection Amendment*, Senate Joint Resolution 1, introduced 2005, 109th Congress.

[25] M Howell, 'The Future of Sexuality Education: Science or Politics?' *Transitions*, March 2001, viewed on 26 May 2007, <http://www.advocatesforyouth.org/PUBLICATIONS/transitions/transitions 1203.pdf>

[26] American Civil Liberties Union (ACLU)), 'ACLU Applauds Federal Government's Decision to Suspend Public Funding of Religion by Nationwide Abstinence-Only-Until-Marriage Program,' 22 August 2005, viewed on 19 June 2007, <http://64.106.165.214/news/08.22.05%20SilverRing.pdf>

[27] "Abstinence-only" programs teach abstinence as the only safe protection against STDs and pregnancy and do not give any information about other forms of contraception and protection.

[28] SIECUS, Advocates for Youth, 'Toward a Sexually Healthy America: Roadblocks Imposed by the Federal Government's Abstinence-Only-Until-Marriage Education Program,' 2001, viewed on 13 March 2007, <http://www.advocatesforyouth.org/publications/abstinenceonly.pdf>, p.6.

[29] Howell, op. cit., p.1.

[30] Section 510(b) of Title V of the *Social Security Act*, P.L. 104-193. These requirements can also be referred to as part of the *Personal Responsibility and Work Opportunity Reconciliation Act of 1996* or PRWORA, SEC. 101, depending on the context and time frame in which they are referred to.

[31] Nonewmoney.org, 'A Brief History of Abstinence-Only-Until-Marriage Funding,' 2006a, viewed on 22 March 2007, <http://www.nonewmoney.org/history.html>

[32] ibid.

[33] National Fatherhood Initiative, 'NFI History,' 2007, viewed on March 22 2007, <https://www.fatherhood.org/history.asp>

[34] U.S. Department of Health and Human Services Administration for Children and Families, 2006a, p.7.

[35] ibid., pp.7-11.

[36] See Santelli et al., op. cit., p.74.

[37] SIECUS, 'Special Report: It Gets Worse: A Revamped Federal Abstinence-Only Program Goes Extreme,' 2006b, viewed on 23 March 2007, <http://www.siecus.org/policy/SpecialReports/Revamped_Abstinence-Only_Goes_Extreme.pdf>

[38] ibid.

[39] U.S. Department of Health and Human Services Administration for Children and Families, 2006a, p.12.

[40] ibid., p.5.

[41] SIECUS, 2006b.

[42] ibid.

[43] Mathematica, 2007.

[44] Nonewmoney.org, 'Harmful Consequences,' 2006b, 23 March 2007, <http://www.nonewmoney.org/harmful.html>

[45] Santelli et al., op. cit., p.79.

[46] ibid., p.79.

[47] H A Waxman (prepared for), *The Content of Federally Funded Abstinence-Only Education Programs*, December 2004, viewed on 22 May 2007, < http://oversight.house.gov/documents/20041201102153-50247.pdf>, p.I-II.

[48] Union of Concerned Scientists, *Scientific Integrity in Policymaking: An Investigation into the Bush Administration's Misuse of Science*, March 2004, viewed on 23 March 2007, <http://www.ucsusa.org/assets/documents/scientific_integrity/RSI_final_fullr eport_1.pdf>, p.11.

[49] ibid., p.12.

[50] Nonewmoney.org, 'A Brief History of Abstinence-Only-Until-Marriage Funding: Spending for Abstinence-Only-Until-Marriage Programs (1982-2008),' 2007, viewed 21 June 2007, <http://nomoremoney.org/historyChart.html>

[51] S Coontz, 'No Sex for You,' 6 November 2006, viewed on 23 March 2007, <http://www.tompaine.com/articles/2006/11/06/no_sex_for_you.php>

[52] S Jayson, 'Abstinence Message Goes Beyond Teens,' *USAtoday.com*, 31 October 2006, 23 March 2007, <http://www.usatoday.com/news/washington/2006-10-30-abstinence-message_x.htm>

[53] Coontz, op. cit.

[54] Nonewmoney.org, op.cit.

[55] J E Darroch, Jacqueline E., S Singh and J J Frost, 'Differences in Teenage Pregnancy Rates Among Five Developed Countries: The Roles of Sexual Activity and Contraceptive Use,' *Family Planning Perspectives*, November/December 2001, 33 (6): pp.244-281, p.244.

[56] Nonewmoney.org, 'On Our Side: Public Support for Comprehensive Sexuality Education,' 2006c, viewed on 23 March 2007, <http://www.nonewmoney.org/public.html>

[57] Dailard, op. cit.

[58] W J Clinton, 'Radio Address of the President to the Nation,' St. Thomas, Virgin Islands, 4 January 1997, quoted in T C West, 'The Policing of Black Women's Sexual Reproduction' in K M Sands (ed), *God Forbid: Religion and Sex in American Public Life*, Oxford University Press, Oxford, New York, 2000, p.138.

[59] G W Bush, 'National Sanctity of Human Life Day, 2002: A Proclamation by the President of the United States of America,' 18 January 2002d, viewed on 18 June 2007, <http://www.whitehouse.gov/news/releases/2002/01/20020118-10.html>

[60] G W Bush, 'State of the Union Address,' 20 January 2004, viewed on 18 June 2007,<http://www.whitehouse.gov/news/releases/2004/01/20040120-7.html>

[61] G W Bush, 'President Announces Welfare Reform Agenda,' 26 February 2002b, viewed on 18 June 2007, <http://www.whitehouse.gov/news/releases/2002/02/20020226-11.html>

[62] G W Bush, 'President Discusses Welfare Reform and Job Training,' 27 February 2002c, viewed on 18 June 2007, <http://www.whitehouse.gov/news/releases/2002/02/20020227-5.html>

[63] Bush, 2002b.

[64] White House, *Working Toward Independence*, 2002, viewed on 16 February 2009, < http://georgewbush-whitehouse.archives.gov/news/releases/2002/02/welfare-reform-announcement-book.pdf>, p.1.

[65] White House, 2002, Table of Contents.

[66] White House, *President George W. Bush: A Remarkable Record of Achievement*, August 2004, viewed on 24 March 2007, <http://www.whitehouse.gov/infocus/achievement/Achievement.pdf>

[67] ibid., p.36, emphasis in the original.

[68] ibid., p.37, emphasis in the original.

[69] ibid., p.38, emphasis in the original.

[70] www. 4parents.gov

[71] Kaisernetwork.org, 'Nearly 150 Advocacy Groups Send Letter to HHS Secretary Criticizing Government Sex Ed Web Site as Biased, Inaccurate,' April 1, 2005a, viewed on 11 May 2007, <http://www.kaisernetwork.org/daily_reports/rep_index.cfm?DR_ID=29069>

[72] Kaisernetwork.org, 'HHS Abstinence Web Site for Parents of Teens Contains Inaccurate, Misleading Information, Review Says,' July 14, 2005b, viewed on 11 May 2007, <http://www.kaisernetwork.org/Daily_reports/rep_index.cfm?DR_ID=31365>

[73] ibid.

[74] U.S. Department of Health and Human Services Administration for Children and Families, 'HHS Unveils "Parents Speak Up" National Campaign PSA Campaign, New Web Site Help Parents Talk to Kids About Waiting to Have Sex,' 21 June 2007, viewed on 2 July 2007, <http://www.acf.hhs.gov/news/press/2007/parents_speak_up.htm>

[75] The content of 4parents.gov was renewed in late spring 2007 and these booklets can now be downloaded in an updated version slightly different from the one used here.

[76] Waxman, op. cit., p.i.

[77] ibid., p.i.

Chapter 6
Abstinence and Creationism

Abstinence may at first appear as just one out of many issues that constitute the conservative Christian agenda. A closer look, however, shows that it is at the heart of many other conservative Christian discourses and that it is part of a complex ideological framework whose various segments mutually reinforce each other.

The next six chapters seek to explain how a seemingly single, rather obscure issue was in the past decade at the center of American conservative Christian ideology and politics. It will prove a surprising cohesion and systematicity of conservative thinking and show how various issues and conservative Christian narratives are linked through the demand for sexual abstinence before marriage.

To begin with, the presence of the creationist narrative in pro-abstinence discourses will be analysed as well as the interaction between this narrative and the one of abstinence. I then move on to explore how pro-abstinence discourses and the polarised vision of sexual morality they provide enable conservative Christians to actualize their experience of sexuality through a clear set of reassuring guidelines.

In Chapters 7 and 9 I investigate how pro-abstinence discourses strengthen the conservative Christian narrative of the "superiority" of the traditional patriarchal family cell, as well as their defense of the right of parents to control every areas of their children's life.

Finally, Chapters 10 and 11 look in detail at the promotion by pro-abstinence discourses of a vision of welfare and poverty based on the cultural narrative of success, as well as at the instrumental role of abstinence programmes in promoting this vision. It also underlines how pro-abstinence discourses through their focus on children's sexual innocence contribute to maintain the impression that conservative Christians are in the middle of a "culture war."

Though both topics are high on the conservative Christian agenda, the link between abstinence and creationism is not necessarily an obvious one. Yet it is clearly made by both the LaHayes and Rebecca Hagelin, who explain to their readers that teaching creationism is crucial to achieving the goal of "raising virtuous children."[1]

Starting with the Scopes trial in 1925, the visibility of creationism as one of the key narratives of American fundamentalist Christianity remained high throughout the century even after a drop before its revival in the 1960s. It even regained momentum after the arrival of the Bush administration to power with the support of the president for the teaching of both evolution and creationism[2] and particularly in 2005 with the controversy over the concept of "intelligent design" (ID).[3] As for abstinence, it has been the object of growing media attention at home and abroad in the past decades, particularly in view of the important support it received from the two G. W. Bush administrations.

It is interesting that these two issues which are at the core of the media and self-image of conservative Christians are brought together by both the LaHayes and Hagelin. The quotes in which they do so look very similar. The first one, by the LaHayes, is taken from the second chapter of their book entitled "How To Raise Virtuous Children," which formulates various pieces of advice and principles for parents to follow in the education of their offspring. This advice ranges from loving children to teaching them "early about sex," from sending them to Christian schools to teaching them moral values and from keeping them active in the church to not making them delay marriage for too long. The quote by Hagelin comes from an article with a similar intent, entitled "The Culture War: A Five-Point Plan for Parents." These five points are: "envision the type of adult you want your child to become"; "commit to the daily battle" against contemporary culture; "teach your child that he has intrinsic value in God's eyes"; "improve your family life"; and "take a hands-on approach with your child's education."[4]

Both quotes revolve around the same idea, the link between the belief in creationism and children's "self acceptance." For the LaHayes, self acceptance

> is a problem for children because public educators reject or omit all references to God and teach children they are biological accidents - the result of 'random chance as products of evolution.' We know better. Our children are creatures of God! They need to know that. Talk about improving self-image! Children who know they are creatures of God have much less trouble understanding 'Who am I?' or 'Where do I come from?' than those children who mistakenly think they evolved.[5]

Hagelin explains that

> The greatest gift we can give our children is to let them know that there is a God who loves them and knows them by name. We must teach our sons and daughters that the God of the Universe is intensely interested and familiar with every aspect of their lives and wants what is best for them. Today's culture teaches even the young child that he is here by accident, and that he is just another creature on a big, impersonal planet, no different from any other animal.

It's no wonder that kids today are experiencing depression
and loneliness in record numbers.[6]

For both Hagelin and the LaHayes, teaching children through evolution that
they are "biological accidents - the result of 'random chance as products of
evolution'", "just another creature on a big, impersonal planet, no different
from any other animal", leads to poor self-acceptance. On the other hand,
they argue that creationism provides children with a sense that they are
"creatures" of a God "who loves them and knows them by name" and "is
intensely interested and familiar with every aspect of their lives and wants
what is best for them", which provides them with a strong sense of self-
confidence and worth. Both reinforce their point by blaming the "record
numbers" of teenagers who "today are experiencing depression and
loneliness" due to problems of "self-acceptance" on the teaching of
evolution.

The Institute for Creation Research (ICR),[7] one of the foremost US
creationist organisations, holds similar views as the LaHayes and Hagelin.
The ICR was created (with the help of Tim LaHaye) in 1970, by H. M.
Morris who is often credited for the renewal of the creationist movement in
the 1960s. The ICR defines Darwinism as a "pessimistic, antitheistic, and
nihilistic"[8] theory which sees the human mind as nothing more than - and
here they quote the science columnist C. Raymo - "a computer made of
meat."[9] For them such a pessimistic vision of humanity is not what children
should be taught.[10]

The ICR, and creationists in general, identify two major negative
consequences of Darwinism. First, it questions the inerrancy of the Bible by
invalidating the story of the Creation told by Genesis. In their view, this
amounts to robbing the Gospel of its foundation, since to question one
passage of the Bible is to question and invalidate the whole of the Christian
faith.

Second, Darwinism, by putting animals and humans at the same
level, denies man a "special superior status" in the Creation and thus refutes
the existence of man's immortal soul. In his book *L'Amérique entre la Bible
et Darwin* (America Between the Bible and Darwin) French philosopher D.
Lecourt explains that for creationists that if the soul of man is not immortal, it
is not submitted to the Last Judgment and consequently Christian morality
collapses, since the absence of judgment makes the need for morality void.[11]
As a matter of fact for the ICR, the sheer immorality implied by the
"atheistic" evolutionist stance witnesses to the fact that this theory is "Satan's
lie,[12]" "the anti-Gospel of anti-Christ."[13] Lecourt underlines that for
creationists, evolutionism is a trick devised by Satan to draw humans towards
immediate physical pleasures and away from God. For, they argue, if we are

just animals and there is no God and no Last Judgment, what is the point of being moral and resisting physical temptations?[14] In Tim LaHaye's words,

> [t]he doctrine of evolution has led naturally to the destruction of the moral foundation upon which this country was built. If you believe that man is an animal, you will expect him to live like one. Consequently, almost every law required to maintain a Bible-based, morally sane society - such as those involving marriage and divorce or sexual matters such as pornography and homosexuality - has been struck down so that man may follow his animal instincts and appetites.[15]

To raise "moral" children it is therefore indispensable to educate them in the belief of the Genesis' story of creation.

Likewise, in their advocacy of abstinence, the LaHayes explain that if children need to know that they are "children of God and coheirs with Jesus Christ - John 1:12; Romans 8:17"[16] before anything else, they also need to be told that they are their parents' children. Drawing a parallel with their argument on creationism, they explain that "it is reassuring to children to know they were wanted by their parents and are loved by them."[17] In their view, children should know that they are neither random "biological accidents" nor the outcome of the random sexual encounter of their parents. On the contrary, they need to understand that they are the fruit of a loving relationship sanctified by marriage. Following this idea, out-of-wedlock birth can be assimilated with the theory of evolution, as according to this logic children who have no "proof" of the love of their unmarried parents, might be exposed to problems of self-acceptance and see themselves as an "accident," a "mistake." To understand fully the weight of this argument it is indispensable to keep in mind that for abstinence proponents, as a famous advocacy group put it, "True Love Waits", and that individuals who cannot wait until marriage to have sex do not genuinely love each other.

In their advocacy of abstinence, the LaHayes also use creationism to reassert the fact that Christians are "children of God" and that according to St Paul "their body is not their own but is 'the temple of God' and should be kept holy."[18] For the LaHayes, when a child "received" Christ (usually through baptism or a born-again experience) he/she becomes the "temple of God." This means that God has "a wonderful plan" for the life of this child and this plan is "his road to true happiness."[19] But it can only be fulfilled through "sexual purity or virtue." For as St Paul writes,

> [t]he body is not meant for sexual immorality, but for the Lord… Do you not know that your bodies are members of

Christ himself? Shall I then take the members of Christ and
unite them with a prostitute [immoral person]? Never! Do
you not know that he who unites himself with a prostitute is
one with her in body? For it is said, "The two will become
one flesh." But he who unites himself with the Lord is one
with him in spirit - 1 Corinthians 6:13b 15-17.[20]

It is interesting to note here how the LaHayes cautiously add the commentary
that a prostitute stands for "immoral persons" in general, therefore preventing
their readers from a literal, uninterpreted reading of the passage. They also
warn their readers that "nothing circumvents the 'perfect will of God' for a
person's life like the sexual sins of fornication and adultery."[21] For the
LaHayes, "fornication" includes premarital sex: "young people need to
realize that premarital sex is not some harmless activity like baseball or
tennis. The Bible calls it 'fornication.'"[22]

But children are not only part of God's body, they are also part of
the body of their earthly family, to which they are accountable. Thus, the
LaHayes argue that when a child behaves in a promiscuous way s/he not only
defiles "Christ's body" or "God's temple," but is also "a reproach to the
whole family."[23] Through this discursive link between creationism and
abstinence, the analogy between God and the family of Christians on the one
hand and parents and earthly family on the other is reinforced, as is the
authority of both over the child. As will be analysed in greater detail further
on, abstinence discourses are heavily involved in this discursive project of
reinforcement of parental and religious authority.

The LaHayes and Hagelin also draw a parallel between creationism
and abstinence by their reference to children's lack of "self-acceptance,"
"depression and loneliness." Along with the theory of evolution and out-of-
wedlock births, they see premarital sex as both being a potential cause and
consequence of such negative states of mind. In Meg Meeker's words:

Studies find that kids who are depressed gravitate towards
sex, since sex acts as a drug, numbing a hurt, filling a void,
keeping their minds altered, if only for a moment. But
sexual activity also leads to depression.[24]

The parallel made here by Meeker between premarital sex and drug use is a
common rhetorical device in pro-abstinence discourses. It reflects the
commonly held view that the use of addictive substances, like alcohol and
drugs, can occasion a lack of control and a suspension of inhibitions, which
may lead to sexual activity. It also emphasises the vision of teenage sexual
activity as another "risk behavior" threatening youth's physical and mental
health on the same negative level as drug or alcohol abuse.

This position is further reinforced by Elayne Bennett's foreword to Meeker's first book, where she states that,

> [m]any adolescents do not hold themselves in high regard, and the absence of self-worth can be a serious handicap, which makes them more vulnerable to negative peer pressure, early sexual activity, drug and alcohol abuse, and violent and aggressive behavior.[25]

Here again the causal link between lack of "self-worth" and premarital sex is drawn, a lack of self-worth caused, for the LaHayes, by a lack of parental love.[26] But another link that the attentive reader will most likely not fail to make is that those children, who so much lack self-worth that they look for it in sex, were probably not taught creationism but evolution. Following the creationist argument, children who believe that they were created by a loving God who has "a wonderful plan" for them would not need to find reassurance in sex. On the contrary, children who think that they are just animals, the random result of natural coincidences, develop a low level of self-confidence and do not acquire the moral values necessary to behave differently from animals and practice sexual abstinence. This is the view held by John Morris, who asks if "teaching more evolution" is the solution or the cause of the "malfunctions" of US public schools.

> Decades of teaching students that they evolved from animal ancestry by purely random processes like mutation and natural selection, that there is no Creator to whom they are responsible, that there are no absolutes in morality, has brought us to this point. Can evolutionists legitimately blame the situation in today's schools, whose students murder classmates and teachers with no remorse, where premarital sex and sexually transmitted diseases are common, where suicidal thoughts plague many, on lack of *better* evolution teaching?[27]

Following Morris, the LaHayes and Hagelin, creationism, by boosting self-confidence and morals, helps prevent premarital sex and is consequently reasserted as being an indispensable tool in children's education. Conversely, abstinence defined as the appropriate attitude towards one's own body and therefore Christ's, reasserts the creationist idea that humans are children of God. Both creationist and pro-abstinence discourses thus confirm each other in a circular pattern.

This pattern of confirmation does not stop there, as abstinence is related to creationism through yet another argument. As hinted at by Hagelin and confirmed by the ICR, creationism reinforces the notion of the adamant difference between human and animal nature. If humans are children of God conceived in his likeness, they are of a divine nature, not "just another creature on a big, impersonal planet, no different from any other animal."[28] On the contrary, creationism views Darwinism as a theory stating that humans are "descended from the ape" and therefore do not owe their superiority to an essential difference in nature with other animals but to natural coincidences. As stated earlier, if humans believe that they are just animals and consequently do not believe in God, their sense of morality collapses and they will succumb to earthly temptations particularly to sexual immorality. Additionally, the heavily sexually connoted image of the ape, which is strongly connected to the popular vision of Darwinism, reinforces the link between animality and sexuality.

The notion that sex undermines the difference between humans and animals is central to a tradition which claims "that human development occurs through a shift away from the animal bodily calls of physicality to the higher planes of reason and the mind."[29] An example of this can be found in the early American fear of miscegenation, which lasted well into the twentieth century. The idea that a white "civilized" man or woman could have sex with an "uncivilized" black slave or Native American, who were considered closer to animals than to humans, was threatening for colonial and 19th-century religious authorities. Indeed, at that time and until the beginning of the 20th century, blacks were seen as standing at the bottom of the scale of "races" only followed by the orangutan. Given their different sexual and social practices, among them polygamy, blacks and Native Americans were considered much more sexually oriented than whites who, by regulating their sexuality through monogamous marriage, could control their sexual urges which bore witness to their more divine nature. As mentioned in Chapter 1, similar arguments were also used later in American history to differentiate between "civilised" Anglo-Saxons and "uncivilised immigrants."[30] However, not all forms of sex were considered degrading, marriage was considered by Puritans as "an expression of love and fellowship"[31] only "fornication" or illicit sex was seen as "unclean" and "disorderly" and as pulling them away from God and spirituality.

This last idea is also defended by the LaHayes, who claim that "premarital sex destroys our children's spiritual life"[32] through the guilt they feel after disobeying God. The LaHayes also confirm the idea that extramarital sexuality is of an "animal" nature by stating that a boy who says he cannot wait until marriage to have sex is not in love but "in heat."[33] By controlling their sexuality through abstinence before marriage, Christians reassert their divine status and deny their animality, which is also the purpose of creationism.

Another additional common feature of pro-abstinence and creationist writings is their similar wish to counteract the decline of "traditional American values" through a pro-family agenda. For the Heritage Foundation, as well as for the G.W. Bush administration while it was in office, abstinence is part of a larger plan to reassert the traditional family. In Heritage's view "the basic unit of society is the family and the cornerstone of the family is marriage"; "as an institution, marriage is the foundation of a harmonious and enriching family life and the basic building block of our society."[34] This position is similar to the one promoted in the *Personal Responsibility and Work Opportunity Reconciliation Act of 1996*, which stated that "marriage is the foundation of a successful society [and] an essential institution of a successful society which promotes the interests of children." The G.W. administration, like the Heritage Foundaation, considered that teenage sexuality endangers marriage for two reasons. First, because it reduces the need for this institution by refusing to see it as the only frame for sexual activity; second, because it increases the likelihood of having different sexual partners throughout one's life. By its refusal of the model of traditional lifelong monogamous marriage as the only legitimate frame of sexual activity, teenage sexuality also opens the way to non-traditional sexualities (extramarital sex, homosexuality) and non-traditional family cells (single-parent families, gay families).

On the contrary, abstinence-only programmes support the traditional family by teaching that:

> - Abstinence from sexual activity outside marriage [is] the expected standard for all school age children.
> - A mutually faithful monogamous relationship in context of marriage is the expected standard of human sexual activity.[35]

Moreover, as explained in Chapter 4 and developed further on, the Heritage Foundation promotes the idea that abstinence "reduce[s] risk behaviors and instill[s] moral character."[36] Thus, it constitutes a crucial tool in the fight against what it defines as "behavioral poverty," and for the reassertion of "traditional American moral values" that Heritage, along with most conservative Christians, sees as "declining."

The idea of the "decline" of America and its "traditional values" is also at the heart of Morris' creationist discourse. Grounding his argument in his literal reading of the Bible, Morris argues that, eventually, all nations will be evaluated by God along five criteria and then "He" will part the "good" ones from the others. Those five criteria are "righteousness"; the extent to which those nations see God through the "evidences" he left in his Creation which amounts to their belief in creationism; whether these nations are friends with Israel, God's chosen nation; the extent of their missionary work; and finally how they respect the biblical injunction to

> *"[b]e fruitful, and multiply, and replenish the earth, and subdue it and have dominion . . . over the earth"* - Genesis 1:26. This mandate implies a large population and every honorable occupation - science, commerce, education, etc. This "dominion mandate" amounts in effect to a magnificent divinely-commissioned stewardship for man over God's great creation - to understand its processes and develop its resources to the glory of God and the good of men.[37]

Following these five criteria, Morris continues by asking if the United States will be among the "chosen" nations.

> What about our own nation? We have been the best friends of Israel and have also contributed more than most other nations to the dominion mandate. Our nation was founded in large measure to serve the Lord, and has sent out the largest number of missionaries in modern times. In the past, at least, our moral standards were relatively high.[38]

Using the recurring complaint of conservative discourses that moral standards were higher in the past, a past identified as antedating "recent decades," Morris suggests that the main failing of the United States concerning God's requirements is on the "moral" level. This is reinforced by the idea that the "recent decades" to which he is referring have been marked by the sexual revolution and the women's liberation movement. Though he adds in the next paragraph that "our positions relative to all five of the criteria have badly declined",[39] he still puts the emphasis on the "moral" one, in most of his articles and in the remedies he offers against this decline.

As a solution to this crisis, and also to insure that the United States will be among the "chosen," he offers "true Biblical revival."[40] That is, a revival which must be based on creationism. As explained further above, for ICR analysts the Christian faith has been corrupted by evolution, as even part of the church adheres to it. But evolution is not only the cause of the collapse of morality. Using the contentious link between Darwinism and eugenics, they also add that with its defense of the notion of the "survival of the fittest" the theory of evolution is at the root of "racism, imperialism, and economic exploitation"[41] - and this in spite of the fact that conservative Christians have rarely convincingly opposed any of these.

Emphasising that calling for changes in law will not solve "moral problems" like abortion, homosexuality or suicide, ICR analyst Kenneth Ham concludes that

> [o]nly this realization - that all of Biblical doctrine has its foundation in the book of beginnings, the book of Genesis - will enable Christians to come back to the fulfillment of God's ultimate plan and purpose for mankind. The church will then return to the understanding of its moral values and responsibilities - that marriage means one man for one woman for life, that homosexual behavior is an abomination to the Lord, that the family is the first and most fundamental of all human institutions as well as the backbone of society, and that the immorality that is pervading the world today is causing a schism between God and man which can be healed only by a return to God's Word, beginning with the book of Genesis and continuing through the belief in the "one mediator between God and men, the man Christ Jesus" - I Timothy 2:5.[42]

Here again, the emphasis is put on sexual morality and the "collapse" of the "traditional family" as the core of the necessary Biblical Revival. In this quote, Ham raises the exact same concerns raised by pro-abstinence discourses: the challenge to the traditional family cell. Similar to the LaHayes' discourse, which explains that abstinence or "sexual purity and virtue" are the only way to fulfil God's "wonderful plan,"[43] for Ham fulfilling "God's ultimate plan"[44] means going back to a traditional vision of lifelong monogamous and heterosexual marriage.

To fulfil this plan, abstinence and creationism both work at the same level: education. The strategies used to promote creationism and abstinence are similar and are very much representative of the grassroots activism developed by conservative Christians. Advocacy groups for both causes advise their followers to act on the level of school boards by running for membership and lobbying for the censorship of explicit books, of sexual education programmes, or for the inclusion of creationist materials in biology courses. The ICR provides clear guidelines to its members. They first suggest that creationists should get information on which authorities in their state are responsible for decisions regarding school curriculum. Then, they should try to obtain permission to speak at the next board of education meeting.

> Finally, creationists should petition the state (or district) board of education to pass a resolution to teach both the scientific evidence for creation and the scientific evidence

for evolution, in any course dealing with origins. And creationists should request the state (or district) textbook commission to select only texts presenting both scientific creationism and evolution, or else to require supplements presenting scientific creationism to be attached to the inside back cover of texts presenting only evolution.[45]

The type of strategy offered by abstinence proponents is similar. They usually target either sexually "explicit" books in literature programmes, sex-education programmes and pedagogical tools. With these types of clear guidelines any convinced creationist, or abstinence proponent, can easily get involved in promoting his cause in his school district.

This method has been particularly efficient in the past thirty years; as in most cases proponents of comprehensive sex-ed and of evolution are much less organised and less systematically involved in school-boards. This type of local activity is in fact the major focus of Pat Robertson's Christian Coalition, one of the foremost conservative Christian organizations. Linda Kintz explains that

> [t]he Christian Coalition conducts School Board Training Seminars around the country, and in conjunction with those seminars publishes a sophisticated leadership manual that consists of the following sections: "Dealing with Teacher's Unions," "Education Reform and School Choice," [...] "Winning as a Religious Conservative," "Developing Your Campaign Plan and Message." Also available for purchase and use in one's church group are a set of videotapes entitled *Targeting Voters and Building Coalitions, Building an Effective Grassroots Organization, Developing Your Campaign Plan and Message,* [...][46]

Rebecca Hagelin, among others, is featured on one of these Christian Coalition tapes. It is this type of activism which regularly brings cases to federal courts where, for example, the creationist curriculum imposed by a local school-board is challenged by proponents of evolution.

Another type of activism is used at the national level by prominent think-tanks and organisations. However, so far, this strategy has been much more efficient for abstinence than for creationist education, which has been repeatedly declared unconstitutional by the courts. On the contrary, since the Reagan administration, abstinence has enjoyed an increased support from Republican Congresses and administrations which was translated in increased federal funding for abstinence-only programmes.

Creationism and abstinence proponents also put forward similar arguments to defend their position. Both argue that parents, not the federal state, have the right to decide what their children are being taught; and that sex education and evolution, by going against their religious and moral beliefs discriminates against them. This logic is well illustrated by the following quote from the ICR which argues that

> [t]he First Amendment of the Constitution protects free exercise of an individual's religion from government abridgment. [...] Abridgment of this constitutional right to religious freedom occurs when a governmental program puts a burden on religious exercise and when no compelling reason justifies that burden. [...] Classroom instruction that presents only evolution without an alternative theory puts a burden on religious freedom. Teaching only one theory of the origin of life and man indoctrinates creationist students in that evolutionary theory, and the Supreme Court has ruled that public schools cannot undermine religious beliefs.[47]

Abstinence proponents follow a similar line when they consider that sex-education in public schools draws their children to immoral behaviors and go against the moral and religious values of their families. The LaHayes even claim that in some cases school administrators and teachers force children to take sex education.[48] This assertion is questionable for, as W.S. Pillow underlined, "unlike many components of sex education courses, abstinence-only programmes require no notification to parents or permission from parents for their children to participate."[49] And yet in many cases the movies and pictures which abstinence-only programmes present of STD symptoms, for example, can be considered as "shocking" as images displayed in sexual education classes.

The idea that creationist and pro-abstinence parents and their children are being discriminated against, though questionable, carries a strong potential for mobilisation. This is well illustrated by Hagelin, who lyrically encourages her fellow conservatives to "commit to the daily battle" to defend their children against a "killer culture" which threatens Christian standards of morality, decency and faith.[50]

Reversing the terms of discourses is a crucial tool in conservative Christian strategy. In the same manner as they present themselves as pro-life or pro-family, instead of as anti-abortion or anti-gay, to give a more positive and inclusive connotation to their movement, they reverse the arguments of their opponents who consider them as discriminating against gays and women to put themselves in the position of the discriminated-against minority. Though conservative Christians often claim to be part of a "moral majority," the way they construct themselves as a persecuted minority whose values and beliefs are threatened by a "perverted" culture has been powerful and instrumental in their appeal. Thus, they draw a parallel between the persecuted Pilgrim Fathers who escaped England to redeem the Protestant faith, and themselves as a "righteous" persecuted minority which tries to save this Puritan heritage and preserve "traditional American values" through the promotion of creationism and abstinence.

Another interesting aspect of the conservative Christians' activism at the public school level is the fact that they loudly encourage parents to withdraw their children from public schools to put them in private schools or homeschool them. Consistent with their conservative advocacy of minimal state intervention, they argue that the state has no right to impose a certain type of education on children but that this choice belongs first and foremost to parents. Consequently, the Heritage Foundation, for example, advocates school vouchers to enable poorer parents to send their children to private schools if they want to. But if conservative Christians do not put their children in public schools, why then lobby for the inclusion of abstinence and creationism in those schools' programmes? Undoubtedly, one could argue that homeschooling and private schools are not necessarily a viable option for all parents and that some conservative Christians might have to send their children to public schools. Moreover, as Tim LaHaye argues, conservative Christians might also want to redeem what they think was formerly "the greatest educational system in the world",[51] which has now been "taken over by secularists."[52]

However, in light of the following quote from the Heritage Foundation, creationist and pro-abstinence activism at the public schools level take on another dimension:

> The greatest changes in policy occur because of fundamental changes in public attitudes. Therefore, the policymaker's foremost job is to be an entrepreneur of ideas. Once public attitudes are changed to support conservative policies, legislative passage becomes far easier. By contrast, legislative victories without a change in underlying ideas are likely to have a marginal effect. [Consequently] at least half of legislative proposals should be crafted exclusively with the intent of altering the terms of debate; actual passage of such proposals is not important.[53]

Likewise, local and national activism aiming at imposing the teaching of abstinence and creationism in public schools can be seen not only in terms of their actual efficiency but also in the way they alter the nature of debates on education. For creationism and abstinence are not only educational issues in their own right, but they also are both tools in the "culture war" waged by conservative Christians against what they define as "secular humanism" or "liberalism." Thus, both creationism and abstinence operate as ideological tools in the conservative Christian attempt to bring back religion in the schools and in politics on the state and federal levels. By advocating abstinence education programmes that promote a "restrictive" sexual ideology, as well as creationist teaching, conservative Christians influence school curricula by their religious beliefs. Moreover, the debates often generated by these attempts on local, national, educational or judicial levels, provide a public platform for their discourses which through carefully directed media exposure often make conservative Christians appear more numerous and powerful than they actually are. Thus, they strengthen their influence and visibility on the public stage through both creationism and abstinence discourses.

Finally, another important similarity between creationism and abstinence, which can help to account for their appeal, is the fact that they both provide "comforting" answers to fundamental human anxieties about life, love and happiness. The main contention of creationism is the faith in the inerrancy of the Bible. As explained in Chapter II, proponents of creationism believe that the Bible can only be true in its entirety, not only partly. Believing in creationism therefore ensures the credibility of the Bible even regarding the question of our origins. Thus creationism substitutes the "comforting" notion that humans and earth were created by a purposeful and loving God to the apparent arbitrariness of the answers provided by evolution to questions such as "'Who am I?' or 'Where do I come from?'"[54] Abstinence provides a similarly comforting pattern by ensuring its proponents that, by being abstinent, they will be sure to marry their "true love" with whom they will live "till death do they part," a life free of concerns like divorce, teen pregnancy or STDs. As W. S. Pillow argues,

> [a]bstinence-only programmes promise to offer a definitive answer to the problem of teen sexuality and teen pregnancy, to bring clarity to ongoing debates about sex education, and to address the decline of values and welfare dependency seen as rampant in some communities. The solution is simple, teach kids not to have sex until marriage.[55]

As will be further examined in the coming chapter, such unquestionable statements, like the religion to which they also belong, have a growing appeal in a postmodern society of uncertainties which fails to soothe the anxieties of individuals already weakened by difficult economic conditions and metaphysical uncertainty.

This chapter has shown that the rhetorical arguments deployed around the two conservative narratives of creationism and abstinence follow similar patterns and confirm each other. Both discourses reassert the authority of God and of the family over children. Creationism, in the way it is described as boosting self-confidence, is defined as an important tool in the prevention of premarital sex, while abstinence reinforces creationism by stating that Christians are children of God who should not defile their bodies by "fornication." They also both state forcefully the adamant difference of nature between animals and humans. Creationism and abstinence education are also used by conservative Christians as tools to counteract the decline of "traditional American values" through a pro-family agenda. They both operate, by using similar grassroots and national strategies, on the same level: education. Moreover, those two issues contribute to the instrumental self-representation of conservative Christians as a "persecuted minority" waging war to redeem America by bringing back religion to the school and the nation, and help them shift the public debate on education in a more religiously and conservatively oriented direction. Finally, creationist and pro-abstinence discourses answer postmodern anxieties about life, love and happiness by religious certainties. But what is more significant for this study is how the more recent conservative Christian discourse on sex-education and abstinence took over the older issue of creationism both to strengthen its own statements and to rejuvenate the creationist discourse. Thus, pro-abstinence discourses reinforce and give new appeal to the conservative Christian belief in creationism. Likewise, as will be examined in the next chapter, pro-abstinence discourse gives new dimension to teenager's and the community's need for faith, certainties and religious authority in postmodern American society.

Notes

1 LaHaye, 1998a, p.31.
2 In a Roundtable interview on August 1, 2005, President Bush answered the following to questions regarding the teaching of Intelligent Design and evolution: "THE PRESIDENT: [...] I felt like both sides ought to be properly taught. Q: Both sides should be properly taught? THE PRESIDENT: Yes, people - so people can understand what the debate is about. Q: So the answer accepts the validity of intelligent design as an alternative to evolution? THE PRESIDENT: I think that part of education is to expose people to different schools of thought, and I'm not suggesting - you're asking me whether or not people ought to be exposed to different ideas, and the answer is yes." *The*

Washington Post, 'Transcript of Roundtable Interview,' *Washington Post.com*. 2 August 2005, viewed on 27 February 2007, <http://www.washingtonpost.com/wp-dyn/content/article/2005/08/02/AR2005080200899_5.html>
[3] The Discovery Institute, to which most intelligent design proponents are affiliated, explains on its website that "the theory of intelligent design holds that certain features of the universe and of living things are best explained by an intelligent cause, not an undirected process such as natural selection" (www.discovery.org). On December 20, 2005, the United States District Court for the Middle District of Pennsylvania ruled in *Kitzmiller v. Dover Area School District* that teaching intelligent design violated the Establishment Clause of the First Amendment to the Constitution of the United States because it cannot be defined as science and "cannot uncouple itself from its creationist, and thus religious, antecedents," U.S. District Court for the Middle District of Pennsylvania, *Kitzmiller v. Dover Area School District: Memorandum Opinion*, 20 December 2005, viewed on 10 June 2007, <http://www.pamd.uscourts.gov/kitzmiller/kitzmiller_342.pdf>, p.136.
[4] R Hagelin, 'The Culture War: A Five-Point Plan for Parents,' 9 August 2005a, viewed on 15 February 2007, <http://www.heritage.org/Press/Commentary/ed080905a.cfm>
[5] LaHaye, 1998a, p.39.
[6] Hagelin, 2005a.
[7] The ICR defines itself as "an organization devoted to research, publication, and teaching in those fields of science particularly relevant to the study of origins" (www.icr.org). The position it defends is defined as "young earth creationism" and maintains that following Genesis the earth is not billion of years old but only thousands of years old (that it between 6000 and 10000 years).
[8] J Bergman, 'The Effect of Darwinism on Morality and Christianity,' June 2001, viewed on 19 June 2007, <http://www.icr.org/pdf/imp/imp-336.pdf>
[9] C Raymo, *Skeptics and True Believers*, Walker, New York, 1998, pp.187-188.
[10] Bergman, 2001.
[11] D Lecourt, *L'Amérique entre la Bible et Darwin*, Presses Universitaires de France, Paris, 1998, p.26.
[12] K Ham, "Back To Genesis' The Hope For America?' 7 April 1993, viewed on 15 February 2007, < http://www.icr.org/article/731/>
[13] H M Morris, 'The Gospel of Creation and the Anti-Gospel of Evolution,' 1 July 1975, viewed on 19 June 2007, <http://www.icr.org/article/71/>
[14] Lecourt, 1998, p.137.

[15] T LaHaye and D Noebel, *Mind Siege: The Battle for Truth in the New Millennium*, Word Publishing, Nashville, 2000, p.76.

[16] LaHaye, 1998a, p.39.

[17] ibid., p.39.

[18] ibid., p.39.

[19] ibid., p.23.

[20] ibid., p.23, author's brackets.

[21] ibid., p.23.

[22] ibid., p.20.

[23] ibid., p.40.

[24] Meeker, 2002, p.71.

[25] Meeker, 1999, p.ix.

[26] LaHaye, 1998a, p.32.

[27] J Morris, 'Are Schools Teaching Evolution Well Enough?' 1 June 1998, viewed on 19 June 2007, <http://www.icr.org/article/1181/>, emphasis in the original.

[28] Hagelin, 2005a.

[29] G Bhattacharyya, *Sexuality and Society: An Introduction*, Routledge, London and New York, 2002, p.105.

[30] Moran, 2000, p.6.

[31] Godbeer, 2002, p.55.

[32] LaHaye, 1998a, p.20.

[33] ibid., p.163.

[34] Fagan, 2006, p.7.

[35] *Personal Responsibility and Work Opportunity Reconciliation Act of 1996.*

[36] R Rector 'Implementing Welfare Reform and Promoting Marriage,' in S M Butler and K R Holmes (eds), *Priorities for the President*, 2001, viewed on 12 June 2007, <http://www.heritage.org/Research/Features/Mandate/upload/Priorities-for-the-President-pdf.pdf>, p.82.

[37] H M Morris, 'All Nations Under God,' October 2002, viewed on 19 June 2007, <http://www.icr.org/pdf/btg/btg-166.pdf>, emphasis in the original.

[38] ibid.

[39] ibid.

[40] ibid.

[41] Morris, 1975.

[42] Ham, 1993.

[43] LaHaye, 1998, p.23.

[44] Ham, 1993.

[45] W R Bird, 'Evolution in Public Schools and Creation in Student's Home: What Creationist Can Do (Part II),' 1979b, viewed on 18 June 2007, <http://www.icr.org/articles/all/2/>

[46] Kintz, 1997, p.73.

[47] W R Bird, 'Evolution in Public Schools and Creation in Student's Home: What Creationist Can Do (Part I),' 1979a, viewed on 18 June 2007, <http://www.icr.org/article/151/>

[48] LaHaye, 1998a, p.37.

[49] Pillow, 2004, p.183.

[50] Hagelin, 2005a.

[51] LaHaye and Noebel, 2000, p.100.

[52] ibid., p.102.

[53] Rector, 2001, p.90.

[54] LaHaye, 1998a, p.39.

[55] Pillow, 2004, p.183.

Chapter 7
Abstinence, Faith and Religious Authority

Religion is a need of the spirit. People feel so lost in the vastness of the world, so thrown about by forces they do not understand; and the complex of historical forces, artful and subtle as they are, so escapes the common sense that in the moments that matter only the person who has substituted religion with some other moral force succeeds in saving the self from disaster.[1]

In her introduction to the collection of essays *Media, Culture and the Religious Right*, Linda Kintz, drawing on sociologist John Fulton's analysis of the writings of the Italian political theorist Antonio Gramsci, highlights the sense of "agency" provided by religion and how Religious Right leaders understood and used it. One of the main contribution Kintz takes from Gramsci is the idea that he

> avoided the mistakes many Marxist analysts had made, as they too had often dismissed religious belief as unenlightened superstition and overlooked the powerful sense of agency such belief provided. As Fulton argues, Gramsci took seriously "*as a source of power*, the self-understanding of religious groups and the interpretations of the world in which those groups actualize their existence."[2,3]

Gramsci believed that

> [o]ver a certain period of history in certain specific historical conditions religion has been and continues to be a "necessity," a necessary form taken by the will of the popular masses and a specific way of rationalizing the world and real life, which provided the general framework for real practical activity.[4]

He specifies that it is not the official Christianity of the Church which can fulfill this need but what he defines as the "naïve Christianity"[5] of the people. In his view to succeed, new ideologies have to provide a replacement for this popular religion and follow the pattern used by Christianity to achieve hegemonic status.

The leaders of the Religious Right have not tried to replace religion but have instead used its "power," in particular the one derived from the strong emotional nature of evangelicalism, to build their appeal. This is often ignored by academics who dismiss religion as "unenlightened superstition."[6] Kintz remarks that Ralph Reed, former executive director of the Christian Coalition, learnt much from Gramsci.[7] She argues elsewhere that academics are often unable to understand the appeal of the Religious Right because they are

> not used to understanding beliefs that are not expressed according to [their] own scholarly expectations. By dismissing arguments that are not articulated in the terms with which [they] are familiar, [they] overlook the very places where politics come to matter most: at the deepest levels of the unconscious, in our bodies, through faith, and in relation to the emotions.[8]

In this she reflects Gramsci's idea that

> [t]he intellectual's error consists in believing that one [...] can be an intellectual (and not a pure pedant) if distinct and separate from the people-nation, that is, without feeling the elementary passions of the people [...].[9]

Conservative Christians understand this necessity to appeal to faith, feelings and passions in order to yield political power, a necessity analysed by Gramsci in the following terms:

> One cannot make politics-history without this passion, without this connection of feeling between intellectuals and people-nation. In the absence of such a nexus the relations between the intellectual and the people-nation are, or are reduced to, relationships of a purely bureaucratic and formal order; the intellectuals become a caste or a priesthood [...].[10]

This comment can be connected to the very strong trend of anti-intellectualism in American conservatism well exemplified by G.W. Bush's development of his image of simple "Texas cowboy" in spite of the fact that he comes from an old political family and attended an Ivy League school.

Talking about faith, sexuality and family life, conservative Christian leaders ground their discourse in this "passionate" dimension of daily life and "irrationality" instead of actually dealing with more structural and seemingly more remote questions like the economy or social policies. Through pro-abstinence discourses, for example, they construct sexuality as "sacred" and "divine" and use religion to both "rationalize" and elevate the human experience of sexuality. Contrary to the permissive sexual ideology which emphasises freedom of sexual choice rather than traditional morality, through the demand for abstinence and a narrow view of marriage they provide frames that allow conservative Christians to actualize their experience in their own spiritual terms. Abstinence can allow Christians to construct their sexuality in a way that is more relevant to their own experience of the world than that offered by a permissive sexual ideology.

The LaHayes and Meeker illustrate this process when they describe marital sexuality as a "sacred" experience. In the LaHayes' words sexuality is

> the sublime, intimate interlocking of mind, heart, emotions, and body in a passionately eruptive climax that engulfs the participants in a wave of innocent relaxation that thoroughly expresses their love. The experience is a mutual "knowledge" of each other that is sacred, personal, and intimate. Such encounters were designed by God for mutual blessing and enjoyment.[11]

Meeker also explains that "many teens describe sex as being spiritual. [...] Sex is sacred and something extraordinary, during which a connection occurs beyond human comprehension."[12]

In both their glorification of marital sex and their rejection of premarital sex, the LaHayes and Meeker inscribe themselves in a dichotomous vision of sexuality inherited from the Puritans, one very different, for example, from the traditional Catholic vision of sexuality. In his book *Sexual Revolution in Early America* historian Richard Godbeer explains that though Puritans condemned extramarital sex staunchly, they did hold a very positive view of marital sexuality. This contrasts with the vision of sexually repressed Puritans presented by authors like Nathaniel Hawthorne. However, Puritan teachers, Godbeer writes, did warn their pupils "that even marital sex could become illicit if a husband and wife allowed their desire for each other to eclipse their love of God."[13] In his view what Puritans tried to achieve was not

> to repress their sexual instincts but to keep them *within ordained borders*. Although determined to root out "wild love" as unruly and pernicious, they extolled love "of God's own planting" as one of humanity's greatest blessings. Even marital sex had the potential to become "wild" if not appropriately managed: all human affections

> must serve and remain subordinate to spiritual ardor. But a
> symbiotic passion for one's earthly spouse and heavenly
> bridegroom [Christ] was truly a "garden of love and garden
> joy."[14]

Contrary to the Catholic tradition, the Puritans did not extol chastity and disagreed with the idea that "marital sex constituted a necessary evil."[15] Moreover, they considered a fulfilling marital sexual life as the best prevention against extramarital sexuality. This idea of keeping sexuality "within ordained borders" is at the core of contemporary pro-abstinence discourses.

Through these discourses, conservative Christians define the borders within which sexuality can be practiced. For them, as already mentioned, the only appropriate frame for sexuality is a lifelong faithful heterosexual monogamous marriage. Within this union sexuality should be enjoyed, and some forms of contraception can be considered acceptable by some leaders, like the LaHayes. Outside of those borders fall all forms of extra-marital sexuality: premarital sex, infidelity, homosexuality and cohabitation. Divorce could also pose a significant problem; however, conservative Christian leaders tend not to stigmatise divorcees too openly, as doing so might alienate a significant proportion of their followers. Indeed, a 2004 poll led by the evangelical Barna Group found that

> [a]lthough many Christian churches attempt to dissuade
> congregants from getting a divorce, the research confirmed
> a finding identified by Barna a decade ago (and further
> confirmed through tracking studies conducted each year
> since): born-again Christians have the same likelihood of
> divorce as do non-Christians. Among married born-again
> Christians, 35% have experienced a divorce. That figure is
> identical to the outcome among married adults who are not
> born-again: 35%.[16]

Within the boundaries of abstinence and marriage, sexuality is coded as "sacred," "pure," "moral" and as an expression of "true love" and selflessness. Outside those boundaries it takes on the opposite connotations of "promiscuity" and "immorality" and of an expression of "lust" and "selfishness." Hence, sexuality within "traditional" marriage is defined as morally superior to any other form of sexuality, as it is seen as being the expression of God's will and not of human lust and selfishness, God being the only source of morality and not man himself. Besides, it is not only the morality of sexuality which is appraised here, but also the nature of the relationship expressed by it. As noted earlier, for conservative Christians,

"True Love Waits". A love which cannot abstain and wait to be expressed within the boundaries of marriage is not "true", but is in fact selfish and lustful. Hence, in the LaHayes' view, those who do not wait until marriage to have sex will perhaps not give up "true love", since such a statement would make "secondary virginity" irrelevant, but they at least give up the unique sexual communion intended by God for those who respect his will. Not being abstinent would thus "cheapen" their marital sexuality and make it incomplete forever. As the LaHayes sum it up,

> [p]remature sexual expression is the supreme example of sacrificing on the altar of the immediate that which is permanent. It may produce incomparable excitement and thrill for the moment, but in the long run it produces heartache, grief, and sometimes physical pain.[17]

Moreover, they note in *The Act of Marriage* that their findings on this issue in a survey that they compared with a poll by *Redbook Magazine* from 1975, show that premarital sex may hinder sexual adjustment and that Christians seem to have better sex than non-Christians.[18]

In the style of self-help books, abstinence can thus be seen as the surest method to follow to achieve "true love" and marital bliss. This idea is also reasserted by the CBAE extension of requirements of 2006, which repeatedly claimed that there is a direct correlation between sexual abstinence before marriage and marital happiness. For example, it demanded from its grantees that they teach "the importance of abstinence in the teen years to long-term healthy and happy marriages."[19] In a world where marital love, though threatened by divorce, is still seen by many as the ultimate path to happiness, such a certainty can indeed provide a significant sense of agency. Although the Catholic Church defines sexual boundaries in a similar way, its theologians only equate sexuality with "true love" when its procreative dimension is not counteracted. In stating that "*the two dimensions of conjugal union,* the unitive (sic.) *and the procreative, cannot be artificially separated* without damaging the deepest truth of the conjugal act itself"[20], the Catholic Church differs clearly from the LaHayes, who condone contraceptive use within marriage. Positions similar to that of the Catholic Church can also be found inside the conservative Christian community itself, thus emphasising that sexual boundaries are not universal even among conservative Christians.

To help their readers in locating these boundaries, the LaHayes provide an exhaustive description of what is and is not acceptable before and after marriage in matters of sexual practices. In *Raising Sexually Pure Kids* they define what they consider as being abstinence according to the Bible's teaching. For example, they warn teens about the "law of emotional progression" a concept they take from sex advisor George B. Eager.

According to Eager "when a guy and a girl spend time alone together, the relationship tends steadily to move toward greater physical intimacy."[21] In his view, echoed by the LaHayes, the point of "no-return" is reached when couples move from the "simple goodnight kiss" to "prolonged kissing."[22] If teens go beyond this point, he claims, they will inevitably have sex. From this, Eager and the LaHayes deduce that anything more sexual than a "simple goodnight kiss" is reserved to marriage, and to avoid temptation teens should avoid being alone together.

The proscription the LaHayes put on everything that follows this goodnight kiss is, quite logically, extended to homosexual acts, as they are condemned in the Bible and are completely outside the frame of marital sex - Leviticus 20:13. It is extended to masturbation as well.

Masturbation is a complex issue for the LaHayes. And it is, in their writings, made even more complex as they write that: "the Bible is silent on this subject; therefore it is dangerous to be dogmatic."[23] Yet the story of Onan - Gen 38, 8-10 - in the book of Genesis was often used to condemn masturbation, which owes its name "onanism" to this episode. Why the LaHayes do not use this story is confusing and is probably due to the fact that in their book they do not prohibit masturbation radically. After much consideration the LaHayes come to the conclusion that masturbation is not an acceptable practice for a Christian male for the following reason. First, masturbation involves lustful thoughts which are condemned by the Bible. Besides,

> [g]uilt is a universal aftermath of masturbation unless one
> has been brainwashed by the humanistic philosophy that
> does not believe in a God-given conscience or in right or
> wrong.[24]

This guilt will hinder the spiritual growth of the man who masturbates, just as premarital sex will. Masturbation is also a disincentive to marriage. A man who satisfies his sexual drives himself will not feel the need to marry for sexual fulfillment as strongly. The LaHayes argue that there are enough reasons not to marry (financial, social) in our society without adding this one to the list. For these reasons masturbation is also subjected to the requirement of abstinence.

By contrasting different Christian visions on masturbation, the LaHayes pragmatically moderate their interdiction through the conclusion reached by a group of youth pastors that

> if an unmarried man could masturbate for physical release
> only and without entertaining lustful thoughts, it should not

be prohibited or associated with guilt. Even then, it should
not become an addictive habit.[25]

But the door they open is indeed small as the ability of dissociating sexual
fantasies from masturbation seems very illusory. Here, their argument seems
to be more inspired by pragmatism than by theology, probably
acknowledging the difficulty even for Christian males not to resort to
masturbation in times of celibacy. This supposed biological need of an outlet
for the overstock of sperm stored in males' bodies is further acknowledged
by the LaHayes as they explain that God provided men with a "pure" way of
release through "wet dreams." Of course those wet dreams will most likely
be caused by a dream of a sexual nature, but

> [d]reams are subconscious, and a boy need not feel guilt or
> shame when this experience occurs for God knows he has
> no control over his brain while sleeping. However, he
> should be aware that sexually stimulating pictures, movies,
> or stories can create dreams that bring on these experiences
> more frequently.[26]

Echoing "secular" sexual advisors, the LaHayes recommend that
parents talk with their sons about "wet dreams" matter-of-factly, and explain
to them what God intended them for, so that they do not feel guilty about it.
However, their position on masturbation emphasises the fact that for them it
is not only the body which should be kept pure or "abstinent," but also the
mind which has to be kept clear of "lustful thoughts." Consequently, they
strongly condemn pornography as leading to lustful thoughts and - echoing
the arguments of some feminists - to rape and sexual abuse.

Nothing is written by the LaHayes about female masturbation. Most
likely because as women do not "store" sperm they do not have any
"biological need" for sexual release, thus masturbation can never be
considered acceptable, as it would not serve any other purpose than "lustful"
ones. In spite of the fact that the LaHayes explain to girls that not having sex
does not hurt a man physically, throughout their writing they still support the
idea that men have more intense sexual needs than women.

With *The Act of Marriage*, the LaHayes provide Christian readers
with another set of boundaries and recommendations to be applied after
marriage. Through both books they contribute to keeping the sexuality of
their readers and parishioners "within ordained borders." They provide them
with guidelines of what is, according to their faith, acceptable or not
regarding sexual behaviour, thus limiting the possibility for their readers to
negotiate their own relation to sexual morality. Yet if such a strict religious
frame can appear oppressive, one should not overlook its potentially

empowering dimension, as too many possibilities might sometimes prove more of a hindrance to freedom than boundaries that appear justified. Indeed, instead of losing time and energy pondering what one may or may not do in a realm of endless possibilities, abstinence provides clear frames grounded in faith and certainties. This can appear particularly valuable in a postmodern culture of relative sexual freedom where practices not so long ago deemed extreme, like sadomasochism or swapping, are openly represented in the media. For Christians who might feel alienated by such practices and media depiction, framing sexuality, as Rebecca Hagelin or the LaHayes do, by just stating that "sex outside of marriage is just plain wrong"[27] might help them cope with a deeply unsettling environment. Besides, by constructing marital sexuality as "sacred," abstinence can provide, for those who inscribe themselves within conservative Christian sexual boundaries, a reassuring sense of moral and emotional superiority in a postmodern world where hierarchies defined by gender and family roles are constantly redefined. It also provides for religious and conservative leaders the power to establish what is sexually acceptable or not regarding what they interpret as being God's law.

Defining the boundaries of sexual respectability has always been one of the key functions of abstinence before marriage. Through pro-abstinence discourses the authority of the church to celebrate marriage, which defines the threshold of "legitimate" sexual intimacy, is reasserted. Interestingly, this function was already at the heart of the debate on premarital sexuality in colonial America, a debate Puritans had themselves imported from England.

> Indeed, roughly one-fifth of English brides in the late sixteenth and early seventeenth centuries were already pregnant by the time they formally married. Widespread premarital intercourse did not represent a wanton rejection of moral propriety by ordinary people. Instead, it arose from a common belief that the boundary between illicit and licit sex was crossed once a couple became committed to each other. The Church of England, however, insisted that couples should remain abstinent until they were formally wed. Premarital intimacy had political as well as moral implications since it brought into question the authority of the local clergyman - and, by extension, the church as a whole - to control the moment at which a man and a woman became a couple.[28]

The stakes are the same today for abstinence proponents who claim the superiority of God over man and defend the view that it is not the individual who can decide what morally fits him/herself, but rather the Bible and religion, which are the sources of all morality. In this perspective, sexuality should only be marital and sanctioned by God and "His" church, through a sacrament performed by "His" minister.

With their definition of marital sex as "sacred," and thus part of a "spiritual" or religious experience, pro-abstinence discourses reassert the authority of religious leaders over sexuality. By promoting strict codes of sexual behaviors conservative Christian leaders emphasise the difference between their experience of religion and the one promoted by more "pick and choose" types of Christianity. They affirm their literal reading of the Bible and proclaim that the word of God cannot be adapted to fit one's life choices or inclinations. As mentioned earlier, such strict visions of religion can have a significant appeal in our societies, especially as some might see as incoherent the more liberal positions of many churches. It is understandable that some Catholics, for example, might feel alienated by congregations that lead a life far remote from the teaching of the Catechism. This might be why Catholicism, as well as Judaism and Islam, have seen in the past decades a significant development of their radical trends, be it the schismatic movement of Mgr Lefebvre or Salafism. By requiring their followers to be abstinent before marriage in order to obey God's law, religious leaders assert their faith as a source of unquestionable authority and truth, whereas more liberal trends might disturb followers in search of clear boundaries. This insistence on the non-negotiable dimension of religion is at the heart of a conservative Christianity grounded on the inerrant reading of the Bible.

The reinforcement of the authority of the church carried out by pro-abstinence discourses operates both on a spiritual and a pragmatic level. It reasserts not only the spiritual authority of the minister, but the necessity of his function and of his church, among other things, for the celebration of weddings. This more "material" reinforcement of the need for churches and ministers by pro-abstinence discourses is not limited to this but extends to numerous church initiatives and institutions, especially those concerned with children.

This is well illustrated by the LaHayes who, in a chapter entitled "How to Raise Virtuous Children," give a clear description of the role played by the church in keeping children abstinent. First of all, they advise parents to keep their children "active in a Bible-teaching church."[29] If the church they attend is not a "bible-teaching" one, that is one that teaches that the Bible is inerrant, then they should look for a new one to provide the best frame for their children to remain "virtuous." A church which does not interpret the Bible as inerrant might be too liberal regarding sexual boundaries, among other things. The LaHayes also add that parents should "never criticize [their] church within hearing of [their] children"[30] so as not to undermine its authority. In the same manner as parents should not contradict each other in front of their children they should not criticise their church thus establishing it as a key influence in their child's education. The LaHayes also recommend that parents attend religious services regularly and get involved in activities organised by the congregation, a necessary requirement for a church to have any lasting influence on its members. For the LaHayes there is a direct correlation between church attendance and other religious involvement and "promiscuity." Citing statistics claiming that church going youths are less sexually active, they conclude that,

> [e]vidently, the popularly quoted statistic that "51 percent of girls and 63 percent of boys" are sexually active in their teens is so high because many of these teens do not attend church.[31]

They strengthen this statement by the following "dramatic" comment:

> Many of those parents who lamented that they "lost their teens to the world," admitted they became careless about church attendance and involvement. Careless church attendance can be fatal to your children's lives.[32]

In this passage the LaHayes use a syllogism going along the following lines: teens who do not attend church regularly are more sexually active; many sexually active teens die from STDs; therefore many teens who do not attend church regularly will die from a STD. Moreover, one can infer that those odds are increased by other risk behaviors like drug use, etc, that teens who are "lost to the world" are, in the LaHayes' view, likely to practice. Though such reasoning can seem far-fetched, it is interesting to see the way the authors use it as a way to assert that church attendance is literally a matter of life and death, if not of eternal damnation.

Another crucial role of the church can be found in the opportunities it provides for young people to socialise with other Christians who share similar values through church youth groups or youth summer camps. The LaHayes encourage parents to keep their children active in religious groups which, consistently, are bound to be much less sexually oriented than secular environments, and where they will benefit from the teachings and influence of church leaders.[33] The idea that religious youths are less sexually active was supported by the governmental website 4parents.gov, which encouraged parents to keep their children active in religious activities as, it claimed, "teens who are actively involved in a religious organization, who study faith, and pray or worship are less likely to begin early sexual activity."[34]

Finally, the LaHayes advise parents to keep their children out of a public school system controlled by "secular humanists" who teach evolution, and sex-education and are "hostile" to religion and morals, and instead enroll them in Christian schools or homeschool them.[35] Here again one of the arguments is that "unquestionably Christian schools graduate more virgins than do public schools."[36]

Thus, through pro-abstinence discourses, the LaHayes reassert the role of the church in the community and reclaim the role of ministers as educators. This enables them to question the qualification of secular organisations dealing with children in matter of moral education and to attempt to attract more children in their sphere of influence. Advising parents that a religious environment will be more efficient in preserving their children's chastity and even their lives, they also seek to ensure that Christian children are exposed to an all-Christian environment and to enlarge their congregation. If they succeed this is likely to strengthen their influence over younger generations.

By appealing to a radical form of religion strongly grounded in a passionate reading of the scriptures, conservative Christian leaders have succeeded in gathering a significant number of followers. Pro-abstinence discourses play a role in this appeal on the one hand in the way they contribute to the self-definition of conservative Christians as being children of God and not the "random products" of evolution, and on the other hand by contributing to the "actualization" of their experience of sexuality. They do so by providing believers with narratives of human origins and of sexuality they can better identify with than the one offered by the media and popular culture.

The vision of sexuality they offer is inscribed in the Puritan heritage and does not present sexuality as an apparently limitless realm of possibilities but as a space clearly limited by moral and religious boundaries. Likewise, creationism leaves no place for doubt and provides clear-cut answers to metaphysical questions. Within these "ordained borders" conservative Christians can delineate what sexual and non-sexual practices are deemed acceptable or not and be reassured of what "true love" is and what ways and means will enable them to reach it and nurture it. It also provides them with the sense that their sexuality is not only the expression of their animal nature, but the sacred expression of a marriage blessed by God. A feeling of moral and religious superiority can be the outcome of such certainties. This delimitation of love and sexuality, while it can provide believers with a sense of "agency", also constitutes the appeal of conservative Christian leaders and reasserts their influence over their followers. Pro-abstinence discourses provide a practical reinforcement of those leaders' authority by reasserting the literally "vital" role of the church and religious infrastructures in the community and by reclaiming the role of church leaders as educators. They also reassert the need for a strong and respected church leadership which will have a lasting influence over the coming generations.

Notes

[1] A Gramsci, quoted in Kintz and Lesage, 1998, pp.18-19.

[2] J Fulton, 'Religion and Politics in Gramsci: An Introduction,' *Sociological Analysis*, 1987, 48 (3): 197-216, p.214.

[3] Kintz and Lesage, 1998, p.17.

[4] A Gramsci, *A Gramsci Reader*, David Forgacs, (ed), Lawrence and Wishart, London, 1999, p.337.

[5] ibid., p.337.

[6] Kintz and Lesage, 1998, p.17.

[7] ibid., p.17.

[8] Kintz, 1997, p.5.

[9] Gramsci, 1999, p.349.

[10] ibid., p.350.

[11] LaHaye, 1998b, p.26.

[12] Meeker, 2002, p.82.

[13] Godbeer, 2002, p.55.

[14] ibid., p.55, my emphasis.

[15] ibid., p.55.

[16] Barna Group, 'Born Again Christians Just As Likely to Divorce As Are Non-Christians,' 8 September 2004, viewed on 8 March 2006, <http://www.barna.org/FlexPage.aspx?Page=BarnaUpdateNarrow&BarnaUpdateID=216&PageCMD=Print>

[17] LaHaye, 1998a, p.45.

[18] LaHaye, 1998b, pp.32, 291.

[19] U.S. Department of Health and Human Services Administration for Children and Families, 2006a, p.11.

[20] Pontifical Council for the Family, 'The Truth and Meaning of Human Sexuality, Guidelines for Education within the Family,' 8 December 1995, viewed on 19 June 2007, <http://www.vatican.va/roman_curia/pontifical_councils/family/documents/rc_pc_family_doc_08121995_human-sexuality_en.html> , emphasis in the original)

[21] G B Eager *Love, Dating and Sex: What Teens Want to Know*, Mailbox Club Books, Valdosta, 1989, p.64.

[22] ibid., p.64.

[23] LaHaye, 1998a, p.105.

[24] ibid., p.105.

[25] ibid., p. 107.

[26] ibid., p.104.

[27] Hagelin, 2005b, p.149.

[28] Godbeer, 2002, p.3.

[29] LaHaye, 1998a, p.40.
[30] ibid., p.41.
[31] ibid., p.41.
[32] ibid., p.41.
[33] ibid., p.42.
[34] U.S. Department of Health and Human Services, *Parents, Speak Up! Guide for Discussing Abstinence Sex, and Relationships*, 2005a, viewed on 6 March 2007, <http://www.4parents.gov/downloads/parentguide.pdf>, p.4.
[35] LaHaye, 1998a, p.43.
[36] ibid., p.44.

Chapter 8
Abstinence and the Traditional Family Cell

Abstinence is often presented as being part of conservative Christians' "pro-family agenda," and rightly so, since pro-abstinence discourses play a crucial role in the promotion of the traditional family cell in the way they construct marriage as the only possible frame for sexuality and as the base of a healthy society. It is important to keep in mind that the major goal of abstinence education is not so much to forbid premarital sexual activity than to promote marriage and prepare young people to build traditional family structures.

This promotion of the traditional family is performed through two major types of arguments which, on the one hand present the patriarchal family cell as the only possible frame for keeping children abstinent before marriage, and on the other reassert the control of parents over children through the defense of the concept of "parental rights."

One of the central narratives of abstinence-only-before-marriage discourses is the reinforcement of the "fantasy" of the existence of a traditional family cell. The term "fantasy" is apt. As many scholars dealing with the Religious Right underlined, conservative Christian discourses surrounding the traditional family have always pointed toward an idealised past before the sexual and feminist revolution when the traditional "biblical" family was the accepted social norm. According to conservative Christians, to function in a "biblical" way the family has to follow the statement of St Paul that "the head of every man is Christ; and the head of the woman is the man; and the head of Christ is God" (1 Corinthians 11:3). However, this view of the patriarchal family structure as "biblical" has been questioned on several grounds. First, for its historical inaccuracy, which underlines its fantastical nature, sociologist Janice M. Irvine explains that

> the "traditional family" that is so celebrated by conservatives and fundamentalists is less than historically accurate. It is [...] a nostalgic and idealized late nineteenth-century middle-class family in which men and women operated in "separate spheres."[1]

Secondly, this vision has been criticised for its interpretation of the view of the family developed in the Bible. As theologian Rosemary Radford Ruether explains

> "family values" is a misleading and partisan term, used by groups that champion a particular model of family - specifically, one based on male headship and female

subordination. These groups assume that their model of the family is biblical. But actually there is little relationship between this model and the Bible: the historical Jesus in fact appears quite often to have endorsed views that might be characterized as anti-family.[2]

Further on, she explains that the modern nuclear family composed of father, mother and children living together under the same roof did not exist in biblical times, when people lived in "households" that also included other kin, like grandparents, as well as servants and slaves.

In spite of these historical inaccuracies, Irvine notes that the concept of "family values" and the support of the traditional family unit constitute a useful rhetorical tool for conservative Christians.[3] Instead of formulating the opposition to gay rights, feminism and teen sex in negative terms - anti-gay, anti-feminist, anti-sex education - it groups those issues under the positive term of "pro-family," a similar rhetorical strategy as turning "anti"-abortion into "pro"-life. Thus, pro-abstinence activism, instead of being an anti-sex-before-marriage movement, falls under the more positive umbrella of the defense of "family values."

One of the key functions of abstinence-before-marriage is the external control of the sexual life of the human individual. As mentioned earlier, this had already been the issue at stake in debates around premarital sexuality in colonial America, where religious authorities used marriage to establish their power in determining sexual legitimacy. The *Personal Responsibility and Work Opportunity Reconciliation Act of 1996*, supported by a Republican Congress and reauthorized in 2003, required abstinence programmes funded by the government to teach that "a mutually faithful monogamous relationship in context of marriage is the expected standard of human sexual activity."[4] With this statement, all forms of extra-marital sexuality were defined as illegitimate. This did not only include sexually active teenagers, but also cohabiting couples as well as gays and lesbians, and extra-marital relationships involving married persons. Marriage, sanctioned by the state or the church, was thus defined as superior to any other form of relationship involving sexuality. The same text also claimed that "marriage is the foundation of a successful society"[5] a statement echoed by the Heritage Foundation on its website.

For the Bush administration, as well as the Heritage Foundation, even cohabitation, which in most cases corresponds to an unofficial form of marriage, was defined as not being good enough, as it

> is not equivalent to marriage in promoting the well-being of children. [For] by the time they reach age 16, three quarters of children born to cohabiting parents will see their parents

separate, compared to only about one third of children born to married parents. In the last decade, the proportion of cohabiting mothers who eventually marry their child's father fell from 57 percent to 44 percent.[6]

Additionally,

> children growing up without a married mother and father are about twice as likely to drop out of school, over 50 percent more likely to have a child themselves as a teenager, and over 50 percent more likely to abuse controlled substances. As adults, they are over 30 percent more likely to be both out of school and out of work, and tend to have less stable relationships.[7]

On the contrary, "two-parent, married families represent the ideal environment for raising children"[8] who will be "less likely to be depressed, to have difficulty in school, to have behavior problems, or to use marijuana."[9] In the extension of the requirements for CBAE grantees abstinence-only-education programmes are clearly envisaged as "marriage training" programmes by requiring applicants to "teach abstinence in preparation for marriage"[10] and to

> equip participants with skills and knowledge that give them a greater capacity to develop both healthy relationships in the short-term and healthy marriages in the long-term.[11]

Thus, abstinence-only-before-marriage education was, and still is, at the centre of the conservative strategy of promotion of the traditional family cell as it provides an incentive to marriage by constituting it as the only possible frame for sexual expression and reproduction and by coding extra-marital sex as morally wrong. An example of this is given by the governmental website 4Parents.gov, which repeatedly disqualified premarital sex as being a "poor sexual decision"[12] and abstinence as the "best choice emotionally and physically for all teens"[13] as it develops values such as "respect, responsibility, and self-control."[14] Moreover, the site encouraged parents to tell their children that in addition to protecting them from STDs and teen pregnancy, abstinence also allows them to avoid worrying "that the person they are dating is only interested in them because of sex."[15] Through such assertions, premarital sex was equated with lust and irresponsibility. These types of statements coming from the government were problematic as they disqualified the experience of many citizens as "immoral." Moreover, they could be deeply traumatic for youths who might have intended to remain abstinent but had been sexually abused.

The 4Parents website even went as far as asserting that married people "enjoy a better sex life,"[16] yet they did not specify if those same married people had been abstinent before marriage. This argument coming from the government might appear surprising and rather out of place, as it confuses positions of public health with sex advice. Obviously, this discourse contradicts the cliché that sexual pleasure in marriage is killed by the routine of the every day and parenthood. The idea that married people have better sex than the rest of their non-married fellow citizens, though it might be statistically true, appears in this context to be a direct confirmation of the conservative Christian claim that marital sexuality is superior. It underscores the LaHayes' and mid-20th-century belief that premarital sexuality might hinder sexual adjustment in marriage,[17] a view also promoted by the CBAE extension which, for example, required programmes to teach that:

> [N]on-marital sex can undermine the capacity for healthy marriage, love and commitment. [...] non-marital sex in teen years may reduce the probability of a stable, happy marriage as an adult. [...] premarital sexual activity can create a pattern of relationship instability.[18]

In addition to this the LaHayes claim that premarital sex reduces incentive to marry since "a realized need is a demotivator."[19] After having had sex with a woman, they argue, a man will not see the necessity of marrying her anymore.[20] Through such statements, they reinforce the patriarchal cliché of men being reluctant to get "trapped" into marriage and being primarily interested in the sexual dimension of the couple relationship. In short, pro-abstinence discourses construct chastity as an incentive to marriage, defining it as the only appropriate and most gratifying space of sexual expression.

Pro-abstinence discourses promote the traditional family cell by resorting to another argument, the need for increased parental involvement. As mentioned above, marriage is seen by conservative Christians as the ideal living arrangement for raising children, especially as it ensures a greater emotional stability through the presence of both parents. One of the issues addressed by pro-abstinence discourses, which today is at the heart of the conservative rhetoric, is the need for more parental authority and involvement in their children's lives. This need for parents to be the providers of frames and boundaries is, in the view of conservative Christians, crucial in abstinence education, as teenagers need clear guidelines and boundaries to help them resist the messages of sexual promiscuity they are bombarded with in contemporary American society.

Conservatives are not the only ones to underline the relevance of frames and parental involvement after the cultural revolution of the 1960s and its denunciation of the oppressive nature of the traditional family cell. In her work *The Body Project, An Intimate History of American Girlhood*, historian and women's studies professor Joan Jacobs Brumberg provides the following comment:

> According to Tufts University psychologist David Elkind,[21] our current postmodern style of family nurturance pays little deference to the old ideal of protecting children from life's vicissitudes or adult knowledge. Today's "harried parents" expect their "hurried children" to be autonomous, competent, and sophisticated by the time they are adolescents. This pseudo-sophistication leads adults to abandon the traditional position of setting limits and forming values, particularly in matters of sex, that characterized previous generations of parents, teachers and female mentors. Adolescents raised in this permissive environment become extremely stressed precisely because they have been denied a comfortable envelope of adult values that allows them time to adjust emotionally to their developing bodies and new social roles.[22]

In a note on this comment, Brumberg adds that "Elkind proposes that we raise some kind of protective structure once again, a suggestion that echoes conservative critics."[23]

Indeed, Meg Meeker does offer a similar view when she states that

> [m]any parents of our generation give too much freedom too soon to our kids because we want to teach them autonomy. While your intentions may be rooted in love, your teen feels just the opposite - that he is unloved. Remember, *rules and boundaries make teens feel loved*. Parents who abandon too many rules too quickly communicate to their kids that the teens are adult enough to make all their own decisions. Thus, teens begin acting in "adult" ways. To them, this means drinking, doing drugs, and having sex.[24]

Though Meeker's statement may seem exaggerated when she argues that a liberal upbringing will inevitably lead teens to "drinking, doing drugs, and having sex," she does strike a chord especially in a contemporary US society which views teens' attitudes and behavior in rather negative terms. For example, the 1999 study *Kids These Days '99: What Americans Really Think About the Next Generation*, led by the polling organization Public Agenda underlined that most Americans

> are deeply disappointed with "kids these days." More than seven in ten adults resort to words such as "rude," "irresponsible," and "wild" to describe today's teens, and more than half also describe young children disapprovingly. On the whole, high hopes for kids are wanting - no more than two in five adults, parents or teens themselves say youngsters today will grow up to make America a better place.[25]

Yet, sociologist Susannah R. Stern nuances this view by quoting studies which show that although

> some teens may admittedly deserve this characterization, many - if not most - do not.[26] In fact, today's adolescents are highly ambitious and conscientious, with the majority engaged in work, community service, and extracurricular activities, and most aspiring to earn college degrees.[27,28]

Nevertheless, the Public Agenda study also found that a majority of Americans blame parents rather than "social forces" for what they see as the "bad" behavior of children. In their view, most parents "have children before they are ready," divorce too hastily "without regard for their kids," "equate buying things for kids with caring for them"[29] and do not behave as appropriate role models. Hence, the conservative view that "kids today" behave badly and that a lack of parental involvement and parental authority is the source of this problem meets important anxieties of a majority of Americans, conservatives as well as liberals. Since, as liberals tend not to address the traditionally conservative issue of parental authority and are seen as the cause of the weakening of this authority since the 1960s, they leave free play for conservatives to appropriate this important issue.

The fact that many parents, though wanting to get involved, might be prevented to do so by the demands of the job market is not considered by conservatives who defend the traditional model of the male breadwinner and stay-at-home mother, a model which is not accessible to most Americans anymore. Thus, in a pattern typical of conservative policies, a situation caused by economic and social circumstances is blamed on individual shortcomings. This way, Meeker, the LaHayes, and Hagelin, like the Bush administration when it was in office, use pro-abstinence discourses as tools to reassert a conservative vision of parenthood and of the family which, though probably too strict and inaccessible for many Americans, does address crucial needs of contemporary teenagers and feeds on the feelings of guilt and inadequacy harbored by their parents.

Rebecca Hagelin skillfully taps those concerns when she exhorts parents to spend more time with their families.

> Our instincts tell us that individuals who live in loving families that spend time together make for better individuals - but how many of us actually *live* like we believe it? How many moms and dads have forgotten that what kids really want isn't another television or more "stuff"; what they *really* want - and need - is time with *you*. The trips don't have to be expensive or filled with endless planned activities and tours, and the meals don't have to be fancy. They just have to *be*. Whether it's taking the time for a walk in the park or a picnic, biking, or doing something a bit more [un]conventional like providing the perfect environment for apple-bomb wars, you'll be instilling in your children loving memories, values and a sense of security.[30]

According to Hagelin what children need are not "more things" but more parental presence. For, as both Meeker and the LaHayes explain, "children who go home after school to an empty house,"[31] often due to parents' long working hours and the fact of working mothers, are too much left to their own devices and can easily be exposed to bad influences.

One of the most noticeable consequences of this lack of supervision is, in the LaHayes' and in Meeker's view, the loss of either chastity or "reputation" that this will almost inevitably cause

> [u]ntended homes, due to both parents working, provide a dangerous environment that is [...] conducive to "making out" and [...] inciting to sexual relations [...]. Such places should be expressly off limits even for the most trustworthy teens. The Bible instructs us to "avoid every kind of evil" - 1 Thessalonians 5:22. Two teens of the opposite sex in an empty house may not misbehave, but their unsupervised presence together could ruin their reputations and should be expressly forbidden.[32]

The Department of Health and Human Services, in the booklet *Parents, Speak Up! Guide for Discussing Abstinence, Sex, and Relationships* available at 4Parents.gov, expressed the same concerns by telling parents that "'first sex' often happens in an unsupervised area of the house."[33] It is therefore necessary for parents to organize their time so that this cannot happen even if this means, as Jerry Falwell suggested as early as 1981 in his book *Listen, America!*, to buy fewer "things" and to give up one salary:

> Many women today say they must work for economic reasons. Although inflation has placed a financial burden on the family, we are overly concerned about materialistic wealth. Many Americans consider it more important to have several cars in the driveway, a beautiful house, and two color television sets than have a stable home environment for their children.[34]

Consistent with a conservative perspective, Falwell implies that the salary to be given up should be that of the mother, who should return to her traditional role as housewife and nurturer, reasserting in the process the status of her husband as breadwinner. Rebecca Hagelin, as well, likes reminding her readers that "mothers and fathers are not so interchangeable as we moderns would like to believe"[35] and of the importance for women of "putting marriage and motherhood"[36] above their career. Further on, she thanks Beverly LaHaye for providing her in 1987, at a time when this was not common, with the opportunity of telecommuting. This did not entail giving up her salary and her job at Concerned Women for America, but rather allowed her to be at home to take care of her children.

Conservatives blame feminism for the breakdown of the traditional family and the increasing numbers of mothers working outside the home. However, it is not so much the wish of women to emancipate economically, but the current capitalist and "liberal" economy that conservatives promote which makes it less and less affordable for most women to stay at home or for fathers to work less. Contrary to Falwell's assertion of in the 1980s, it is not merely a matter of sacrificing material luxuries, but of survival. In her book *Marriage, a History*, historian Stephanie Coontz comments on a statement of sociologist Frank Furstenberg that

> "it's as if marriage has become a luxury consumer item, available only to those with the means to bring it off. Living together or single-parenthood has become the budget way to start a family."[37] At the very least, marriage is now a discretionary item that must be weighed against other options for self-protection or economic mobility.[38]

In view of this, the traditional family might well not be fit anymore, if it ever was, to solve the problem of the isolation of children after school.

Nevertheless, here Falwell, Hagelin, Meeker and the LaHayes strike an essential point in a time of economic uncertainty when people tend to turn themselves back more and more to their family, the only environment that still seems able to provide them with a sense of recognition and security. Moreover, for today's adults, who increasingly come from divorced families with two working spouses, the fantasy of an ideal traditional family cell that they will succeed in maintaining contrary to their parents, can become increasingly attractive. Linda Kintz highlighted that:

> The ability to mobilize a coherent symbolic message that is passionately grounded in one's family experiences (or at least in one's longing for such intimate and secure family experiences) has been central to the power of [religious conservative] discourse that elides the fact that most families are excluded from its terms [...].[39]

Additionally, the economic impossibility for most young American women today to become housewives even if they wanted to might contribute to an idealisation of this role in contrast to the criticism of feminists since the sixties.

Characteristically, the reassertion of traditional gender roles found in pro-abstinence discourses not only concerns the division of parenting and economic tasks but also the global vision of society of conservative Christians. For abstinence proponents, patriarchal gender roles are necessary to the family equilibrium and a proper development of the child into a chaste teenager. All of the abstinence discourses studied in this book are addressed to both boys and girls. Nevertheless, under this apparent gender neutrality, they all more or less overtly reinforce traditional notions of gender. The necessity for pro-abstinence discourses to promote traditional gender roles is grounded in the fact that for them gender equality and feminism are undermining the appeal of traditional heterosexual marriage. Since the major goal of abstinence discourses is the reinforcement of the latter, the theme of traditional gender roles is necessarily one of its important components.

In the section of her book *Shaking the World for Jesus: Media and Conservative Evangelical Culture*, investigating Christian teen magazines, media studies professor Heather Hendershot notes that similarly to what is often found in secular culture, it is only at puberty that children start to be targeted as "separate species" by conservative Christian media.[40] The LaHayes actually underline gender differences in much younger children as well, but it is really at the beginning of adolescence that they recommend clearly separate teachings for boys and girls in matters of sexuality and different rules concerning dating. Part 3 of their book "How To Teach Your Teens To be Sexually Pure" is divided into parallel sections devoted to girls and boys like "Mother's questions to daughters"[41] or "What boys need to know before they start dating."[42]

The picture of gender roles drawn by the LaHayes, Meeker, Hagelin and the programmes evaluated by the Waxman Report is one directly inherited from the 19th century middle-class theory of the separate male and female spheres. A striking example of this is given by the LaHayes in *Raising Sexually Pure Kids* when they state:

> [G]irls are romantic. From early childhood, their fantasies are of Prince Charming and motherhood, not sex. Ask a five-year-old girl playing with her dolls what she wants to be when she grows up and she will probably say, "a mommy." She automatically thinks of family and childhood. Ask a five-year-old boy, and his answer will almost never be "a father." He thinks in vocational terms of being a fireman, a policeman, or a ball player.[43]

In the LaHayes' view girls naturally know from an early age that the sphere to which they belong is the domestic sphere and their main roles those of nurturers and caretakers. Conversely, boys know "instinctively" that they belong to the public sphere and have to focus on a career that will enable them to fulfil their roles as breadwinners. The fact that those differences might be socially learnt, for example by inducing girls to play with "dolls," and not "natural," is to the LaHayes no more than liberal and feminist "propaganda."[44] For them gender differences and sexual roles are given by God[45] and it is against nature to upset them.

In the above quote, the LaHayes also imply that contrary to boys, girls are romantic and not primarily attracted by sex but by love and motherhood. This view was also reasserted by the CBAE extension which recommended that abstinence-only programmes teach students that "males and females may view sex, intimacy, and commitment differently."[46] The Waxman Report also contained a section citing programmes which promoted "stereotypes that reinforce male sexual aggressiveness."[47] In a passage devoted to teenagers and puberty, Meg Meeker echoes the LaHayes where she states that when

> teens begin to mature sexually, they feel confused about what to do with the strong, unfamiliar sexual feelings washing over them. Boys begin trying to define their own masculinity, comparing it to other boys around them and wondering if they "measure up." Too often, however, they define masculinity as sexuality. Girls begin to fantasize about romance, and use clothing, makeup, and perfume to

define their own femininity. And, too often, these accoutrements become tools to attract the opposite sex, to feel "sexy," to lead to sex.[48]

In her presentation of puberty and the emergence of sexual feelings, Meeker presents sexual activity as something that comes to girls from the outside. It is something they are led to doing by the media and boys or to gain peer approval, not because they feel a strong physical pressure. On the contrary, boys are presented as having "tremendous sexual urges."[49]

Similarly to the LaHayes in *Raising Sexually Pure Kids*, Meeker also completely omits female masturbation, although she does treat the question of male masturbation. This omission is rather coherent in a perspective which considers females as always associating romance and feelings to sexuality. Indeed, the admission that a woman masturbates, i.e. seeks sexual pleasure for its own sake, makes it more difficult to argue categorically that women are first and foremost interested in romantic love and relationships rather than sex. Besides, the possibility that women might seek men for the sole purpose of sexual gratification, like males are assumed to do, destabilises the image of the stable female to whom the fickle male will attach himself for life and who will civilise him by forcing him into monogamy.

This alleged sexual aggressiveness of the male, in spite of its threatening dimension, is associated to his role as leader and protector of his wife. Yet the idea of a man who, while he is supposed to be the responsible head of his family, is completely controlled by his sexual urges, which only marriage can tame, appears somewhat paradoxical. In her insightful book *Fatherhood Politics in the United States: Masculinity, Sexuality, Race, and Marriage*, sociologist Anna Gavanas provides an interesting analysis of this phenomenon within what she defines as the "pro-marriage" branch of the fatherhood movement.[50] This trend defends ideas similar to those of the Heritage Foundation. It has also been closely connected to the Bush administration and abstinence-only programmes through Wade Horn, the co-founder of the Fatherhood Initiative and prominent member of the marriage movement who, as Secretary for Children and Families at the Department of Health and Human Services, oversaw the administration of abstinence programmes from 2001 to 2007. Gavanas argues that as long as it is channeled through heterosexual marriage the Fatherhood Movement considers men's aggressive heterosexual sexuality as a positive force, which defines them as "real men" in opposition to women or gay men. In the tradition of a restrictive sexual ideology, they contend that when it is not channeled, men's sexuality leads to social disorder. Thus unmarried men are a threat to society as they might become sexual predators and delinquents. Consequently, Gavanas explains, marriage proponents, like the LaHayes and the famous Christian male organization Promise Keepers, advocate marriage in order to contain male sexuality through sexual restraint and their responsibilities as husbands and fathers. Such reasoning provides further ground for a traditional vision of marriage and its promotion through abstinence discourses.

Two other types of "deviant" men coexist along with the aggressive single man: the gay man and what Gavanas refers to as the "androgynous" man. By questioning traditional gender roles, these men, together with feminists, endanger the role of the father by making him redundant. Gavanas underlines that for marriage proponents if men are not manly anymore and merge their roles with female roles they will become superfluous. Paradoxically, marriage proponents argue that males need to be "domesticated" to channel their sexual aggressiveness but not so much as to become "sissified."[51] Therefore, the role they have to play in the family is one that is appropriately male and not feminised, for example by practicing "sport, religion, or other 'manly' activity"[52] and recreating a male culture of their own. The notion that parenthood does not need to be divided along strict gender lines is particularly threatening for conservative Christians, since it provides a ground for defending gay or single parenthood as not constituting any threat for the proper development of the child.

Emphasising the strict gender roles promoted by pro-abstinence discourses, the Waxman Report quoted a government funded abstinence-only-education curriculum which listed "'Financial Support' as one of the '5 Major Needs of Women,' and 'Domestic Support' as one of the '5 Major Needs of Men.'"[53] In spite of the fact that female salaries can no more be considered today as "pin money" but are indispensable to maintaining many families' middle-class status, pro-abstinence discourses continue to present the function of the wife as being primarily that of a stay-at-home mother. In doing so they reassert the unique and irreplaceable nature of the male contribution to the household and favor a family structure which precludes divorce by strengthening female financial dependency. Since female employment increased divorce rates by providing women with the possibility to financially afford divorce, conservatives deduce that divorce can best be fought by depriving women of any personal income. By reinforcing, through pro-abstinence discourses, the stereotypes of the family as being constituted of a male breadwinner and a housewife, conservative Christians attempt to influence the coming generation into practicing their vision of traditional marriage.

In a passage worth quoting at length Hagelin evokes similar concerns when she claims that the

> diabolical teachings of the radical feminist movement, [...]
> have robbed our society of many of the blessings God

intended for us to enjoy. The embracing of the selfish
"blame the male," "get out of my way" attitude by the
popular media and an entire generation of women has
directly contributed to the breakup of the traditional family
unit. Instead of teaching the values of courage, forgiveness,
commitment, and honor, the radical feminist movement and
many in the media force-feed America's young women
destructive attitudes of selfishness and disrespect for men
and each other. In so doing, the movement now bears much
of the responsibility for having driven many males from
their traditional role as caretakers, causing much confusion
about exactly how they should approach and treat females.
A natural regression in male attitudes about courtesy and
responsibilities began when the feminists started attacking
them. What once was seen as a service and a courtesy - the
simple act of a man opening the door for a woman -
became an action man had to carefully consider. Soon, the
question of "Do I open the door?" digressed to "Do I really
have to work hard and offer my wife the opportunity to stay
at home with our children?" which further digressed to "Do
I have an obligation to stick around and help raise the
kids?" And who is suffering most from the destruction of
the family caused by the feminist movement? The young
women of today.[54]

In this scathing quote, Hagelin presents an interesting vision of men and
young women as "victims" of radical feminism in particular and second-
wave feminism in general. The image she paints of the movement underlines
what she considers as its lack of "moral values" like "courage, forgiveness,
commitment, and honor" and its selfishness. In her view, by demanding
gender equality and thus denying the "natural" differences between men and
women feminists drove men to forsaking an active role in the family. She
consequently constructs men as victims who "naturally" fled the house when
asked to perform roles that were not gender-appropriate. Like the pro-
marriage wing of the fatherhood movement, she demands that men be given
back a "manly" role in the family to curb its breakup.

The theme of men and particularly fathers being demeaned and
undervalued by today's society is recurring in conservative discourses and is
interestingly the topic of Meeker's third book *Strong Fathers, Strong
Daughters, 10 Secrets Every Father Should Know* (2006). It even evolved in
a worrying trend which through pro-abstinence discourses promotes father-
daughter bonding as the most important link in girl's lives to the exclusion of
mothers. Such attitudes culminate in the successful "purity balls,"[55] created

in 1998 by the evangelical Wilson couple, where fathers take their daughters to a ball where they pledge to protect their purity by being themselves models of integrity and chastity. The girls also implicitly take a chastity pledge on this occasion. While the fact that fathers thus appropriate their daughter's sexuality can appear problematic and archaic, the incestuous implications of the ceremony and of the insistence on the father-daughter bond are also disturbing. These balls, in which mothers do not take part, consist in the pledge, a dance between father and daughter, but also in many cases in the gift of a ring to the young woman by her father, making the whole ceremony evocative of a wedding in which the daughter gives up to her father the sexual agency she will later give up to her husband. In this case, the attempt by conservative Christians to reassert the influence of the father through abstinence discourses as the leader of his family appears to reach potentially dangerous extremes. This is particularly concerning in view of a recent complaint filed with the Inter-American Commission on Human Rights against the United States by a group of mothers and their children, accusing US courts of a failure "to protect the life, liberties, security and other human rights of abused mothers and their children" by "frequently awarding child custody to abusers and child molesters."[56] Paradoxically, while the menace constituted by of an oversexualised society, pedophiles and child abductors has been exacerbated by US media, the much more real question of the role of fathers in child abuse appears to be minimised for the sake of the preservation of the model of traditional fatherhood.

Another danger of feminism and liberalism presented in detail by the LaHayes in *Raising Sexually Pure Kids* is "sex-role confusion,"[57] that is homosexuality, to which Tim LaHaye devoted a whole book: *The Unhappy Gays: What Everyone Should Know About Homosexuality* in 1978. For the LaHayes individuals are not "born" homosexuals, on the contrary "heterosexuality is God's design; homosexuality an abomination or a perversion of that design."[58] In their view homosexuality can be caused by either the absence or lack of connection with the parent of the same sex as the child or the dominance of the parent of the opposite sex which can lead to wrong gender identification, which in both cases amounts to a disruption of the script of the traditional family. Hence, the LaHayes deduce that the best way to "protect" a child from homosexuality is to bring him/her up

> in a Christian home where the father is the loving head of the home, where the mother is supportive of the father's role, and where both parents have a warm and affectionate relationships with their sons and daughters.[59]

In short, according to the LaHayes, if children are raised in a non-traditional family they will run the "risk" not only of being sexually active before marriage but "worse," of becoming gay.

For the LaHayes, homosexuality is necessarily caused by abnormal circumstances, either sexual abuse or homosexual influences. It is not presented as a free choice but a state induced by pressure, the media or the permissive sexual ideology of public schools. Through their construction of homosexuality, or "gender confusion," as abnormal, the LaHayes reinforce the idea that gender roles are natural and God-given. In their view, upsetting these can only lead to "negative" consequences like homosexuality, the breakdown of the traditional family and even child abuse. The LaHaye's pro-abstinence discourses are not the only ones to reject homosexuality; abstinence-only discourses in general by the emphasis they put on pre-*marital* chastity systematically exclude homosexual teenagers from their terms.

In *Raising Sexually Pure Kids*, the LaHayes' claim that the breakdown of the family as well as the delaying of marriage also account for the aggravation of child sexual abuse, as "the present generation [has] more single men than any other generation in history."[60] If men lose interest in a family in which they are made to feel redundant by the lack of gender specific tasks that they alone are able to fulfil, then their sexuality, no longer channeled by matrimony, will inevitably wreak havoc in society.

A feminist perspective would argue that the main beneficiaries of the reinforcement of gender roles promoted by pro-abstinence discourses are males. Yet as illustrated by Hagelin, conservative Christians argue that feminism also harmed women and that they would have much to win from a reestablishment of gender differences. In particular they would benefit from a renewed involvement of males in family life as argued by the fatherhood movement and the Promise Keepers among others. The comforting dimension of strict gender roles in a postmodern society where certainties are collapsing and boundaries are blurred should not be underestimated first and foremost for men, but also for women who might find more reassuring to be "led" by their husband than living up to the independence ideal promoted by feminism. A decade ago, sociologist Judith Stacey expressed the same idea when she wrote: "it is unsurprising [...] that so many today indulge fantasies of 'escaping' from freedom and succumb to the alluring certainties of family-values pieties."[61] Yet even in view of this, it is important to keep in mind the potentially damaging effects, especially for young women and gay teens, of such discourses.

The reinforcement of the "fantasy" or "narrative" of the traditional family cell is at the heart of pro-abstinence discourses. Similarly to the interaction between pro-abstinence discourses and discourses on creationism, discourses on the traditional family and on abstinence reinforce each other in a circular pattern. If the traditional family is required to raise abstinent children, pro-abstinence discourses are also required to uphold the traditional family structure. Pro-abstinence discourses contribute to the construction of marriage as a morally and emotionally "superior" frame for sexual activity and for the upbringing of children as well as the promotion of traditional gender roles. It encourages boys and girls to adopt traditional expectations towards work, career and marriage, which reinforce female financial dependency and limit the possibility to divorce. One could argue that pro-abstinence discourses' major function is not so much to encourage teens to remain abstinent rather than reinforcing the apparent necessity and desirability of traditional family structures.

Notes

[1] Irvine, 2002, p.66.
[2] Radford Ruether, 2001, p.3.
[3] Irvine, 2002, p.66.
[4] *Personal Responsibility and Work Opportunity Reconciliation Act of 1996*, Title V.
[5] ibid..
[6] White House, 2002, p.19.
[7] ibid., p.19.
[8] ibid., p.19.
[9] Fagan, 2006, and also U.S. Department of Health and Human Services Administration for Children and Families, 2006a.
[10] U.S. Department of Health and Human Services Administration for Children and Families, 2006a, p.6.
[11] ibid., p.3.
[12] U.S. Department of Health and Human Services, 2005a, p.4.
[13] ibid., p.1.
[14] ibid., p.2.
[15] ibid., p.6.
[16] ibid., p.8.
[17] LaHaye, 1998a, p.25.
[18] U.S. Department of Health and Human Services Administration for Children and Families, 2006a, pp.8,9.
[19] LaHaye, 1998a, p.164.
[20] ibid., p. 178.
[21] D Elkind, *Ties That Stress: The New Family Imbalance*, Harvard University Press, Cambridge, 1994.
[22] J J Brumberg, *The Body Project: An Intimate History of American Girlhood*, Vintage Books, New York, 1997, p.199.

[23] ibid., p.248.

[24] Meeker, 2002, p.184, emphasis in the original.

[25] Public Agenda, *Kids These Days '99: What Americans Really Think About the Next Generation*, 1999, viewed on 19 June 2007, <http://www.publicagenda.org/research/pdfs/kids_these_days_99.pdf>, p.3.

[26] P Scales, 'The Public Image of Adolescents,' *Society*, May 2001, 38 (4), pp. 64-75, quoted in S R Stern, 'Self-Absorbed, Dangerous, and Disengaged: What Popular Films Tell Us About Teenagers,' *Mass Communication*, 2005, 8 (1), pp. 23-38, p.23.

[27] Independent Sector, *Overview and Executive Summary: Trends Emerging from the National Survey of Volunteering and Giving Among Teenagers*, 2003; B Schneider and D Stevenson, *The Ambitious Generation: America's Teenagers, Motivated but Directionless*, Yale University Press, New Haven, 1999; Shell Oil, 'Teens Under Pressure, Coping Well,' *The Shell Poll*, 1999, 1(4), pp.1-3; U.S. Department of Labor, *Issues in Labor Statistics*, Bureau of Labor Statistics, Summary 02-06, 2002, all quoted in Stern, 2005, p.23.

[28] Stern, 2005, p.23.

[29] Public Agenda, op. cit., p.5.

[30] Hagelin, 2005b, p.224, emphasis in the original.

[31] LaHaye, 1998a, p.19.

[32] ibid., pp.155-56.

[33] U.S. Department of Health and Human Services, 2005a, p.4.

[34] J Falwell, *Listen America!*, Doubleday, New York, 1980 quoted in S Rogers Radl, *The Invisible Woman: Target of the Religious New Right*, Delacorte Press, New York, 1983, p.6.

[35] Hagelin, 2005b, p.161.

[36] ibid., p.149.

[37] F Furstenberg, 'The Future of Marriage,' *American Demographics*, 1996, 18.

[38] S Coontz, *Marriage, a History: from Obedience to Intimacy or How Love Conquered Marriage*, Viking Penguin, New York, 2005, p.289.

[39] Kintz, 1998, p.8.

[40] H Hendershot, *Shaking the World for Jesus: Media and Conservative Evangelical Culture*, The University of Chicago Press, Chicago and London, 2004, p.88.

[41] LaHaye, 1998a, p.124.

[42] ibid.,p.171.

[43] ibid.,p.161.

[44] ibid.,p.80.

[45] ibid.,p.65.

[46] U.S. Department of Health and Human Services Administration for Children and Families, 2006a, p.9.

[47] Waxman, 2004, p.18.

[48] Meeker, 2002, p.180.

[49] ibid., p.178.

[50] Gavanas defines the movement as follows: "since the mid-1990s, the U.S. fatherhood responsibility movement has claimed that fathers have become marginalized in the family, with catastrophic societal consequences. In response to this perceived situation, the fatherhood responsibility movement seeks to reestablish the necessity of men in families, constituting fatherhood as specifically male in differentiation from the feminizing connotations of family involvement," A Gavanas, 'Domesticating Masculinity and Masculinizing Domesticity in Contemporary US Fatherhood Politics,' *Social Politics*, 2004b, 11 (2), pp.247-266, p.247.

[51] ibid., p.251.

[52] A Gavanas, *Fatherhood Politics in the United States: Masculinity, Sexuality, Race, and Marriage*, University of Illinois Press, Urbana and Chicago, 2004a, p.251.

[53] Waxman, 2004, p.17.

[54] Hagelin, 2005b, pp.152-153.

[55] For the website of the Wilsons' "Purity Balls" see: <http://www.generationsoflight.com/>, last viewed on 4 March 2009.

[56] Stop Family Violence, 'Press Release: Mothers File International Complaint Against United States,' 11 May 2007, viewed on 29 May 2007, <http://stopfamilyviolence.org/ocean/host.php?page=471>

[57] LaHaye, 1998a, p.80.

[58] ibid., p.65.

[59] ibid., p.109.

[60] ibid., pp.193-94.

[61] J Stacey, *In the Name of the Family: Rethinking Family Values in the Postmodern Age*, Beacon Press, Boston, 1996, p.9.

Chapter 9
Abstinence and Parental Rights

Putting the blame for the alleged lack of boundaries and sexual precociousness of contemporary children on parents and on the collapse of traditional moral values, while echoing a public opinion that they also contribute to shape, is part of the conservative Christians' strategy to reassert the necessity and desirability of the traditional family as the best possible frame for children's education.

This position was reinforced by the *Personal Responsibility, Work, and Family Promotion Act of 2003,* which added to the previous act a section on the "promotion of family formation and healthy marriage." While due to economic and social factors, the traditional family might not be the solution to what most Americans see as the "bad" behaviour of contemporary children, it is nevertheless the one offered today by American conservatives in order to reassert a patriarchal vision of society. This reinforcement of the traditional family requires, for conservative Christians, the re-establishment of the primacy of the concept of "parental rights" as one of their main agendas.

The coming section focuses on the utility of this concept in reinforcing the traditional family cell by limiting state intervention and reasserting the patriarchal hierarchy within it.

The issue of "parental rights" is particularly strong in the conservative Christian community and lies at the core of pro-abstinence discourses and of debates on sexual education in general. As sociologist Sara Diamond explained in her book *Not by Politics Alone: The Enduring Influence of the Christian Right*, the concept of parental rights comes from "the idea that the government [and secular society] now threate[n] parental control of children."[1] Conservative Christians complain that parental rights are challenged by the public school system, especially in sex education classes and governmental agencies dealing with child protection. For example, CWA, Beverly LaHaye's organization, "supports reform of public education by returning authority to parents"[2] and many conservative Christian parents, like Hagelin, chose to bypass the problem by homeschooling their children.

Sara Diamond underlines that while conservative Christians advocate more government intervention in limiting the availability of divorce,[3] in matters concerning children their opposition to government intervention is adamant. Conservative Christian literature is rich in "horror stories" of governmental infringement of parental rights of varying nature like

> condom distribution against parental consent; laws
> requiring teacher certification for homeschool parents;
> intrusive values clarification tests and surveys; legal
> challenges when parents ground minors as a method of
> discipline; sexually explicit curricula; health care provided
> without parental consent; and prohibition on parents'
> viewing of scholastic tests.[4]

However, these horror stories have to be mitigated in the American context since the United States is the only country in the world, together with Somalia, which refused to sign the *United Nations Convention on the Rights of the Child*. The grounds for this refusal are that the convention undermines parental authority, supports the access of young persons to abortion and forbids the application of the death penalty to minors.[5]

The notion of parental rights is based on the idea that children are their parents' "possession". For conservative Christians, children belong to and are solely the responsibility of their parents who directly care for their physical, emotional and spiritual needs and neither the society nor the government has a right to interfere. This idea is clearly explained by the LaHayes in *Raising Sexually Pure Kids* when they state that a child is his/her parents' "most treasured possession", as much their possession as their "car or boat."[6] In fact children are parents' "possession" by proxy "since [their] children are really the Lord's children on loan to [them]."[7] A parent's duty is therefore to respect the will of God and to help his/her child lead the "purest" life possible according to the Bible's teachings. This entails that one critical right, and duty, of parents is the right to decide which moral values they want their children to be exposed to. For example, they have a right to ensure that what their children are taught at school is in agreement with those values. Hence, Hagelin urges parents to "take a hands-on approach with [their] child's education," that is,

> [w]hether your kids go to private or public schools, you
> should be intimately acquainted with what, and how, they
> are taught. When was the last time you picked up your
> child's English book, or science book, and actually read it?
> Do you know what she is being taught in history? Exercise
> your right to opt your child out of misguided sex-ed
> classes. Challenge the reading lists if the assigned books
> are pop garbage. The point is to remember that you, as the
> parent, have every right - and the ultimate responsibility -
> to make sure your child is taught well, and well taught.[8]

The notion that parents have "every right" regarding their children and that children are their parents' possession has been strongly objected to by human rights advocates, as it raises the fear of child abuse and constitutes an infringement on children's rights, among those reproductive ones.

As Sara Diamond underlines, parental rights are first and foremost a question of power:

> [The] assertion of parental *ownership* of children is more than semantic. It cuts right to the heart of what much of the family values debate has been about. Who will *decide* and who will *control* what happens to children, what children and parents can get away with, what spouses can get away with, what pregnant girls and women can and cannot do, what homosexuals can and cannot do? These are all questions of morality wrapped up with questions of power. These old questions are more pressing today because of ongoing changes in the nature of family and gender relations. The old answers ring less and less certain. The uncertainty fosters fingerpointing and a belief that the family is simply breaking down. [...] No one denies the recent changes in family composition: the debate is about what the changes mean. Should the changes be accepted and considered as factors for future policymaking, or should the changes be feared and blamed on the government and secular culture? Christian Right activism on the full gamut of family matters can best be understood as an effort to fight change and punish those seen as responsible for it.[9]

The concept of parental rights, similar to creationism, is for conservative Christians a tool in the defense of a hierarchic vision of the family and society at large. For them the evolution of the family cell since the 1960s, along with the promotion of "children's rights" by the UN and the federal government, are a threat to what they see as the "God ordained" hierarchy of the family. For Tim LaHaye, for example, emphasising "children's rights at the expense of parental rights" puts parents at risk of raising children who will "becom[e] part of the anti-values generation that rebels against the laws of God and society."[10] For conservative Christians, men are below God, wives should submit to their husbands and children should honor their father and mother (Ex. 21:12); outside of this ordered frame, society can only "break down." Following this reasoning, institutions that put the child first and infringe on parental rights go against the hierarchic vision of the family defined by the Bible and threaten society's equilibrium. Hence, as Diamond underlines "[...] parental rights remain a useful rhetorical device in that it reinforces a view of secular institutions as illegitimate"[11] and reinforces the legitimacy of religious institutions. The emphasis of the Bush administration on the federal subsidization of faith-based organisations as better providers of help to citizens "in need" performed the same function by shifting responsibilities and functions from federal state to religious organisations.

While parents have "rights," it is important to mention the insistence of conservative Christians on the fact that these rights also imply a number of parental "duties," among which are never giving up the task of parenting and being a good role model to raise Christian children. In Hagelin's view it is crucial that parents remain committed to their role and not give up their own responsibilities to the schools or the government. For being a responsible parent entails that

> I cannot give-up or tire-out in the responsibility to use every day to coach my children in values and virtues. In so doing, I will establish them both as productive members of society and as souls who will answer eternally for the decisions they make and the love they share.[12]

This statement echoes the idea that the fault for the failure of "kids today" lies with their parents who do not devote enough time and energy to them and rely too much on the school and the federal systems. For conservative Christians, only responsible parents can bring up responsible children. Hagelin illustrates this point interestingly in the following quotation.

> If you're truly going to fight the culture and raise children who will stand up for what is right, you must teach your sons and daughters that certain language and images are not acceptable.
> I never - even once - heard my father utter a curse word. And my kids have never heard my husband utter one. Guess what? Even though I have three teenagers, I've never heard any of them curse either. The power of example cannot be overstated.[13]

For Hagelin, parents have to set standards through their behaviours, as any lack of consistency between their principles and their actions would undermine the moral principles they want they children to acquire. This requirement applies to every sphere of their lives including matters of sex-education and marriage. Where, for conservative Christians, inconsistency can be most destructive for children's morality because, as Tim LaHaye forcefully states it, "sexual sins are number one!"[14] Therefore, conservative

Christians urge parents to reclaim authority over their children's sexual education.

Since the 1960s, sex-education classes in schools have been at the heart of the parental-rights debate, and logically so, as they threaten parental authority and the hierarchy of the traditional family in two fundamental ways. First, they declare the sexual education provided by parents to be inadequate and insufficient. Second, as Moran explains, through the "neutral morality" they originally sought to convey, sex-education teachers, "urged young people to make their own moral decisions, [and] were implicitly suggesting that adolescents need not accept their parent's authority as absolute."[15] By thus "replacing" parental as well as religious authority and questioning their moral standards, sex-education classes both perfectly focus the anxieties of the conservative Christian community in matter of parental rights and the family, and provide an effective emotional tool in the questioning of governmental intervention.

In her book *Talk About Sex: The Battles over Sex Education in the United States*, sociologist Janice M. Irvine explains that "initiatives to protect children from exposure to allegedly corrupting sex talk, whether from sex education programs or the media, are central to conservative cultural politics."[16] By stirring anxieties over the corruption of the young, conservative Christian discourses have constructed a negative image of liberal education as pornography threatening children's innocence. One of the major discursive tools in this construction has been the use of what Irvine calls "depravity narratives" that is "tales about sex education that rely on distortion, innuendo, hyperbole, or outright fabrication,"[17] which I referred to earlier as "horror stories." For Irvine those narratives draw

> their power from four sources. First, [they] wield enough specific details to sound accurate [...]. Second, like so many other operations of sexual speech deployed by sex education critics, they depend on a compelling condensation of sexual threat, fear, and shame. They succeed because they appeal to a cultural logic that someone, somewhere might have done such a thing. Third, they exist in multiples. Sex education opponents routinely have a litany of such tales whose effect is synergistic. Finally, depravity narratives depend on a lack of information about the practices they describe, in this case about the truly limited nature of sex education in the United States.[18]

The LaHayes, Meeker and Hagelin all use and contribute to the proliferation of such depravity narratives. A good illustration of one of them is provided in the opening of the sixth chapter of Hagelin's book "Parent-directed Education" and is worth quoting at length:

> When was the last time you looked at your child's health textbook? If it's been a while, you'd probably be more than a little shocked by the content of sex education - sometimes referred to as "Family Life Education." Long gone are the days of biology class where kids were taught about their bodies and the basics of reproduction. Today's materials include detailed discussions - complete with graphic illustrations - of raw sex in many forms.
> Think I'm kidding? Some programs are so disingenuous that their very names are lies. They're called abstinence-plus, or abstinence-based, but they're not about abstinence. They're about the mechanics of sexuality. [...] Researcher Robert Rector at The Heritage Foundation tells of a program that lists ways teachers can show kids as young as 13 "how to make condoms fun and pleasurable." One of the ways to do that, it turns out, is to send kids on a "condom hunt" to local stores. They're expected to look over the various types that are offered and ask, "what's the cheapest price for three condoms?"
> The so-called "fun" doesn't stop there. Teachers also are supposed to hold "condom races" between teams of students. "Each person on the team must put the condom on a dildo or cucumber and take it off," the program says. "The team that finishes first wins."
> Such programs offer extensive instruction in how to "satisfy each other" short of intercourse: showering together, full-body massages, etc. Does any rational person think these activities make it less likely they'll graduate to intercourse?[19]

This particular depravity narrative is especially convincing as it does, contrary to others, stick to the truth and relies mostly on the outraged comments of Hagelin and the lack of context provided for the examples she quotes. However, Irvine refers to more extreme cases of stories telling that children in sex-education classes

> were being encouraged to fondle each other, sexual intercourse would be taught in kindergarten, schools would install coed bathrooms with no partitions between stalls,

and youth were being told about bestiality with donkeys and sheep.[20]

Such "horror stories" contribute to the construction of comprehensive sex-education as dangerous for children's "innocence," "health" and moral values and are instrumental in convincing parents that they must take back the role of sex educator. It also reinforces the notion of government as interfering illegitimately in families' lives and reasserts the primary authority of parents. In Hagelin's words, the government

> should focus on teaching our children history, literature, science, mathematics, etc. Providing kids with information on sex - beyond a few rudimentary facts that could be taught in biology class - is our job as parents.[21]

Hence, she advises parents to either opt their children out of sex-education classes, enroll them in a private school or homeschool them.

It is interesting to note that though Hagelin, the LaHayes, Meeker and most conservatives rage against sex-education classes and the government's interference, what the Department of Health and Human Services recommended on its website 4Parents.gov is more parental involvement in teaching children about sex and abstinence. As already mentioned, one of the strategies of conservative Christian rhetoric is to picture themselves as a persecuted minority, a strategy which as Sara Diamond explained "is part of a mindset that keeps activists from becoming complacent."[22] Yet in this particular case their influence was clearly felt, as the recommendations of the governmental website copied almost word for word the advice of faith-based abstinence programs and of the LaHayes, only in a slightly more secular fashion.

For example, considering the creation of the website 4Parents.gov its highly controversial content, the assertion of conservative Christians like the LaHayes, Meeker or Hagelin and the Heritage Foundation that the government is promoting a vision of sexual education in opposition to their own moral values might never have been less accurate than under the Bush administration.

As already discussed in Chapter 1, abstinence curricula answered the need for conservative Christian parents to control the information children would receive about sex in schools, in an era when just not talking about sex did not seem to many to be a viable option anymore. Another important point defended by all pro-abstinence texts, 4Parents.gov included, is the significant influence of parents on their children's sexual decisions. The strong emphasis they place on this fact is best understood in the light of the following remark by sociologist Alan Wolfe in his book *One Nation, After All*:

A feeling that parents have lost control over their children's
sexuality is one of the deepest currents in American public
opinion; according to a 1985 poll, only 3 percent of those
surveyed thought that parents had a great deal of control
over the sexual activity of teenagers compared with 46
percent who thought they had very little control.[23]

To contradict the impression that parents have no control over their
teenagers' sexual choices, 4Parents.gov provided the following figures.
When polled about who influenced their sexual decisions most, teenagers
answered: parents 37%, friends 33%, religious leaders 7%, teachers 4%,
media 5%.[24] Hence, the website stated, parents do have a significant
influence on their children's sexuality and they must use it in order to help
them make the "healthiest choice" that is abstinence.[25]

       Most pro-abstinence authors acknowledge the difficulties and the
feelings of awkwardness faced by parents in talking about sex with their
children, especially if their own parents did not do so. Yet they all agree that
they "owe it" to their children to get involved in their sexual choices. Though
parents might have been educated in a culture that avoided sex talk in
families and feared that speaking about it with children might lead them to
try it out and thus "corrupt their innocence," it is now suggested that parents
need to reclaim this educative realm from "immoral" public schools and the
media. *Parents, Speak Up!*, the booklet offered for download on
4Parents.gov, grounded this necessity in the following remarks:

       Research from the largest study ever done on teenagers
       found that teens who felt closely connected to their parents
       (meaning that they felt warmth, love, and care from their
       parents) were much less likely to be involved in risky
       behaviors like drugs, alcohol, tobacco use, and violence.
       Teens who felt connected to their parents were more likely
       to have their first sexual experience later than teens who
       were less connected to their parents.[26]

This data confirmed the idea of "parental rights" in so far as it reasserted the
parents as the appropriate teachers in the matter of sex education and as the
most meaningful influence in his/her children's lives, far above public school
teachers among others.

       To exercise their parental rights fully and help their children choose
abstinence, the LaHayes, Meeker and Hagelin, as well as *Parents, Speak Up!*,
provide parents with comprehensive guidelines regarding their children's
sexual education and choices. In self-help book style, they ensure readers that
"they can do it!" and that their writings are there to help them plan carefully

an appropriate way to do so. Like Benjamin Franklin, who worked all his life on acquiring the virtues that he considered the most useful by a clearly defined method of self examination, parents will have to work hard to fulfill their wish of preserving their children's virginity until marriage. By emphasising the idea that having sexually abstinent children is a matter of hard work and not only chance, or even an illusion, the LaHayes, Meeker, Hagelin, like the Department of Health and Human Services under the Bush administrations, inscribe their writings in the American ideal of achievement through self-control and hard work. Using this cultural narrative thus helps them build the emotional and ideological appeal of their discourse by inscribing it into a familiar script.

Both the LaHayes and Meeker are in complete agreement with "liberal" sexual educators on the idea that it is indispensable to tell children about sex as early as possible. First of all to protect them from sexual abuse, and secondly to help them develop an attitude towards sex that is in agreement with the moral principles of their parents and to control their access to sexual information. Moreover, as remarked by 4Parents.gov, putting off talking about it until a child is already a teenager can be "too late" as "three national surveys report that one out of five teens 14 and younger has had sex at least once."[27]

For conservative Christians, in a contemporary society where public schools do not teach "morality" anymore and where the access to sexual information is extremely easy, parents need to start early teaching their children about sex to ensure that they are their "authoritative" and primary source of knowledge on this issue. Consequently, sexual education should start as soon as possible by answering honestly the first questions that the young child has about sex. Of course the information given should be appropriate to the child's age. As the LaHayes explain,

> [d]o not be like many parents who wait until they think their kids are old enough for "the big sex talk" and then dump the whole load on them in one session. [...] Just remember to be gently aggressive and occasional.[28]

Parents should take the initiative of talking about sex and use the occasion of their children's sex-related questions to teach them about it. The LaHayes explain that parents should answer their children in a "casual" and "healthy" way, devoid of any guilt so as to present them with "a positive biblical attitude toward this beautiful subject."[29] In the LaHayes' view, parents should not reveal everything about sex right away, but make the child feel that the "conversational door" is always open and that s/he is free to ask any question s/he might have on the subject. This openness should be cultivated early on as starting too late might make it more difficult. This way when "it's

time to talk about tough topics, you and your teen will have built a
relationship that allows those conversations to sink in and have meaning."[30]

To convince their children of the relevance of abstinence, Meeker
and the LaHayes also advise parents to teach their children about "the joys
and dangers of sexual attraction"[31], that is, about the beauty of the sexual act
and the pleasure of sexual stimulation but also about emotional hurt, STDs
and teen pregnancy. An example that the LaHayes give of the negative
consequences of premarital sex is that a bride or groom might be exposed to
the risk of having either to tell his virgin spouse that he has not kept himself
pure for his wedding night or to lie and feel guilty. This, the LaHayes
conclude, would start "their marriage off on a very unhappy note."[32]

Meeker's advocacy of abstinence on the other hand is based more on
a medical perspective than the one used by the LaHayes, though the latter
also write about the potential medical consequences of premarital sex. For
Meeker STDs and teen pregnancy are the main issues at stake. She warns
parents that letting children be sexually active before marriage makes them
run the risk of dying from it or dragging heavy physical consequences
through their whole married life. Sterility is one of the examples she uses
most often. She also writes about diseases like genital herpes, which makes
sexual contact difficult. Meeker also emphasises the fact that these diseases
do not only affect the people directly infected by them but can have
consequences for later generations. She refers, for example, to the possibility
of congenital conditions that STD-infected parents pass on to their offspring,
as in the case of the three year old Erin, whose father had contracted herpes
as a teenager and passed it on to his daughter.

> Unlike half of all babies born with herpes, [Erin] survived.
> But a brain scan taken when she was several weeks old
> showed damage to her brain tissue. Today, at age 3, she
> suffers from developmental delay. She walked late, talked
> late, and has a seizure disorder that requires daily
> medication. She'll be able to go to school, but we don't
> know how the disease affected her cognitive abilities, or
> what neurological problems await her in the future.[33]

In a less "dramatic" style *Parents, Speak Up!* succinctly advised parents to
tell their children that if they choose abstinence they

> will not have to worry about getting pregnant or getting
> someone pregnant. They will not have to worry about
> STDs, including HIV/AIDS. [Moreover] experiencing sex
> outside of marriage can jeopardize the likelihood of a
> happy marriage.[34]

The booklet placed a particular emphasis on STDs and on teen pregnancy the consequence of which were presented as particularly bleak, consistent with the belief in a "teen pregnancy epidemic" draining the resources of the welfare state.

> Many teen mothers never finish high school. Teen mothers
> and their babies are more likely to have health problems.
> And families started by teen mothers are more likely to be
> poor and end up on welfare.[35]

Meeker, *Parents, Speak Up!*, the LaHayes and the government also insist on the fact that parents should make it clear that abstinence is not limited to genital intercourse exclusively but concerns any close physical contact leading to sexual arousal. In the LaHayes's view, even "French kissing" has to be prohibited as "this can be very stimulating and, therefore, should be saved for marriage."[36] According to what the LaHayes call "the law of progression,"[37] physical intimacy always calls for more and anything more than a light good-night kiss will inevitably lead to sexual intercourse. Premarital abstinence advocates generally agree that teens need clear-cut rules to avoid these temptations. Echoing Meeker, *Parents, Speak Up!* asserted that

> rules protect and encourage. And even though most teens
> may not admit it, they like to have rules that are enforced.
> Rules give structure to their lives and help them feel cared
> for and secure.[38]

This is why *Parents, Speak Up!* provided parents with examples of what they call "house rules," or as the LaHayes put it "dating guidelines" to help their children stay out of situations that might lead them to sexual activity. Consistently, the LaHaye's guidelines contain a religious dimension which was absent from the rules of *Parents, Speak Up!* These rules, both in their secular and religious version, provide an excellent frame for reasserting the notion of parental rights and re-establishing a practical parental control over their children's sexual and dating lives.

The LaHayes claim that dating, like any other events in children's social lives, needs to be prepared and to follow certain rules. Though the guidelines they give may seem very strict to many parents, a fact the LaHayes are aware of, they explain that children need those guidelines for their protection. The LaHayes acknowledge that enforcing those dating rules can sometimes be difficult but that it is also indispensable:

> At times, your popularity as a parent will drop to an all
> time low if you enforce standards such as [our own], but if
> you do not, both you and your teenagers may live to regret
> it. Popularity will be meaningless then.[39]

The first of those rules is that "dating is for fifteen-year-olds and over" and sixteen would even be better, they add. They also argue against too-wide age differences between the dating teenagers, especially in the case of young girls who in their view are more exposed to this situation. *Parents, Speak Up!*, which advised parents to set an age for dating as well, also insists on this last point. They argue, with the help of statistics, that the larger the age difference, the greater the likelihood of sexual intercourse. They strengthen their point by underlining that

> In many states, it is illegal for a young teen to have sex
> with someone three or more years older, even if the
> younger teen "consents" to sex. The older person can be
> charged with "sexual assault" or other crimes.[40]

Their reason for giving this information, they claimed, was to protect younger teenagers from sexual abuse; however, in doing so, they also provided parents with an important tool to control their teens' dating choices: the possibility to sue an older partner of their child, even if both were consenting, and to oppose certain dates on the ground that they would be illegal and would involve risks for the older partner.

The LaHayes add to this first age requirement that "until high school graduation, only double dating is permitted"[41] to avoid any opportunity for the young couple to stay alone. They justify this standard as follow:

> There is safety in numbers - not much, but some. The main
> reason for this, however, is to force the teenagers to make
> plans in advance and to avoid long periods of time when
> they can drift into "heavy couple talk." Under the romance
> of the moment, young people can easily make premature
> love statements and commitments they do not really mean.
> The presence of another Christian couple greatly reduces
> this possibility, though it does not eliminate it altogether.[42]

The authors recognise that this is probably the most difficult rule to enforce and that it can be materially difficult to organise. This idea of double dating well illustrates the fact that the LaHayes consider dating as an exciting part of teens' social life, of which they should not be deprived, but which should also be framed by clear guidelines.

As hinted at in the above quote, the LaHayes believe that Christian teens should only date other Christians. First to avoid the potentially "'corrupting' influence"[43] of non-Christians and secondly to prevent Christian teens from having to make choices such as choosing between their boy/girlfriend and their faith.

To decide whether the person the teen wants to go out with is a proper candidate, the LaHayes suggest that fathers interview their daughters' date. They explain that it is not necessary in most cases for the mother to interview her son's date since the parents of suitable girls would have proven their daughter's eligibility by interviewing the boy. They give an example of how a predating interview could proceed and explain that this presents a number of advantages, like putting off unworthy candidates and ensuring that the boy is a Christian. Finally, during this predating interview, the dating guidelines that the young couple should follow have to be stated clearly and agreed to by the boy who will not be an acceptable date otherwise. If after all this the father is convinced that the boy is a suitable date he should tell him so while reasserting that, if he does not abide by his rules, this permission will be withdrawn. If the father is not convinced, he should tell the boy that he needs to discuss the matter with his wife and will call him to let him know their decision. Through this process the parental right to judge who their children can socialise with is again strongly reasserted, as their will and judgment prevails on their children's; this also extends to the kind of activities the couple can take part in on a date.

Parents, Speak Up! agreed with the LaHayes that parents have to know what their children are doing on a date. The LaHayes explain that "all dating activities must be approved of in advance"[44] and give examples of acceptable and non-acceptable activities:

> [...] approved dating include[s] all church activities and
> outings, chaperoned parties, sport events, and special
> occasions they wished to request. The don't-bother-to-ask
> list include[s] movies, dances, unchaperoned private
> parties, and activities where drinking takes place.[45]

As double dating is not a hundred percent safe way to make sure that the young dating couple will not find themselves alone, it is coupled with a limitation to group activities with adults in charge and the exclusion of activities that might encourage sexual arousal like going to the movies, which can display sexually stimulating content and ensures a degree of privacy by the darkness of the projection room, as well as dancing or drinking which weakens the individual's self control.

Consistently, this rule is followed by the interdiction to "park" their car in isolated corners warning about the dangers of the intimacy provided by "lover's lane" and to "never go to a home or confined quarter without a responsible adult in attendance."[46] As explained earlier, *Parents, Speak Up!* and the LaHayes agreed on the fact that children, even when dating or especially when dating, should never find themselves in unsupervised situations, as this would almost inevitably lead to too much intimacy.

Parents, Speak Up!, like the LaHayes, also recommended teaching teenagers "refusal skills" to help them face potential sexual demands from others. Such skills include: saying "no" clearly, "not 'maybe' or 'later'";[47] changing the topic of conversation; going away; planning in advance what to say in such situations; avoiding putting yourself in situations where such demands might be more likely to be formulated like going to the back seat of a car or to unsupervised parties. *Parents, Speak Up!* added that parents should try to be available "to pick up your teen if he or she calls in an uncomfortable or threatening environment or situation."[48]

As previously explained, the LaHayes advise parents to plan a special evening at the restaurant with their child, when (s)he will be encouraged to make a commitment to virtue and will be presented with a "virtue ring" or pendant to symbolize this pledge to God. The LaHayes explain that "your children's commitment to virtue should be the biggest event in their life since their conversion to Christ."[49] For the LaHayes, "this event will help [children] celebrate their emergence into the adult world of hormones, drives and passions."[50] To make this event especially significant in the child's life, the LaHayes advise parents to plan it very carefully in advance. It should also be a time to answer any questions the child might have about sex, and make sure that he or she has understood all the elements of the sexual education so far, among which the importance of abstinence before marriage. The LaHayes explain that this event

> is not a welcome into the world of dating. That too could be
> the cause of a special night out when your child is fifteen or
> sixteen (whatever is your set time for dating). The only
> kind of dating they should be doing after the commitment
> to virtue is group dating such as church youth activities.
> Dating, like getting your driver's license, should be a set
> time, but it should not be confused with the commitment to
> virtue that should occur two or three years earlier. Your
> children need the time in between to realize the seriousness
> and importance of this commitment.[51]

The LaHayes understand that this commitment to virtue "may sound like a lot of fluff to those of us who had no such custom when we were teens"[52] but they stress its importance. For them, this commitment and its symbol, a ring or pendant, can be decisive reminders to children to stay pure in moments of temptation. The commitment to virtue should also include the future spouse of the child:

> [E]ncourage your teen to set as his goal to wear that ring until his wedding night, when he will give it to his new mate as a symbol that he has kept himself pure.[53]

The child and his/her parent should then pray that God help his/her future spouse to remain chaste before marriage, too.

Though for the LaHayes, or in the Purity Balls mentioned earlier, parents play a crucial role in demanding from their children and organising the chastity pledge, it is to be noted that other pro-abstinence discourses do not directly involve parents in this event. The pledge can also be taken by the teenager alone, with their dating partner, or with peers in important gatherings. This does not mean that they are not influenced by their parents, or other authority figures, but the involvement of their parents in their choice might be less direct and directive. The LaHayes' version, on the contrary, seems to leave little, if any, possibility of refusal to the child and involves parents in his/her sexual life and choices to an extent which can appear disturbing to proponents of a permissive sexual ideology. In particular, the idea that a girl pledges to preserve her virginity before her parents to make a gift of it to her future husband evokes traditional notions of women as men's sexual properties with no sexual agency of their own. Yet it is fully consistent with the idea of parental rights and of the child as his/her parent's possession.

The idea of the chastity pledge, when it is forced on the child, can legitimately be objected to as an infringement on personal choice and the vestige of an outmoded vision of parental authority; however it might not be as irrelevant as it appears to sexual liberals at first sight. It is my contention that the chastity pledge can also be understood as a valuable ritual for a child coming of age and participates in the process of identity construction. This last idea is supported by social researchers Peter S. Bearman and Hannah Brückner, who define the virginity pledge movement as an "identity" movement especially in cases where pledges are taken in group gatherings.[54]

The chastity pledge can play a significant role in marking the entrance into the adult world, as practiced in non-western societies at the time of menarche or of the boys' coming of age by "community rituals of initiation or exclusion."[55] Actually, such a pledge might take on an empowering dimension. For, as Brumberg explains many

> different kinds of social critics now agree that American girls make the trip from menarche into adulthood without either knowledgeable guides or appropriate protective gear. For that reason, we may want to borrow at least one

operating principle from our Victorian ancestors and
consider the idea that young women deserve to be eased
into womanhood more slowly than is the case today.[56]

Brumberg is not a proponent of abstinence and would most likely
disagree with the chastity pledge offered by the LaHayes. Yet in view of this
quote, it may be relevant to consider the possible benefits of the moral frame
that the chastity pledge constitutes. As the LaHayes and Meeker often argue,
abstinence in general and the chastity pledge in particular can make teens feel
in control of their sexual lives, as they are not only led by their urges but
have a clear line set for themselves to follow in this matter. The fact that their
parents take a clear stand in matters of sexuality and do not leave them alone
in their questioning can also feel reassuring at a time when teens usually feel
unsafe. The chastity pledge can also offer a privileged moment for dialogue
between parents and child and provide the mentoring evoked by Brumberg.
Finally, telling teens that they can also legitimately "say no" to sex without
feeling like a "geek" in a society where sex might be too often presented as
the only road to happiness can also help them to figure out what they want
for themselves. But this might only work if they are given the free choice that
the LaHayes and Meeker exclude by promoting abstinence only.

Though the idea of a chastity pledge may seem very demanding on a
teenager, we need to remember that the LaHayes leave a door open for
"repentant" teens who would like to take a pledge of "renewed virginity."
This door is also left open by Meeker, as well as *Parents, Speak Up!* and the
CBAE extension of requirements, which also argued that it is never too late
to do well and make "healthy choices."

As mentioned earlier, "parental rights" also entail "parental duties,"
duties which extend to sexual behaviour as well. Hence, Meeker and the
LaHayes advise parents to send their children a coherent message by clearly
stating their position on premarital sex and by practicing the pro-abstinence
principles they promote. Meeker explains, for example, that for her,
ambivalence is permission. Parents should make clear that they want their
children to remain abstinent; if they leave room for doubt by silence on the
subject or by a display of contradicting attitudes, teens will see it as an
acceptance of premarital sexual activity. For her, parents should also avoid
telling their children that they had sex before marriage, even if this had been
the case. Meeker explains "while you don't want to hide anything, your
business is private and it just might encourage your teen to make mistakes
that could cost her dearly."[57] The apparent contradiction and hypocrisy of
this statement underlines the fact that, for Meeker, it would be preferable if
parents would have nothing "to hide." That is why both she and the LaHayes
maintain that parents should behave in agreement with their pro-abstinence
stance. For Meeker one major problem is that

[t]ime and time again teens tell me that their single mother or father warns them that they should not be sexually active, but that same mother or father is living, unmarried, with a sexual partner - often one of a long line of partners. What teens in this situation ask me is that since their mother or father is clearly sexually active, why shouldn't they be? In fact, the kids have an excellent point. If a parent really wants his or her teen to stay away from sex, there are some serious decisions to make. If a parent stops having sex in order to provide a good example for their teen, believe me, that teen will sit up and take notice![58]

Though the trust that Meeker places in this method might seem excessive for some, coherence does indeed make the pro-abstinence stance more convincing and fairer. But what makes this statement a particularly interesting one is how the requirements of abstinence are not here limited to teens, but are also extended to the sexual life of their parents, in particular single ones. This is evocative of the Administration for Children and Families' extension of abstinence programs to adults up to twenty-nine years old.[59] To have children who remain abstinent outside of marriage, parents should be abstinent outside of marriage as well. This example shows that abstinence not only concerns teens but all non-married persons. Besides, this quote further stigmatises non-traditional family cells by presenting single and divorced parents as more concerned about their sexual and emotional life than about their children's.

This idea of parents having to stand as models is defended in a slightly different way by the LaHayes, who put the emphasis on the idea that parents should send their children signals that they "genuinely" love each other. For example, they suggest that parents take "mini-honeymoons" away from their children regularly, "to cultivate their love not just for themselves, but also for their children."[60] If children feel that their parents are really in love and faithful to each other, it will give them a positive vision of marriage and will keep them away from immorality. On the contrary, the LaHayes explain,

[i]t is devastating to the moral practices of Christian youth when their parents are immoral. Many a girl has traded her virtue more out of revenge for her father's unfaithfulness to her mother than as an act of passion.[61]

To strike the reader's mind, the LaHayes give the example of parents who lost their children as a consequence of their unfaithfulness to their spouse. "No small price to pay for sin",[62] they conclude, confirming once again that those who stride out of "God's path of virtue" will have to pay for it. For the LaHayes, like for Meeker, to have virtuous children parents need to set a model of virtue by their own lives.

The model of morality set up by abstinence as a barrier to the immorality inherited from the 1960s is not only concerned with children's but also with adult's sexual behaviour. Abstinence thus provides rules for teenagers and adults and demand consistency from parents. To reclaim their "parental rights", parents, if they want to be consistent with their beliefs, have to become completely independent from government's interference in raising their children and provide these with a traditional familial frame. This influence of abstinence discourses over individuals of all ages is further reinforced by the focus of abstinence discourses on educating children to fulfill the traditional family model as adults. As argued in this chapter, pro-abstinence discourses and their support of the traditional family cell as a superior and autonomous structure operate as tools in reasserting the illegitimacy of the government and of secular institutions and in reinforcing the feeling of conservative Christians that they belong to an oppressed minority. They are also instrumental in re-establishing a hierarchical system of power with God and the Church at its apex followed respectively by men, women and children, the government being only peripheral to this structure. Such a system of family, gender and community interaction and the strict rules and limited worldview it provides to bind its followers to this hierarchy can appear and, certainly is, oppressive to a significant extent. Yet, as observed by Linda Kintz

> [c]oncentrating on only the negative effects produced by such rigidity, and there are many, risks overlooking the important sense of confidence and security such training provides for many people. The problem is its exclusivity.[63]

To reach a deeper understanding of the identity and mechanisms of the conservative Christian community it is necessary to take into account the "comforting" dimension of the choice to sacrifice a certain degree of autonomy to, as Gramsci formulated it, "sav[e] the self from disaster,"[64] in a postmodern society where only rigid systems of belief seem to be able to provide certainties anymore.

Notes

[1] Diamond, 1998, p.115.
[2] CWA, 2007.
[3] Diamond, 1998, p.1.

[4] ibid., p.119.
[5] M Piekarec, 'Droits des enfants: le déni américain,' *Le Devoir*, 8 May 2002, viewed on 29 March 2007, <http://www.ledevoir.com/2002/05/08/376.html#>; HUMAN RIGHTS WATCH, 'Questions and Answers on the UN Special Session on Children,' 2006, viewed on 29 March 2007, <http://www.hrw.org/press/2002/05/unchildrenqa0502.htm>
[6] LaHaye, 1998a, p.151.
[7] ibid., p.138.
[8] Hagelin, 2005a.
[9] Diamond, 1998, pp.114-115, emphasis in the original.
[10] LaHaye and Noebel, 2000, p.52.
[11] Diamond, 1998, p.116.
[12] Hagelin, 2005b, pp.202-203.
[13] ibid., pp.174-175.
[14] LaHaye, 1998b, p.64.
[15] Moran, 1999, p.192.
[16] Irvine, 2002, p.1.
[17] ibid., p. 54.
[18] ibid., p. 54.
[19] Hagelin, 2005b, pp.98-99.
[20] Irvine, 2002, p.55.
[21] Hagelin, 2005b, p.108.
[22] Diamond, 1998, p.5.
[23] A Wolfe, *One Nation, After All: What Middle-Class Americans Think About: God, Country, Family, Racism, Welfare, Immigration, Homosexuality, Work, The Right, The Left, and Each Other*, Penguin Books, London, 1999, p.120.
[24] U.S. Department of Health and Human Services, 2005a, p.2.
[25] ibid., p.1.
[26] ibid., p.2.
[27] ibid.p.5.
[28] LaHaye, 1998a, p.35.
[29] ibid., p.73.
[30] U.S. Department of Health and Human Services, 2005a, p.5.
[31] LaHaye, 1998a, p.44.
[32] ibid., p.26.
[33] Meeker, 2002, p.41.
[34] U.S. Department of Health and Human Services, 2005a, p.6.
[35] ibid., p.7.
[36] LaHaye, 1998a, p.157.

[37] ibid., p.49.
[38] U.S. Department of Health and Human Services, 2005a, p.4.
[39] LaHaye, 1998a, p.150.
[40] U.S. Department of Health and Human Services, 2005a, p.5.
[41] LaHaye, 1998a, p.154.
[42] ibid., p.154.
[43] ibid., p.151.
[44] ibid., p.154.
[45] ibid., p.154.
[46] ibid., p.155.
[47] U.S. Department of Health and Human Services, 2005a, p.9.
[48] ibid., p.4.
[49] LaHaye, 1998a, p.136.
[50] ibid., p.136.
[51] ibid., p.137.
[52] ibid., p.147.
[53] ibid., p.140.
[54] Bearman and Brückner, 2001.
[55] Brumberg, 1997, p.33.
[56] ibid., p.200.
[57] Meeker, 2002, p.219.
[58] ibid., pp.219-220.
[59] U.S. Department of Health and Human Services Administration for Children and Families, 'FY 2007 Program Announcement, Section 510 Abstinence Education Program,' 2006b, viewed on 27 March 2007, <http://www.acf.hhs.gov/grants/pdf/ACYF-FYSB-AE-01-06updated.pdf>
[60] LaHaye, 1998a, p.33.
[61] ibid., p.34.
[62] ibid., p.34.
[63] Kintz, 1997, p.53.
[64] A Gramsci, quoted in Kintz and Lesage, 1998, p.19.

Chapter 10
Abstinence and Welfare

For the US government under President G.W. Bush and the Heritage Foundation abstinence was, and still is for the latter, presented not only as a religious or family issue but first and foremost as a question of social "welfare" and public health. However, the vision of social services that abstinence education implies is deeply influenced by a conservative view of welfare grounded in the cultural "narrative of success." It is also, like the narrative of the "culture war," a recurring theme of pro-abstinence discourses explored in the next chapter, grounded in the idea that the cause of major "social problems" like out-of-wedlock pregnancy, STDs, delinquency and teenage promiscuity in general is the sexual revolution of the 1960s. Considering this cultural phenomenon as the source of all social problems results in an idealisation of a pre-1960s past when, contrary to today, promiscuity was supposedly not rampant and where the traditional family and religious faith were guaranteeing social morality and stability.

This chapter is devoted to showing how sexual-abstinence-only-before-marriage programmes and discourses are a tool in the promotion of a conservative vision of welfare society consistent with the American cultural narrative of success. In the conservative view, the major cause of poverty in America is not structural but moral. The poor are poor because they lack the type of moral values promoted by religion. By helping the poor financially, the welfare system maintains them under a dependency, which erodes their work-ethic and their morality. For conservatives, sexual-abstinence promotes morality, marriage and self-control as well as religion. In direct line with American narratives of achievement through self-improvement and hard work, they also claim that the self-discipline learnt from being sexually abstinent brings success in every area of life: in studies and work, health and marriage.

Contemporary pro-abstinence discourses play an important role in the promotion of a conservative vision of welfare, which in the past twenty-five years has shaped approaches to questions of premarital sexuality and teenage pregnancy in the USA. This vision, promoted by the Heritage Foundation, the G.W. Bush administration, and before that the Reagan administration, was well illustrated in a volume entitled *Priorities for the President* published by the Heritage Foundation in 2001, in which the think-tank suggested to the new Republican government a number of guidelines regarding social services. The vision of poverty, welfare and the family developed by Heritage researcher Robert Rector - who participated in the drafting of the *Personal Responsibility and Work Opportunity Reconciliation Act of 1996* - clearly highlights the role that abstinence can play in promoting conservative moral values and marriage.

Rector's idea of welfare is directly inspired by the "social Darwinism" of the Gilded Age, which significantly influenced the views of businessmen like Carnegie or Rockefeller. In accordance with this tradition, which promotes a "survival of the fittest" ethos, Rector claims that L.B. Johnson's "war on poverty", started in the 1960s, was an utter failure. According to Rector, there are two philosophies of welfare: a "permissive philosophy of welfare entitlement"[1] promoted by Johnson and "liberals" after him, and a "morally constructive philosophy of welfare."[2] For Rector "there is little true material poverty in the United States," but rather what he calls "behavioral poverty."[3] In opposition to the liberal vision, which states that poverty generates destructive behaviours, Rector argues that, in fact, it is the destructive behaviours of the "underclass" that create poverty. Johnson's "war against poverty" was therefore bound to fail as it

> sought to prop up material living standards artificially while ignoring the behaviors that lead to material poverty. By contrast, the morally constructive philosophy is directly concerned with the culture of the underclass, which can be defined by an erosion of the ethos of marriage, work, and education. Underclass culture also involves deterioration in the ethos of self-control (as evidenced in drug and alcohol abuse); a loss of respect for others (as seen in crime, domestic abuse, child abuse); and a weakening of the ethos of self-transcendence (or linkage to something larger than self). Morally constructive welfare seeks to eradicate this culture of self-destruction and thereby open the doors to opportunity for millions cut off from mainstream society.[4]

For Rector there are few "deserving poor," but a significant number of individuals who, through destructive behaviour, maintain themselves in a state of poverty, out of which they could easily climb if they had better moral values. He argues that two of the major consequences of the "underclass'" lack of morals are the growth of illegitimacy and divorce which are "powerful factors contributing to virtually every other social problem facing the nation."[5] In Rector's opinion, children who due to divorce or illegitimacy grow up without fathers are deprived of an indispensable "moral" leadership. Consequently, they will almost inevitably grow up to be single parents or divorcees themselves, as well as delinquents or drug addicts depending on welfare for survival. His reasoning reflects the ideas of the fatherhood movement, which claims that fathers bring a unique and irreplaceable contribution to the upbringing of their children. Consequently, for Rector "policies to reduce out-of-wedlock childbearing and strengthen marriage should be at the center of all future welfare policies."[6]

One of Rector's colleagues, Pat Fagan, whose views were explained by Hagelin in an online article, made this statement even clearer:

> America must create a "Culture of Belonging," [Fagan]
> says. And the formula for that is "work, wedlock and
> worship." According to the social science data, if these
> three fundamentals are in place, government social policy
> is virtually unnecessary.[7]

In this motto, which might sound to some as coming from another age, Fagan summons the image of righteous and hard-working citizens abiding by the laws of God and the land. He relates his view of society to an ideal American past, evoking the Puritans as well as Jeffersonian agrarianism. As will be seen in the next chapter, such images are part of the conservative idealisation of a better past to which the American society should strive to return. Thus members of the "underclass" must be incited to work, marry and be religious in order to put an end to welfare. Yet Fagan seems to ignore the fact that contemporary US society is far from full employment and that the "right" to work is an issue today.

As seen in the previous chapter, for the Heritage Foundation, marriage is the basis of a "successful society." The Heritage Foundation researchers also underline that it contributes significant "benefits" to men, women and society at large. These include economic benefits. For example they claim that married men will be encouraged to be more productive to provide for their families and that marriage guarantees a greater financial security to women and children.[8] Or, as formulated by Senator Rick Santorum in a lecture at the Foundation, marriage also provides a "civilising" influence on men by making them more family-oriented and less prone to violence and crime.[9]

Thus, abstinence easily finds its place in Rector's recommendations concerning welfare as it promotes marriage as the only appropriate frame for sexual activity, "reduce[s] risk behaviors and instill[s] moral character"[10] while being grounded in conservative Christian ideology. For the Heritage Foundation abstinence is not an end in itself, but a tool in the defense of the traditional heterosexual family unit. It is with the same idea in mind that the Bush administration supported the extension of the support of pro-abstinence education programmes with the *Personal Responsibility, Work, and Family Promotion Act of 2003* along with the integration of a new section entitled: "Promotion of family formation and healthy marriage." However, as underlined by sociologist Scott Coltrane,

> [n]ew data from the 2000 census confirm what sociologists
> have been saying for some time: married couples with

children make up only about one-fourth of U.S. households. The so-called traditional family of breadwinner dad, stay-at-home mom, and two children is even more rare.[11]

If the "traditional" or nuclear family cell is losing ground it does not follow that marriage itself is endangered. Coltrane points out that "because 9 of 10 Americans are projected to marry - a rate much higher than that of most nations - one can safely conclude that recent trends in cohabitation and divorce are not a threat to the institution of marriage."[12] In his view,

> the recent trend toward diversity in family forms is inevitable, and [...] national campaigns to promote idealized father-headed families will have little influence on marriage rates or fathering practices.[13]

For Coltrane, the "marketing of the 'marriage' solution" to solve issues of welfare does not stem so much from the will to curb poverty rather than from "white men's insecurity and their fear that women no longer need them."[14] By reasserting the traditional family cell and the uniqueness of fatherhood, conservative think-tanks and the Bush administrations affirm the relevance of fathers as "males" to the contemporary family.

Marriage promotion and its correlate, abstinence, are also buttressed by discourses supporting the provision of social services by religious organisations. Rector, like Fagan, also emphasizes the role of religion in the moral reform of the "underclass" through the place he gives to faith-based institutions arguing that they

> can perform a unique and indispensable role in combating the destructive culture of the underclass. Clearly, private faith-based groups can and regularly do transform the inner moral character of individuals in positive ways that would be inconceivable in a government bureaucracy. Faith-based groups will also be essential to the vital task of rebuilding marriage in socially devastated communities.[15]

In Rector's view, faith-based organisations are especially well suited to change poor citizen's attitude towards marriage. Support of a greater role of religion in the public arena is one of the Heritage Foundation's major missions, in their view "religious practice is a vital private and public good, and public policy should recognize the important civic contribution of religious institutions and individual religious practice."[16]

The main function of Rector's discourse, is to displace the problem of poverty from a structural level that needs to be dealt with by society in general and the government in particular to the individual level of private morality. Theologian Rosemary Radford Ruether provides an insightful perspective on this matter when she explains that this view can be

> traced to a U.S. culture that lacks a critical education on economic and class structures and conceives of wealth and poverty primarily in individualistic and moralistic terms, as a matter of hard work and personal discipline versus laziness and the wrongful expectations of "getting something for nothing." This individualist and moralist culture renders older generations of middle-class white Americans blind to the roots of their own success (e.g., the extent to which it was based on government subsidies such as the GI Bill, which supported education and housing) and uncomprehending of the difficult times faced by their own children, as well as endemic poverty of those seen as "other" - that is the nonwhite poor. This myopia underlies the punitive responses to the dilemmas of those nonwhite poor, who are presumed to be the cause of their own poverty due to their lack of moral discipline.[17]

Abstinence discourses play an important role in the maintenance of this vision of poverty as they construct sexually active teens and especially teenage mothers as the group in need of moral education. Such a discursive construction is especially useful as it is easier, under the guise of child protection, to morally re-educate teenagers and teenage mothers through legislation than to overtly legislate the moral "re-education" of non-white poor adults.

The first federal use of abstinence to buttress this conservative vision of welfare was the *Adolescent Family Life Act* (AFLA) of 1981, also dubbed the "Chastity Act," which inaugurated government funding of abstinence programmes. As sociologist J.M. Irvine explains, this act was passed without debate as part of the *Omnibus Budget Reconciliation Act of 1981*.[18] It was aimed at making possible the funding of conservative types of sexual education aimed at the "prevention of adolescent premarital sexual relations"[19] and teenage pregnancy, a token of acknowledgement to the Religious Right which had contributed to the election of President Reagan.

An important achievement of the AFLA was to provide funding to religious organisations providing sexual education. One of the requirements of the act was that

services encouraged by the Federal Government should
promote the involvement of parents with their adolescent
children, and should emphasize the provision of support by
other family members, religious and charitable
organizations, voluntary associations, and other groups in
the private sector.[20]

This way, the greater involvement of religion in public policy later
recommended by Rector would be fulfilled.

As mentioned in Chapter 1, in order to support teenagers' access to
contraception and sex information, sexual liberals created the myth of a teen
pregnancy epidemic arguing that to protect young women, and by extension
society, from poverty, the inevitable outcome of teen pregnancy,
contraception and abortion should be made easily accessible. However, this
strategy backfired when conservatives started claiming that it was the
increased availability of contraception and abortion which had caused the
epidemic. As a consequence, the AFLA defended a strictly anti-abortion
stand, denying funding to programmes that provided abortion "or abortion
counseling or referral" and promoted "adoption as an alternative for
adolescent parents."[21] The act also reasserted the notion of parental rights
and further limited teenagers' access to contraception and abortion by
requiring parental notification and assent for providing most services to
minors.

In this context, when teen birth rates were actually steadily
decreasing since 1960,[22] discourses on teen pregnancy became inextricably
linked with discourses on the welfare system. Conservatives started
defending the idea that teenage mothers and especially the black "welfare
queens" described by Ronald Reagan, were draining the welfare state of its
funds, calculating that making babies enabled them to live off welfare
benefits without working and thus generating a cycle of poverty and welfare
dependency. As pointed out by educational policy professor Wanda S.
Pillows in her book *Unfit Subjects* (2004), blaming teenage mothers for
draining a welfare system funded by tax money enabled the government to
make the issue a taxpayer's concern. Thus it justified a more important state
regulation of teenage sexuality through a restricted access to contraception
and abortion and the promotion of abstinence.

This need for regulation was further reinforced by defining the
teenage family, particularly the unmarried family, as an inappropriate
environment for raising children. The AFLA formulated this negative vision
of teenage pregnancy in the following passage

pregnancy and childbirth among unmarried adolescents,
particularly young adolescents, often results in severe

adverse health, social, and economic consequences including: a higher percentage of pregnancy and childbirth complications; a higher incidence of low birth weight babies; a higher infant mortality and morbidity; a greater likelihood that an adolescent marriage will end in divorce; a decreased likelihood of completing schooling; and higher risks of unemployment and welfare dependency.[23]

As seen in the previous chapter, such statements were at the heart of the pro-marriage and pro-abstinence rhetoric of the G.W. Bush administration, and are still crucial for the Heritage Foundation and other abstinence proponents. However, this vision is revealed to be more ideologically motivated than fact-based. Indeed, W.S. Pillow notes that since the 1980s, research has shown that the burden of being a single-mother persists whether one is a teenager or older and that poor single mothers are usually already poor before having a child. Besides

several researchers question the assumed link between teen pregnancy and long-term social, educational, and economic failure of the unwed mother, arguing that the long-term effects of teen pregnancy are not as dire as previously assumed and longitudinal studies indicate that a majority of teen mothers catch up to their peers in educational and economic attainment by age twenty-five.[24,25]

Yet constructing single pregnant teenage girls as irresponsible and engaged in an unstoppable cycle of failure and welfare dependency was a useful strategy for conservatives. First, it allowed for the regulation of teenage sexuality under the guise of teenage pregnancy being the taxpayer's problem, since teenage sexual irresponsibility had repercussions on the spending of the welfare state. Second, it displaced the cause of poverty. Instead of being structural, poverty could be interpreted as a question of personal behavior. Third, it polarised racial anxieties by putting the blame for poverty in the US first and foremost on the black population and on black women in particular. Such a construction of the black "welfare queen" abusing taxpayers' money and living outside the patriarchal structure was especially effective, on several grounds. With the publication in 1965 of the *The Negro Family: The Case For National Action* most widely known as the "Moynihan Report," the black family had already been pinpointed as dysfunctional, given the high birthrates to unmarried black mothers. The idea of black single mothers as immoral and irresponsible was also reinforced by age-old stereotypes of black sexuality as uncontrollable. Finally, the higher birth rate of racial minorities also reinforced the fear of what Pillow calls a "browning" of America.

Most importantly, this construction of teenage mothers as welfare mothers reasserted the need for the traditional family as the best frame for the rearing of children and as the best remedy against welfare dependency. Putting the blame for poverty on teen pregnancy and the decline of the traditional family was a means to criticise changes in the family in the population at large. As hinted at by Religious Studies professor K. M. Sands, whereas it was difficult to blame supposedly rational adults for the changes occurring in the family, like cohabitation or single parenthood, teen pregnancy offered the opportunity to declare these changes harmful for a part of the population arguably made less rational by raging hormones.[26] Indeed, Sands points out that teenage mothers represent a crucial challenge for the traditional family:

> Although criticized for "dependence," it would be in some sense more accurate to say that impoverished single mothers are stigmatized for their independence. Whether by choice or by circumstance, they are rearing children outside marriage, evidently (though not always truly) without the support or supervision of men.[27]

This question of the dependence/independence of teenage mothers is crucial as the AFLA and further legislations, while aiming at making teenage mothers self-sufficient economically, deprive them of power-making decisions by, among other things, making financial help conditional on going back to school or living with their parents. Blaming black teen mothers for poverty and welfare dependency was strategically efficient, as it implicitly equated blaming the breakdown of the traditional patriarchal family. Therefore to solve the problems of poverty and welfare dependency of the nation, the changes in the family caused by the sexual revolution and buttressed by the "lower" moral standards of the "underclass" had to be reversed.

Up to the present day, discourses surrounding teenage pregnancy and illegitimacy have continued to develop along the same conservative lines as in the 1980s in spite of scientific investigations arguing that illegitimacy is not in and of itself the main cause of poverty in the nation and that pro-marriage policies have small likelihoods of lifting single mothers out of poverty. This is particularly true as "non-marriage is often a result of poverty and economic insecurity rather than the other way around"[28] as explained by historian Stephanie Coontz and economist Nancy Folbre of the Council on Contemporary Families. Yet these discourses were even reinforced by President Clinton in the mid-1990s when he repeatedly raised the issue of teen pregnancy to top priority of the government in his State of the Union Addresses, and when he launched in 1996 the National Campaign to Reduce Teen Pregnancy, stating in a radio address that

> we have to make it clear that a baby doesn't give you a right and won't give you the money to leave home and drop out of school. Today we are moving to make responsibility a way of life, not an option.[29]

That same year the *Personal Responsibility and Work Opportunity Reconciliation Act* (PRWORA), while providing funds for abstinence-only education programmes, reinforced this vision of teen mothers as irresponsible by making it a requirement for them to live with a parent or guardian and to attend school or job training to be eligible for social help. The objective of the law was to make teenage mothers financially independent through work and to prevent them from basing their household budget on welfare money. However, as convincingly argued by psychologists Wendy M. Limbert and Heather E. Bullock, such measures fail to acknowledge that

> living wage jobs are largely unavailable to poor women, that child care services are insufficient to meet families' needs, that many low-income children would benefit more from a full-time caregiver, and that the non-poor benefit from poor women's low-wage work [...]. Moreover, these arguments reinforce belief in meritocracy and individualism by constructing poverty as an issue of personal rather than collective responsibility [...].[30]

The previous chapter on abstinence and the family already shed light on the strong opposition of the G.W. Bush administration and of the Heritage Foundation to unmarried families as being a major root of poverty and a bad environment for child rearing. The Bush administration's position on teenage pregnancy and the means to prevent it was well summed up in its pamphlet *Working Toward Independence* (2002).

> The sexual revolution that began in the 1960s has left two major problems in its wake. The first is the historic increase in non-marital births that have contributed so heavily to the Nation's domestic problems including poverty, violence, and intergenerational welfare dependency. The second is the explosion of sexually transmitted diseases (STDs) that now pose a growing hazard to the Nation's public health. To address these problems, the goal of Federal policy

> should be to emphasize abstinence as the only certain way
> to avoid both unintended pregnancies and STDs.[31]

For the Bush administration, abstinence was the one and only means to prevent teen pregnancy and STDs, another financial burden on the health care system. 4Parents.gov reminded its readers that "STDs in young people cost more than $6.5 billion a year." Like the Reagan administration, the Bush administration did not only want to reduce teen pregnancies and STDs but more generally wanted to reduce teenage sexual activity. It thus promoted a vision of premarital sex as, to take up J.P. Moran's image, a "hazard"[32] to teenagers themselves and to the nation's economy and social equilibrium.

    Like the Reagan administration, the Bush administration was strongly pro-life. Consequently, it promoted adoption and tried to limit teenagers' access to contraceptives and abortion. As explained in Chapter V, G.W. Bush himself was committed to repealing *Roe v. Wade* and considered abortion akin to terrorism. His two administrations supported several anti-abortion laws among others the *Unborn Victims of Violence Act of 2004*, which became Public Law of the Land that same year and the *Child Interstate Abortion Notification Act*, which ruled that

> whoever knowingly transports a minor across a State line,
> with the intent that such minor obtain an abortion, and
> thereby in fact abridges the right of a parent under a law
> requiring parental involvement in a minor's abortion
> decision, in force in the State where the minor resides, shall
> be fined under this title or imprisoned not more than one
> year, or both.[33]

This did not apply if the abortion was necessary to save the life of the minor or in case of parental incest. The respect of the parental right was here again at the core of this law. The Bush administration was also involved in numerous measures to restrict access to contraception, like reserving the over-the-counter delivery of emergency contraception (EC) to women over eighteen. Thus to obtain EC, minors needed to have access to a medical doctor willing to prescribe it.

    Contrary to discourses over teenage pregnancy in the 1980s, contemporary discourses on abstinence present themselves as racially "neutral." This is probably due to the sharp criticism the rhetorical image of the black "welfare queen" provoked in the past twenty years and, as mentioned by Ashbee, to the wish of the Bush administration to convey a more sympathetic image of "compassionate conservatism."[34] Race is nowhere mentioned in these writings, but in the texts by the LaHayes, Meeker and Hagelin, this "neutrality" rather suggests an erasure of racial differences under the hegemony of whiteness as being the norm than a real inclusion of diversity. The LaHayes, for example, describe a homogenous middle-class Christian environment which appears to be only populated by the smiling Caucasian youths featured on the cover of their book. Meeker's discourse evokes a similar middle-class homogeneity in spite of the fact that the cover of one of her books presents a light-skinned African-American teenage boy and a dark-haired girl who could almost be Latina. 4Parents.gov featured the most inclusive type of discourse. Though race was nowhere mentioned, the pictures featured on the website displayed the greatest possible racial variety, including Asians, Latinos, African-American and Caucasian. This racial "neutrality" in the discourse, paired with racial variety in the images featured, is common to many abstinence websites like those of the Silver Ring Thing or Great to Wait. Yet in spite of this variety it can be argued that for a public influenced by the racist welfare discourses of the past twenty years, racial minorities might still be seen as primarily responsible for teenage pregnancy rates.

In an article entitled "'Children Having Children:' Race, Innocence, and Sexuality Education," Jessica Fields uncovers how, without mentioning race openly but by referring to the contaminating influence of "sexually and socially deviant" youths, abstinence debates revolve around racialised assumptions. She underlines that while "'deviant' is ostensibly race-neutral; [...] it is also a category that sexuality educators too often construct as comprising African-American mothers and poor and low-income people."[35]

Likewise, using her analysis of Senate and Congress hearings on abstinence education and teen pregnancy in 1996, W.S. Pillow argues that the image of the "black family" of the 1980s had been replaced by that of families coming from the "inner city."[36] In a similar document of 2004, a "Special Hearing before a Subcommittee of the Committee on Appropriations of the United States Senate" in Pennsylvania the term "inner city" does not appear. References are made to a "high risk population"[37] and two of the students testifying are African-American boys who explain that abstinence programmes helped them refocus their lives and achieve academic success when before, they were close to being expelled from their schools due to discipline problems.[38]

This idea that abstinence can be a way for black teens to be empowered is widespread in pro-abstinence discourses. It is also often described as a means for African-Americans to reverse the age-old racist image of blacks as irrepressibly promiscuous. For A.C. Green, former NBA player and leader of an abstinence program targeted by the Waxman report, if

> [o]ur youth are taught, through abstinence-based curriculum, that they have the power to control themselves and to change their lives in the process, the result may be

less promiscuity and increased personal effort to step out of
the cycle. [...] For inner city teenagers, a curriculum
empowering students in a society that infers through sex
education and condom distribution that they are powerless
might well be the answer.[39]

Green, who is himself African-American and focuses on children from
disadvantaged communities, takes up the term "inner city" teenagers and
evokes the particular echo that abstinence programmes can have in such
communities. For Green, abstinence is a means to step out of a "cycle," the
nature of which he does not specify, but which in the context of pro-
abstinence discourses evokes ideas like poverty or welfare dependency.

Social personality psychologists April Burns and Maria Elena Torre
investigated the unique impact that pro-abstinence discourses can have on
African-American girls. Through interviews, they discovered that African-
American girls expressed their desire for personal and social success in terms
that relied "heavily on a strong sense of personal responsibility and delayed
gratification (of all desires) as strategies" to achieve these goals.[40] Burns and
Torre explain that "given their lived realities of limited social privilege, these
strategies were experienced as the most available and seemingly viable."[41]
They argue that

> [i]nundated by "true life stories of how easy it is to "lose
> everything" [...], working-class girls and girls of color are
> constantly reminded of the fragility of their success.
> Dipping into the waters of sexual desire, they are
> repeatedly warned, will only lead them off-track and into
> disaster. Abstinence-only programmes exploit these
> feelings of anxious achievement by capitalizing on the
> danger and extreme consequences of knowing and/or acting
> on sexual desire.[42] They purposely create a climate of fear
> and anxiety so that youth can recognize the "safety" in
> "making the right choice" of disengaging their sexual
> desire.[43]

In this case while the abstinence programmes themselves might not be openly
marked by notions of race and class, they enable their users to play on the
fact that they take on a different dimension for girls whose social
circumstances create heavier consequences and social stigma in case of out-
of-wedlock pregnancy in particular.

Though featuring apparent racial neutrality pro-abstinence
discourses in connection with discourses on teen pregnancy and welfare, still

contribute to the promotion of racial stereotypes and this even when formulated by members of the African-Americans community.

The association of the prevention of teen pregnancy, abstinence and religion made by the AFLA and recommended by Rector was also present in the Bush administration legislations and discourses. In fact the G.W. Bush administration created in 2001 the White House Office of Faith-Based and Community Initiatives (White House OFBCI) aimed at establishing

> policies, priorities, and objectives for the Federal Government's comprehensive effort to enlist, equip, enable, empower, and expand the work of faith-based and other community organizations to the extent permitted by law.[44]

Through CBAE funding the Bush administration also supported faith-based pro-abstinence organizations like the Silver Ring Thing, or others mentioned in the Waxman report, and insisted on the role played by religious leaders regarding teens' sexual choices. Indeed, though texts on abstinence issued by the government featured a rather secular discourse they were not devoid of references to religion. The 4Parents website, for example, repeatedly advised parents to encourage faith in teens and to refer them to religious leaders. This is justified by the website's claim that "teens who are actively involved in a religious organization, who study faith, and pray or worship are less likely to begin early sexual activity."[45]

Like the Reagan administration in the 1980s, the G.W. Bush administration, similar to the Heritage Foundation, relied on its defense of abstinence as a means to prevent teen pregnancy, STDs and teen sexuality, to promote a conservative vision of welfare based on the idea of poverty being a moral matter.

Abstinence discourses played a crucial role in this promotion, since one of their major arguments was that abstinence guarantees teenagers a better professional and emotional future whereas promiscuity inevitably dooms them to a life of disease, emotional instability and welfare dependency.

Pro-abstinence discourses, though they present sexual choices in terms of morality, do not openly construct an image of sexually active teenagers as immoral but rather present an image of premarital sex as immoral. In their words, teenagers are pressured into wrong sexual choices by, among other things, the sexual revolution, lack of parental presence, peer pressure or "promiscuous media." For conservative Christians "children" are therefore not immoral per se, but innocent victims of a "sex-crazed" society,[46] or as Hagelin bluntly puts it:

> [O]ur children are paying - with their bodies - for the sins
> of their parents, who shed their own morals during the
> sexual revolution of the seventies and are passing on their
> brand of immorality through the media, education, and the
> culture in general.[47]

The sexual revolution is being held responsible by Hagelin, but also the LaHayes, Meeker, the Heritage Foundation, as well as by the now defunct Bush administration, not only for teen pregnancy and STD rates but for many of the problems facing the American society today. Pro-abstinence discourses are so centred on this notion of the moral decay of society as being the cause of teenage promiscuity that when children refuse to acknowledge the fact that sex might be wrong for them and persist in being sexually active, the cause must be in their view, that they are in "deep psychological pain [and] use their risky sexual behaviors to cope with this pain" because generally "their emotional needs are not being met."[48] Hence teenagers must be rescued from the negative influence around them and be told, as 4Parents.gov asserted that premarital sex is a "poor sexual decision"[49] and that abstinence is the "best choice emotionally and physically"[50] as it develops values such as "respect, responsibility, and self-control."[51]

Teenage "promiscuity" is also associated in those discourses with substance abuse. For example Hagelin quotes a study by the National Campaign to Prevent Teen Pregnancy which found that

> [s]exually experienced children were far more likely than
> virgins to engage in other risky behavior. They were six
> times more likely to drink at least once a week. They were
> three times more likely to smoke and four times more
> likely to use marijuana.[52]

According to Meeker all these substances contribute to sexual arousal and lift inhibitions.[53] The Heritage Foundation reinforces this dramatic picture by asserting that: teenage sex is related to higher rates of depression and suicide attempts; 67% of sexually active teenagers wish they would have waited to have sex; the earlier a woman has sex, the greater her risks of becoming pregnant, having an abortion, catching a STD, having multiple sex partners and being in an unstable marriage.[54] Many of these views were also promoted in the extension of CBAE program requirements of 2006.

But if premarital sex is presented by pro-abstinence discourses as leading to personal failure, abstinence is, on the contrary, defined as the key to personal, social and professional success. This is made especially clear by a conference paper entitled "Teenage Sexual Abstinence and Academic Achievement," delivered at the Heritage Foundation by Robert Rector and

Kirk A. Johnson and which, SIECUS argues, provided the base for the extension of CBAE program requirements. In this paper based on the results of the *National Longitudinal Study of Adolescent Health* Rector and Johnson state that abstinent teenagers are

> less likely to be depressed and to attempt suicide; to experience STDs; to have children out-of-wedlock; and to live in poverty and welfare dependence as adults [and] more likely to have stable and enduring marriages as adults.[55]

Moreover,

> teens who abstain from sex during high school years are substantially less likely to be expelled from school; less likely to drop out of high school; and more likely to attend and graduate from college.[56]

Which leads them to the conclusion that as better educational achievements usually lead to higher incomes; abstinent teens can expect to have an income 16 percent higher than non-abstinent teens from similar socio-economic backgrounds, meaning "an average increase of $370,000 in income over a lifetime."[57] But why would this be so? For two reasons, according to Rector and Johnson, first,

> teens who abstain will be subject to less emotional turmoil and fewer psychological distractions; this will enable them to better focus on schoolwork. Second, abstinence and academic achievement are promoted by common underlying character traits. Teens who abstain are likely to have greater future orientation, greater impulse control, greater perseverance, greater resistance to peer pressure, and more respect for parental and societal values. These traits are likely to contribute to higher academic achievement. [...] In short, teen virgins are more likely to possess character traits that lead to success in life. Moreover, the practice of abstinence is likely to foster positive character traits that, in turn, will contribute to academic performance.[58]

Read between the lines, this quote depicts by inversion a bleak image of the "promiscuous" teenager as having little capacity for long-term planning, as favoring instant gratification and being more easily influenced by peers than by meaningful adults, while being averse to societal values and thus possibly delinquent. This way sexual activity is equated with a host of undesirable behaviours while premarital abstinence is defined as the proper path to social integration and success.

The idea that sexually active teenagers are involved in "self-destructive" behaviours and that they do not respect themselves, their bodies and others are also recurrent in pro-abstinence discourses. Thus in spite of the fact that children are described as victims of a society that surrounds them with bad values, in pro-abstinence discourses the image of the "bad" teenager still coexists with the image of the "good" teenager, the existence of one being conditional on the existence of the other. However, as previously explained, even the "bad" teenager can repent and choose secondary virginity.

The assertion by SIECUS that this article provided the background for the CBAE requirements is confirmed by a comparison between the two texts. Similar to Rector and Johnson, the Department of Health and Human Services states that

> teen sexual activity is associated with decreased school completion, decreased educational attainment, and decreased income potential [...] teens who are sexually active are also more likely to engage in other risk behaviors such as: smoking, alcohol abuse, drug abuse, violence, and crime.[59]
> [...] abstinence is beneficial in preparation for successful marriage and significantly increases the probability of a happy, healthy marriage.[60]
> [...] abstinence is a means of developing discipline, self-awareness, and goal-setting behaviors.[61]

The connection of sexual abstinence, and other type of abstinence for example from alcohol, with personal and professional success and morality is nothing new and is central to the American narrative of success, the idea that hard-work, delayed gratification and self-control lead to success whereas laziness and instant gratification lead to moral laxity and failure. This was best illustrated by America's most famous self-made man: Benjamin Franklin. In his autobiography (1771-1790) Franklin explains how his early practice of temperance and hard work helped him rise above his initially poor circumstances and become a prominent public figure. In particular, Franklin recounts his very methodical attempt to acquire the thirteen virtues he had defined as essential, among them were temperance, frugality, moderation, and chastity under which he specified: "rarely use venery but for health or Offspring; Never to Dullness, Weakness, or the

Injury of your own or another's Peace or Reputation."[62] Though he did not succeed in mastering all these virtues, and came to the conclusion that if he had mastered them, such a perfect character would have been displeasing to his friends, he ascribed to this endeavour much of his later success in life and good public character.

Though Franklin was a deist, his belief in discipline and hard work was strongly grounded in America's religious heritage. Protestantism, as it was and is still practiced in the US, is based on the idea that material success in earthly life shows whether an individual is chosen by God. The key to success was the "puritan work ethic" of hard work, continence, and frugality. Abstaining from action on one's physical desires and overcoming them would enable the believer to invest all his energy on achieving material success. Therefore, as Americanists Michel Rezé and Ralph Bowen explain,

> [v]agrancy, gambling, habitual drunkenness, sexual dalliance and other unproductive uses of God's precious gifts of time and physical strength were unceasingly denounced from the pulpit and rigorously punished by the magistrate.[63]

The 19th-century Male Purity movement mentioned in the first chapter was part of this heritage when it promoted discipline and chastity as means to avoid immorality and poverty. Similarly, contemporary abstinence proponents advocate the idea that abstinence will lead teenagers to success in both their private and public lives while promiscuity will lead them to professional, personal and moral failure. The LaHayes, Meeker, Hagelin, like 4Parents.gov, also ensure their audience that if they work hard enough for it and follow their advice they will succeed in "raising sexually pure kids." The narrative of success and the Puritan work-ethic explain how the conservative vision of welfare advocated by abstinence proponents can be powerful, in spite of the fact that to work it relies on, as pointed at by Radford Ruether, an ignorance of "economic and class structures."[64] As argued by Burns and Torre, one of the consequences of the emphasis laid by pro-abstinence discourses on personal responsibility and delayed gratification is that

> pregnancy, disease, and the lack of academic success for youth with the fewest options all become coded in the public imagination as individual failures rather than as the social and political abandonment of young people.[65]

While for privileged youths the impact of such discourses might be rather insignificant, since their affluence better enables them to prevent the visible outcomes of their sexual activity like pregnancy, for working class and minority young people they can be devastating, particularly in their impact on welfare policy.

Contemporary pro-abstinence discourses are instrumental for the promotion of a conservative vision of welfare grounded in the traditional family structure and deeply influenced by cultural and historical visions of success, work and religious commitment. Abstinence education fits particularly efficiently in this vision of welfare, as it reinforces many of its central tenets. Thus, pro-abstinence discourses promote self-control, delayed gratification and the sublimation of sexual energy towards higher purposes. They also advocate a return to the traditional heterosexual family cell and challenge what conservatives see as the cause of its erosion: the sexual revolution. Moreover, they question some of the sexual revolution's major gains, access to abortion and contraception, and seek to increasingly involve faith-based organisations in children's reproductive choices and in federal education programmes.

Through pro-abstinence discourses, conservatives disturbingly equate sexual promiscuity, immorality and poverty. Thus they stigmatise the poor in general, especially African-Americans, and poor unmarried women in particular. This use of abstinence raises the ghost of social Darwinism and of a vision of welfare where the necessarily immoral poor should be denied financial support and only provided with moral re-education. Such a vision supports itself by the stigmatisation of poor single mothers who, they claim, face poverty as a consequence of their promiscuity while promoting a liberal economy, which scarcely provides unmarried mothers with means of achieving self-sufficiency.

Notes

[1] Rector, 2001, p.72.
[2] ibid., p.73.
[3] ibid., p.73.
[4] ibid., p.73.
[5] ibid., p.81.
[6] ibid., p.81.
[7] R Hagelin, 'Creating a Culture of Belonging,' 1 August 2006, viewed on 15 February 2007,
<http://www.heritage.org/Press/Commentary/ed080106b.cfm>
[8] R Santorum, 'Heritage Lecture: The Necessity of Marriage,' 20 October 2003, viewed on 18 June 2007,
<http://www.heritage.org/Research/Family/HL-804.cfm>
[9] ibid..
[10] Rector, 2001, p.82.
[11] Coltrane, 2001, p.390.
[12] ibid., p.406.

[13] ibid., p.391.

[14] ibid., p.390.

[15] Rector, 2001, pp.79-80.

[16] HERITAGE FOUNDATION, 2006, p.13.

[17] Radford Ruether, 2001, p.192.

[18] Irvine, 2002, p.90.

[19] *Adolescent Family Life Act of 1981*, United States Code /Title 42, The Public Health and Welfare Chapter 6A - Public Health and Service/Subchapter XVIII - Adolescent Family Life Demonstration Project, 97th Congress.

[20] ibid..

[21] ibid..

[22] J P Moran explains that "the birthrate for women age fifteen to nineteen had actually been declining from its all-time high of 91 per 1,000 in 1960, to 69,7 per 1,000 in 1970 and 55.6 per 1,000 in 1975," in Moran, 2000, p.200. The decrease remained constant in the next decade; however what did increase was the likelihood that these women were giving birth outside of marriage, a tendency also present in the rest of the population.

[23] *Adolescent Family Life Act*, 1981.

[24] Here Pillow refers the reader to the following:
K Luker, *Dubious Conceptions: The Politics of Teenage Pregnancy*, Harvard University Press, Cambridge, 1996; A Phoenix, 'The social Construction of Teenage Motherhood: A Black and White Issue?' in A Lawson and D L Rhode (eds), *The Politics of Pregnancy: Adolescent Sexuality and Public Policy*, Yale University Press, New Haven, 1993; D L Rhode, 'Adolescent Pregnancy and Public Policy' in Lawson and Rhode, 1993.

[25] Pillow, 2004, p.116.

[26] K M Sands, 'Public, Pubic, and Private, Religion in Political Discourse' in K M Sands (ed), *God Forbid: Religion and Sex in American Public Life*, Oxford University Press, Oxford, New York, 2000, p.78.

[27] ibid., p.77.

[28] Coontz and Folbre, 2002.

[29] Clinton, W. J., 'The President's Radio Address, May 4th 1996,' 1996, viewed on 18 June 2007,
<http://www.presidency.ucsb.edu/ws/index.php?pid=52768>

[30] W M Limbert and H E Bullock, ''Playing the Fool': US Welfare Policy from a Critical Race Perspective,' *Feminism and Psychology*, 2005, 15(3), pp.253-274, p.261.

[31] White House, 2002, p.22.

[32] Moran, 2000, p.216.

[33] *Child Interstate Abortion Notification Act*, H.R. 748, introduced 2005, 109th Congress.

[34] Ashbee, 2007, p.63.

[35] J Fields, ''Children Having Children:' Race, Innocence, and Sexuality Education,' *Social Problems*, 2005, 52 (4), pp.549-571, p.561.

[36] Pillow, 2004, p.202.

[37] U.S. Congress, Senate, *Abstinence Education: Special Hearing before a Subcommittee of the Committee on Appropriations of the United States Senate*, 108th Congress, 2nd sess., 16 February 2004, p.22.

[38] ibid., p.32-33.

[39] ACGreen.com, 'Abstinence Curriculum,' 2007, viewed on 15 March 2007, <http://www.acgreen.com/default.aspx?pageid=3939>

[40] A Burns and M E Torre, 'Shifting Desires: Discourses of Accountability in Abstinence-only Education in the United States' in A Harris (ed), *All About the Girl: Culture, Power and Identity*, Routledge, New York and London, 2004, p.129.

[41] ibid., p.129.

[42] D L Tolman, *Dilemmas of Desire: Teenage Girls Talk About Sexuality*, Harvard University Press, Cambridge, 2002.

[43] Burns and Torre, 2004, pp.130-31.

[44] G W Bush, 'Executive Order: Establishment of White House Office of Faith-Based and Community Initiatives,' 29 January 2001, viewed on 18 June 2007, <http://www.whitehouse.gov/news/releases/2001/01/20010129-2.html>

[45] U.S. Department of Health and Human Services, 2005a, p.4.

[46] LaHaye, 1998a, p.10.

[47] Hagelin, 2005b, p.33.

[48] Meeker, 2002, pp.222-223.

[49] U.S. Department of Health and Human Services, 2005a, p.4.

[50] ibid., p.1.

[51] ibid., p.2.

[52] Hagelin, 2005b, pp.33-34.

[53] Meeker, 2002,p.160.

[54] R Rector, 'Abstinence Promotion,' in HERITAGE FOUNDATION, *Issues 2006: The Candidate's Briefing Book*, 2006, viewed on 18 June 2007, <http://www.heritage.org/research/features/issues/pdfs/BriefingBook2006.pdf>, p.100-101.

[55] R Rector and K A Johnson, 'Teenage Sexual Abstinence and Academic Achievement,' 27 October 2005, viewed on 19 June 2007, <http://www.heritage.org/Research/Welfare/upload/84576_1.pdf >

[56] ibid..

[57] ibid..

[58] ibid..
[59] U.S. Department of Health and Human Services Administration for Children and Families, 2006a, p.10.
[60] ibid., p.8.
[61] ibid., p.12.
[62] B Franklin, *The Autobiography and Other Writings*, Penguin Books, London, 2003, p.83.
[63] M Rezé and R Bowen, *Key Words in American Life: Understanding the United States*, Armand Colin, Paris,1998, p.95.
[64] Radford Ruether, 2001, p.192.
[65] Burns and Torre, 2004, p.133.

Chapter 11
Abstinence and the "Culture War"

The concept, or narrative, of a "culture war" that would be dividing the United Sates into two starkly opposite groups of conservatives and "liberals" is familiar to observers of US politics at least since the early 1990s, when it was popularised by Pat Buchanan at the Republican National Convention. The purpose of this chapter is to examine how the narrative of the "culture war" is used by pro-abstinence discourses to promote traditional family hierarchies and maintain the commitment of conservative activists, and how the sense of being under siege is reinforced by pro-abstinence rhetoric. Before going further in my argumentation I will give a short overview of what is understood by the term "culture war," look at some of its historical roots and question the actual existence this phenomenon. Further on, I will analyse the narrative of the "culture war" within pro-abstinence discourses through the following questions: By whom and against whom is the "culture war" supposed to be waged? On which fronts is it taking place? Why? And what are the weapons that conservative Christians can use to win this war? Finally, I will ask what is really at stake in this narrative and what purpose it serves within these discourses.

The widespread use of the "narrative" of the culture war" in US political discourse is usually dated back to an oft-quoted speech delivered in 1992 by Pat Buchanan at the Republican National Convention, where he stated that,

> [t]here is a religious war going on in our country for the soul of America. It is a cultural war, as critical to the kind of nation we will one day be as was the Cold War itself.[1]

Buchanan would have himself borrowed the expression from *Culture Wars: The Struggle to Define America* a book by sociologist James Davison Hunter published in 1991[2], which described the increasing opposition between an "orthodox" and a "progressist" America on moral issues like abortion, women and gay rights, funding of the arts, etc.

Political scientist Morris P. Fiorina, who questions the existence of such a polarisation, explains that

> [m]ost commentators use the culture war metaphor to refer to a displacement or supercession of the classic economic conflicts that animated twentieth-century politics in the advanced democracies by newly emergent moral and religious ones.[3]

The narrative of the "culture war" is centered on "moral" or "cultural" issues. For conservative writers it corresponds to the erosion of the "traditional American values" of self-sufficiency, hard-work, self-control and religious observance, resulting in a moral decline of the nation. This erosion was, in their view, caused by the 1960s "counterculture," especially the feminist and sexual revolutions. Therefore, they usually point to the 1950s as the ideal era to which they want to return. However, as pointed out by Jeffrey Weeks, the changes they oppose were not only the product of the 1960s but the outcome of a historical process that spanned over several decades.[4] As underlined previously, the ideal of the 1950s traditional American family has little historical accuracy.

The narrative of the "culture war" and the denunciation of a decline of America through the erosion of morality have deep roots in US history. "Culture war" discourses inscribe themselves in the tradition of what Sacvan Bercovitch dubbed the "American Jeremiad." The jeremiad was a form of speech or sermon that puritans brought with them from Europe and adapted to the American context. It was then taken on and altered by following generations into a more secular form of speech up to the present day.[5] English professor Donna M. Campbell explains that the jeremiad

> accounts for the misfortunes of an era as a just penalty for great social and moral evils, but holds out hope for changes that will bring a happier future. It derives from the Old Testament prophet Jeremiah, who in the seventh century B.C. attributed the calamities of Israel to its abandonment of the covenant with Jehovah and its return to pagan idolatry, denounced with "lurid and gloomy eloquence" its religious and moral iniquities, and called on the people to repent and reform in order that Jehovah might restore them to his favor and renew the ancient covenant.[6]

Likewise, discourses dealing with the narrative of the "culture war" denounce the moral decay that followed the 1960s and the state of decline of the United States and offer various solutions to remedy them - teaching creationism, for example, as seen at the beginning of this chapter, promoting traditional marriage, opposing abortion and gay rights, etc.

In contrast with the conservative Christian notion of an ideal past of cultural consensus, it has to be noted that the feeling of crisis entertained by "culture war" discourses is not recent, but rather is part of a long-lasting American cultural tradition. It is therefore legitimate to ask if the "culture war" described by contemporary media as irremediably dividing US citizens is really more than discursive. For political scientists Alan Wolfe and Morris Fiorina it is not. In his book *One Nation After All: What Middle-Class*

Americans Really Think About God, Country, Family, Racism, Welfare, Immigration, Homosexuality, Work, the Right, the Left, and Each Other, published in 1998 Wolfe explains that by

> moving beyond polls and surveys to more ethnographic attempts to uncover people's belief, I have found little support for the notion that middle-class Americans are engaged in bitter cultural conflict with each other over the proper way to live. [...] Above all moderate in their outlook on the world, they believe in the importance of leading a virtuous life but are reluctant to impose values they understand as virtuous for themselves on others; strong believers in morality, they do not want to be considered moralists.[7]

In his book *Culture War: The Myth of a Polarized America*, which focuses mostly on the 2000 and, at the time of writing upcoming, 2004 elections, Fiorina draws similar conclusions, arguing that it is not the ideological divide within the population which causes a divide in politics, but the contrary: "the political figures Americans evaluate are more polarized. A polarized political class makes the citizenry appear polarized, but it is only that - an appearance."[8] For Fiorina the "myth" of the "culture war" is fed by misinterpretation of polls and statistics, deliberate bias by activists and "selective coverage by an uncritical media more concerned with news value than with getting the story right"[9] since conflict sells better than consensus. Using the "culture war" at the heart of pro-abstinence discourses also "sells." As will be analysed now, presenting debates over sex-education as "struggles" in which conservatives have to prevail to protect their children, their family and their country contributes to the appeal and strategic relevance of pro-abstinence discourses.

The vision of conservative Christians as a minority waging a "culture war" against "liberal" forces to rescue traditional American values is at the core of the LaHaye's and Hagelin's pro-abstinence rhetoric and is important in Meeker's writings as well. It was also present, although in less extreme terms, in the discourses of the G.W. Bush administration. This discursive strategy is best illustrated by most of Tim LaHaye's books, including the *The Battle for the Mind* (1980) and its reviewed version *Mind Siege: The Battle for Truth in the New Millenium*, or through his fiction writing like the *Left Behind* series. All these works denounce a "secular humanist" plot inspired by Satan and led by the American Humanist Associaton - a secular organization which promotes the advocacy of ethical behavior independently from notions of retribution and punishment - to destroy Christianity, morality and America and promote among others, atheism, immorality, communism and world government.

Secular humanists are just one of the culprits for the "culture war" identified by some conservative Christian writers. In the framework of their pro-abstinence discourses, the major "enemies" identified by the LaHayes, Meeker and Hagelin are the media and the fashion industry, as well as SIECUS, liberal sex-educators, and the pharmaceutical or "medical" industry.

In the tradition of the American jeremiad, the LaHayes, Meeker and Hagelin blame the 1960s "counterculture" for the moral decline they have to fight. The LaHayes inscribe themselves in this discursive tradition even more literally, in their references to the bible and their belief in a "pre-tribulationist"[10] apocalyptic worldview. For example, they claim that the STD epidemic, which is the result of the sexual revolution, "begins to resemble the end-time plagues described in the Book of Revelation."[11] Pro-abstinence authors also recurrently point back to a pre-60s era, when their own childhood took place, as an ideal state to restore. Hagelin provides a good illustration of this vision when she argues that,

> Americans once shared a collective understanding that ours is a society based on faith in God and His immutable laws of unconditional love, decency, and the simple but powerful concept of treating others as we would be treated. Our schools once taught biblical principles. Our families gathered regularly in churches and synagogues. Prayer was a standard part of life - both private and public. Americans were taught the Ten Commandments and the rich Judeo-Christian heritage of our country.
>
> But that all changed in the 1960s when there began to be a steady removal of God and His absolutes from the public square. As a nation we forgot, as President Lincoln once said [...], "that the fear of the Lord is the beginning of wisdom." Schools were purged of prayer and biblical values, leaving a vacuum that was soon filled with the preaching of moral relativism, sexual anarchy and a trashing of U.S. history. Now, about forty years later, there is no collective understanding of our Judeo-Christian heritage and the values that once permeated our halls of government, our schools and our lives.[12]

Through this dramatic depiction of contemporary US society, these authors warn parents that their task in keeping their children abstinent is harder than that of any generation before their own. Ignoring the long tradition of conflicts over sexual norms in American history[13] they present parents with a struggle of an unequalled scale, which requires a mobilisation never seen before, and in which defeat implies moral mayhem and countless deaths. While Meeker reminds her readers that when they were teens in the 1960s a simple shot could cure most identified STDs, today there might be no cure at all.[14] As for the LaHayes, they draw an epic picture of the task to be taken on by parents:

> you can raise virtuous children in this permissive society, but you will have to work harder at it than any generation before you. Our culture is one of the most sex-crazed this world has ever known. It is impossible to shield your child from it, for it is everywhere, from TV programming and commercials to school curricula to unbelievably early childhood conversation. Because of society's overemphasis on sex, your children will probably show curiosity about it much earlier than you want them to.[15]

All these pro-abstinence authors see themselves as being in the middle of a "war," or fight against the "culture," that they sometimes openly refer to as "culture war." The LaHayes use the expression several times in their books and recurrently denounce the "culture" as Christian families' enemy. One of Hagelin's articles is explicitly entitled "The Culture War: A Five-Point Plan for Parents"[16] and Meeker blames the STD "epidemic" on a culture in which, she claims, "teens are literally being trained into sexual activity, indoctrinated into a lifestyle that can kill them."[17] President Bush echoed this type of discourses when he explained in his 2004 *State of the Union Address* that,

> [a]bstinence for young people is the only certain way to avoid sexually-transmitted diseases. Decisions children now make can affect their health and character for the rest of their lives. All of us - parents and schools and government - must work together to counter the negative influence of the culture, and to send the right messages to our children.[18]

The "culture" they refer to is one that, in Hagelin's words, menaces to invade homes "through the Internet, television, the radio" and books.[19] It is a culture of "depravity" deprived of the "civilizing" influence of religion and whose main heralds are Hollywood, MTV and brands like Abercrombie & Fitch.[20] In the view of abstinence proponents, the field in which the "culture" has the most "negative influence" is sexuality, for "sexual permissiveness has been at the core of that culture war."[21] Particularly, in their view, because sex "sells"[22] and is consequently at the heart of the business of the entertainment and fashion industry of which children and teens are a major target.

The major culprits that pro-abstinence writers hold accountable for what they see as the current state of "oversexualisation" or "promiscuity" of the nation can be divided into two major groups that they both blame for attacking children's "innocence" and "parental rights": on the one hand the entertainment industry or "media" and the fashion industry, and on the other hand SIECUS and sex-educators along with the medical industry.

Be it the LaHayes, Meeker, Hagelin or 4Parents.gov all promote, or in the case of the latter promoted, the idea that the media, along with the fashion industry are overly displaying "sexual" materials as a marketing strategy and have therefore a negative influence on children's sexual behaviour or lack thereof. Hagelin and Meeker both report occasions when they were shocked by the content of advertisements or magazines teens are exposed to. Hagelin, for example, asks her readers to

> think about some of the slogans kids encounter: "Just do it." "Why wait?" "Obey your thirst." "No boundaries." "Got the urge?" In other words, be selfish, instantly gratify yourself, regardless of the consequences.[23]

Indeed, taken out of context these slogans might appear overtly sexual. However, the products they sell are not, *per se*: sport accessories, high-speed internet connection, soda, cars or shampoo;[24] which reinforces the idea that nearly everything is "sexualised" by the "culture" in order to sell. This feeling is also conveyed by Meeker who shares that

> I often feel the media and I are at war. They seduce [teens] to get sick; I try to keep [them] well. Think I'm exaggerating? Check out the magazine covers at the supermarket next time you're there. Here's what […] girls […] are reading: "10 Dates before Sex? And Other Secrets of Love that Last and Last"/ "Ultra Orgasm"/"Love Positions"/"Lust advice.com"/"Five Sex Moves Every Woman must Know"/"20 Earth-Quaking Moves That Will Make Him Plead For Mercy and Beg For More" […] You get the picture. The gorgeous beauties gracing the covers were sexy, seductive, and staring right at the viewer. None wore visible wedding rings. One article included pictures of the different positions couples should try during intercourse.[25]

In Meeker and Hagelin's view the "media" encourage selfishness, instant gratification, promiscuity and "immodesty" - as witnessed by Meeker's sexy models "staring right at the viewer" - using sex to sell everything.

The Bush administration contributed to this rhetoric with comments like the following from one of the pamphlets available at 4Parents.gov:

> It comes from everywhere... advertising, friends, movies, TV shows, songs, and books. BUT STOP. . . AND THINK. Will having sex really make you more popular, more mature, or more desirable? No.[26]

Or the recommendation from the CBAE guidelines that abstinence-only programs should teach:

> [H]ow to avoid settings that involve potential interaction with pornography (e.g., explicit movies, TV, magazines, Internet) [and provide] understanding of media influence on sexual behavior and skills for resisting negative media influences.[27]

For the LaHayes, Meeker and Hagelin the entertainment industry only sees teens as a lucrative market and does not care about children's health.[28] In their pro-abstinence writings, they therefore advise parents to protect their children from sexual content in the media and to take actions like boycotting to fight "the negative influence of the culture."[29] Meeker even goes as far as demanding a legislative ban on

> all sexual content from advertising, movies, and magazines promoted to teenage and younger audiences. Prime time television should not include sexual content. Movies rated PG-13[30] should not have sexually explicit content, whether or not they make reference to contraception.[31]

They also advise parents to screen and monitor what their children watch, listen to, read and wear. In her list of "weapons" to fight the "culture war" and protect children's "innocence," Hagelin recommends internet and DVD filters[32] as well as retailers of "modest" clothing for girls, like "Modest Apparel USA"[33] or "Modest by Design," "clothing your father would approve of."[34,35] The LaHayes and Meeker, like 4Parents.gov and the CBAE requirements, provide similar recommendations.[36]

Parents are thus encouraged to exercise their parental rights and reclaim their legitimate status as the most important influence in their children's lives that the culture is trying to rob from them. Hagelin assures them that they "can win"[37], and Meeker closes her book by stating that "there is no question that [their children] will survive the battle. They will if we enter it with them and help them through the fight."[38] As for 4Parents.gov, it attempted to convince parents that contrary to what they might think, statistics prove that they have the most influence on their children's sexual decisions.[39]

The fact that an outside source like the media might yield a considerable influence on their children on such a crucial issue as standards of sexual morality is necessarily disturbing for conservative parents who are concerned that their sons and daughters acquire the same values as theirs in order to uphold their parental authority. The control they advocate over their children's access to the media is therefore not only motivated by legitimate parental care but also provides them with a ground for asserting their control over their children's interactions with the world outside the family. By permanently stating that the media are threatening their child's morals and health, they justify a control which, especially in the case of older teens might be considered problematic in terms of civil rights.

This condemnation of the media also enables them to develop a discursive strategy around the theme of the protection of children's innocence. The theme of children's sexual "innocence" or "purity" underlies most pro-abstinence discourses. It is closely related to the question of access to "the culture" since it is the culture which is deemed to be stealing their innocence, especially by exposing them to sexual materials inappropriate for their age. Hagelin develops this theme of innocence further. In her book *Home Invasion* she argues that families are menaced by what she calls "cultural terrorism" which destroys the innocence of their children.[40]

This theme of sexual innocence is crucial to the condemnation of the second culprit designated as a major enemy in the "culture war": the "coalition" formed by SIECUS, sex-educators and the medical industry.

SIECUS appears to be one of pro-abstinence writers' favorite targets. The LaHayes, Meeker and Hagelin all devote at least a page to condemn the organisation[41] and retell various "horror stories" concerning it. Each of them details, more or less comprehensively, the recommendations of SIECUS to sex-educators in order to shock parents and make them react on the inappropriateness of sex-education programs in public schools. The recommendations they are the most incensed by as constituting major threats to children's "innocence" are those that underline the positive dimension of masturbation and homosexuality, and the potential recourse to "outercourse" (non-genital sex) as disease and pregnancy prevention.

The LaHayes accuse SIECUS of teaching "promiscuity" to obtain "billions of tax dollars"[42] and, quoting James Dobson of Focus on the Family, they claim that "bureaucrats, researchers and Planned Parenthood types" encourage teenage sexual activity because it generates money through abortion, contraception and medical care.[43] While Meeker does not overtly blame the lack of opposition to teenage sex on mercenary interests, she goes as far as arguing that SIECUS is at the heart of a conspiracy

> operating behind the scenes of public schools sex education. [...To] maintain sexual freedoms rather than prevent disease, maximize psychological health, and ensure healthy sexuality among our teens.[44]

It seems ironical that Meeker blames sex-educators for not ensuring "healthy sexuality among [...] teens" when healthy sexuality for her amounts to no sex at all. Besides, while she underlines the agenda of this conspiracy she does not underline its aim very clearly. In Meeker's view, sexual liberals believe in sexual freedom as a matter of "inalienable personal rights"[45] on which even younger individuals have to make independent choices, a position that she opposes. She concludes that

> it seems clear that SIECUS places sexual freedom for teens above their health. As long as the idea of sexual freedom remains the driving force behind national sex education, the STD epidemic will continue.[46]

For her, as for the LaHayes or Hagelin, "sexual freedom" amounts to a sort of religious belief from their "liberal" opponents, since they defend it despite the danger it constitutes and not necessarily with any apparent reason. They see "sexual liberalism" as being part of the essence of being a "liberal." An interesting vision of the "nature" of liberalism is provided by journalist Thomas Frank who analyses what he sees as conservative's vision of the motivation of liberal activists.

> Liberals tell the news and interpret the laws and publish the books and make the movies the way they do not because it sells ads or it pleases the boss or it's cheaper that way; they do it simply because they are liberals, because it helps other liberals, because it promises to convert the world to liberalism.[47]

Formulating the debate in such absolutes allows abstinence proponents to present it as a matter of "faith" on both sides that cannot be reconciled in any way, thus reasserting the feeling that they are indeed in the middle of war against either other believers or "ruthless" money-makers. The concept of "sexual freedom" which is at the heart of comprehensive sex-education is, as seen previously, especially threatening for conservative Christians in the way as the LaHayes put it, it does not respect parents' rights "to be the primary teacher of this subject" to their children.[48] It is therefore a particularly efficient catalyst for the outrage necessary to motivate the feeling of being involved in a "culture war."

The concept of "children's innocence" and the "horror stories" that accompany it are also heavily resorted to in order to muster outrage at sex education and reinforce the feeling of being under siege. The LaHayes describe sex-educators as perverted and particularly oppose the fact that classes are coeducational which in their view "destroys the moral mystique that naturally exists between the sexes."[49] The opposition to coeducational sex education was also conveyed in the extension of the requirements for CBAE grantees which explained that

> [g]raphic images of genitalia for purposes of illustrating the effects of sexually transmitted diseases (STDs) are inappropriate for certain age groups, especially if classes are not gender separated.[50]

Along similar lines, Hagelin recounts the story of a mother who was "devastated" when she learned that her son was told in fifth grade how girls attach sanitary pads to their underwear;[51] and the regrets of a father who let his daughter attend a sex-ed class where she was handed out condoms. Hagelin concludes that "he knows better now, but [his daughter's] innocence has been lost."[52] Meeker follows the same line of arguments by explaining that one of her young patients was disgusted by the explicitness of sex-education in eighth grade, which subsequently hindered her relationships with boys until college.[53]

As exposed previously, parents are consequently strongly encouraged to take back control of their children's sexual education, demand explicit information on the content of the sex-education classes in their children's schools, and if necessary opt them out of these classes, homeschool them or send them to private schools. These solutions are advocated by pro-abstinence discourses as "weapons" in the "culture war" to protect children's innocence.

If the "culture war" has to be waged on the abstinence front in order to protect children's innocence and parental rights, it is also fought in order to save the nation. Like creationists who advocate the belief in the Genesis story of creation to redeem the United States from the moral decay it is subjected to, the LaHayes see in the STD epidemic a "penalty for discarding God's clear teachings on sexual matters" since the sexual revolution[54] and claim that whereas in the past the church was "the conscience of the nation" today "Hollywood and Broadway have more influence on the morals of society."[55] Meeker sees this epidemic as a threat to "the future of our country", as it menaces the health and survival of the coming generations.[56] The Bush administration echoed these concerns when it wrote, as quoted earlier, that the "explosion" of STDs caused by the 1960s sexual revolution poses "a growing hazard to the Nation's public health" along with the increase in out-of-wedlock pregnancies that "have contributed so heavily to the Nation's domestic problems including poverty, violence, and intergenerational welfare dependency."[57]

Comparing contemporary sexual debates with those occurring in early America, Richard Godbeer remarks insightfully that

> [t]he fundamental issues driving [the] sexual debate remain the same, however: competing sexual codes that stress either exclusive or more inclusive standards for judging intimate relationships still struggle to coexist; Americans continue to frame that debate in terms of the correlation between sexual mores and the character of society as a whole; and as the great republican experiment continues into the twenty-first century, the quest for personal freedom still collides with a hankering after moral community.[58]

Similarly to their forefathers, many contemporary Americans, and particularly conservative Christians, still place the premarital sexual behavior of youths at the heart of their appraisal of society's moral standing. In our western world, youths always represent the future of a nation, the coming generation. Professor of Education Nancy Lesko explains that at the beginning of the 20th century

> adolescence was reformulated in psychological and sociological terms as "the promise of individual or collective regeneration." During the decade 1895 to 1905 the new adolescent was invented as turbulent, as the "seed of new wealth for the future," as the source of progress for the race.[59]

The fact that this "seed" might be endangered by moral "corruption" and STDs through premarital sexual activity must therefore be a major concern for the nation. Abstinence and the way it attempts to limit sexual expression to the boundaries of marriage can consequently only be at the core of the "culture war", since as Weeks put it "as sex goes, so goes society."[60] Teens are thus constructed by pro-abstinence discourses as the guardians of the nation's "morality" since their sexual choices can endanger the nation at large, its health, its social equilibrium, its morality and its future. Hence, for conservative Christians, abstinence constitutes a crucial tool in the preservation of the nation.

For pro-abstinence writers, inscribing their discourses into the narrative of the "culture war" and the tradition of the American Jeremiad also fulfills another function. It contributes to stirring their followers' anxiety, and thus maintains their commitment to the cause of abstinence and to the "culture war." Bercovitch explains that the function of the American jeremiad

> was to create a climate of anxiety that helped release the restless "progressivist" energies required for the success of the venture. [… T]he American Puritan jeremiad […] made anxiety its end as well as its means. Crisis was the social norm it sought to inculcate. The very concept of errand, after all implied a state of *un*fulfillment. The future, though divinely assured, was never quite there, and New England's Jeremiahs set out to provide the sense of insecurity that would ensure the outcome. Denouncing or affirming, their vision fed on the distance between promise and fact.[61]

Similarly, abstinence discourses maintain a permanent sense of crisis. The "culture" will always menace their children's "innocence" and their parental prerogative, victory is "never quite there." To confirm this feeling, pro-abstinence writers systematically diminish the successes of their cause. Like Hagelin or the LaHayes, they argue that "inefficient" comprehensive sex-education is overwhelmingly present in public schools, while abstinence-only is under funded. For example, Hagelin claims that in 2005

> the federal government [spent] about $167 million to teach kids the abstinence-only approach. […] A noble goal, indeed. But it's one that will prove quite an uphill climb for many parents, especially when you consider the fact that the federal government spends about 12 times as much on "comprehensive" sex ed (sometimes dubbed "abstinence-plus" to fool unsuspecting parents) as it does on abstinence-only sex ed.[62]

They also present the media as mostly "perverted" and "oversexualised", in spite of the very rich market of Christian publishing, radio and TV shows; and the fact that even Hollywood increasingly seeks to cater to conservative Christian needs with movies like *The Chronicles of Narnia* (2005) an adaptation of the books of C.S. Lewis, a favorite author of the conservative Christian community, or *Amazing Grace* (2006), the story of a British preacher and abolitionist, which was strongly recommended by Hagelin and CWA. The 20th Century Fox company even developed its own "morally driven, family-friendly" label, which produces and distributes movies that must have an "overt Christian content or be derived from the work of a Christian author."[63] In fact, conservative Christian standards of propriety increasingly influence the productions of Hollywood as well as what can be said or not regarding sexuality in the public place.

By fuelling the sense of anxiety and unfulfilment necessary to maintain the feeling of being under siege, the theme of the "culture war" strengthens pro-abstinence discourses. Conversely, pro-abstinence discourses reinforce the belief that "culture war" is happening by centering the debate on the highly symbolic issue of children's sexuality.

To conclude, the functions that the integration of the theme of the "culture war" into pro-abstinence discourses fulfils are threefold. It contributes to the promotion of parental rights through the need to protect children's innocence against a corrupted culture. It also strengthens the position of abstinence as a central issue of the "culture war" while conversely, the integration of abstinence into "culture war" discourses fuels the sense of threat necessary to maintain the feeling of being under siege that justifies conservative Christians' involvement in the cultural fight.

Within pro-abstinence discourses, the narrative of the culture war and the narrative of success as antidote to welfare dependency are both strengthened and given greater cultural currency. In conservative Christian discourses, both these narratives revolve around a conservative view of history based on the idealisation of a pre-"sexual revolution" era when the "American" values of "work, wedlock and worship" were supposedly better respected. This use of an idealised past enables abstinence proponents to condemn the social, cultural and familial changes, many of them inevitable, which occurred during and after the 1960s, in order to promote a societal order based on traditional hierarchies. Both these narratives also contribute to maintaining a sense of threat and decay, which prevents conservative Christians from, as Sara Diamond put it, becoming "complacent."[64]

The purpose of Chapters 6 to 11 was to underline how pro-abstinence discourses, while seemingly being focused on a single issue, enable their producers to convey much wider ideological messages to their audiences. The strategic interest of the theme of abstinence lies, for conservative Christian leaders, in the way it coalesces most of their core agendas like creationism, parental rights or the culture war. Pro-abstinence discourses also give greater cultural relevance and strength to issues with which it might have become difficult for them to mobilise their followers. Additionally, while creationism or the culture war, by themselves, might appeal only to the most radical fringes of the conservative Christian constituency, abstinence and the anxiety it stirs over the highly sensitive issue of child sexuality might be more suitable to attract broader audiences.

Unlike creationism or parental rights, abstinence can also be justified through medical arguments and is thus more easily dissociated from religious types of discourses, which enables it to attract non-Christians as well. All the more so since abstinence, when it is coupled with information on contraception and abortion, is already supported by many American parents. Hence, if abstinence discourses are formulated in a secular enough way they have the potential to constitute a bridge between conservative Christians and other groups and to attract less open opposition than highly contentious issues like abortion or creationism.

Conversely, abstinence enables politicians to address broad conservative Christian concerns in an implicit manner with a smaller risk of alienating more moderate supporters. However, in this regard the pro-abstinence discourse of the Bush administration, especially in the administration's second term, had become so radicalised - for example with its stricter requirements and the extension of abstinence to people aged up to twenty-nine years old - that this dimension of abstinence discourses was drastically undermined.

In consequence, sexual abstinence before marriage and the discourses it generates should not be dismissed as a question of little political relevance as they constituted, during the Bush era, a crucial locus for the interaction between the government and conservative Christian lobbies as well as a privileged instrument for the extension of traditionally conservative Christian concerns to a mainstream arena.

Notes

[1] P J Buchanan, 'Republican National Convention Speech,' 17 August 1992, viewed on 5 March 2007,<http://www.buchanan.org/pa-92-0817-rnc.html>
[2] J D Hunter, *Culture Wars: The Struggle to Define America*, Basic Books, New York, 1991.
[3] M P Fiorina, S J Abrams and J C Pope, *Culture War: The Myth of a Polarized America*, Pearson Longman, New York, 2005, p1-2.
[4] Weeks, 1986, p.92.
[5] S Bercovitch, *The American Jeremiad*, University of Wisconsin Press, Madison, 1978.
[6] D M Campbell, 'Forms of Puritan Rhetoric: The Jeremiad and the Conversion Narrative,' February 21, 2006, viewed on 5 March 2007, <http://www.wsu.edu/~campbelld/amlit/jeremiad.htm>
[7] Wolfe, 1999, p.278.
[8] Fiorina et al., 2005, p.5.

[9] ibid., p.5.
[10] For a definition of this term see Chapter 2.
[11] LaHaye, 1998a, p.204.
[12] Hagelin, 2005b, pp.7-8.
[13] Godbeer, 2002, p.339.
[14] Meeker, 2002, p.15.
[15] LaHaye, 1998a, pp.9-10.
[16] Hagelin, 2005a.
[17] Meeker, 2002, p.211.
[18] Bush, 2004.
[19] Hagelin, 2005b, p.XIII.
[20] ibid.
[21] LaHaye, 1998a, p.16.
[22] ibid., p.16.
[23] R Hagelin, 'Selling Selfishness to Children,' July 27, 2004b, viewed on 15 February 2007, <http://www.heritage.org/Press/Commentary/ed072704c.cfm>
[24] "Just do it" was a slogan for Nike; "Why wait?" for an internet provider; "Obey your thirst" for Sprite; "No boundaries" for Ford and "Got the urge?" for Herbal Essence shampoo.
[25] Meeker, 2002, pp.120-121.
[26] U.S. Department of Health and Human Services, *Teen Chat: A Guide to Discussing Healthy Relationships*, 2005b, viewed on 6 March 2007, <http://www.4parents.gov/downloads/teenchat.pdf>, p.12.
[27] U.S. Department of Health and Human Services Administration for Children and Families, 2006a.
[28] Meeker, 2002, p.69; Hagelin, 2005b; LaHaye, 1998a, p.16.
[29] Bush, 2004.
[30] PG-13 is a rating category of the Motion Picture Association, which corresponds to "parents strongly cautioned; some material may be inappropriate for children under 13." However, it is important to keep in mind that American ratings are already considerably stricter on sexual contents than ratings in European countries.
[31] Meeker, 2002, p.140.
[32] R Hagelin, 'Parenting II: We're All in This Together,' 3 September 2003, viewed on 7 March 2007, <http://www.heritage.org/Press/Commentary/ed093103a.cfm>
[33] <www.modestapparelusa.com>, last viewed on 10 March 2009.
[34] <www.modestbydesign.com>, last viewed on 10 March 2009.

[35] R Hagelin, 'Fashioning a Response to Immodest Clothing,' 23 August 2005d, viewed on 7 March 2007, http://www.heritage.org/Press/Commentary/ed082305a.cfm>

[36] LaHaye, 1998a, p.58; Meeker, 2002, pp.140-142; U.S. Department of Health and Human Services, 2005a, p.4.

[37] Hagelin, 2005b, p.XXI.

[38] Meeker, 2002, p.223.

[39] U.S. Department of Health and Human Services, 2005a, p.2.

[40] Hagelin, 2005b, p.3.

[41] LaHaye, 1998a, p.17 and pp.255-56; Meeker, 2002, pp.26-28; Hagelin, 2005b, pp.107-108.

[42] LaHaye, 1998a, p.17.

[43] ibid., p.38.

[44] Meeker, 2002, p.26.

[45] ibid., p.28.

[46] ibid., p.28.

[47] T Frank, *What's the Matter with Kansas? How Conservatives Won the Heart of America*, Metropolitan Books, New York, 2004, p.132.

[48] LaHaye, 1998a, p.37.

[49] ibid., p.37.

[50] U.S. Department of Health and Human Services Administration for Children and Families, 2006a, p.5.

[51] Hagelin, 2005b, p.107.

[52] ibid., p.106.

[53] Meeker, 2002, p.212.

[54] LaHaye, 1998a, p.207.

[55] LaHaye, 1998b, p.15.

[56] Meeker, 2002, p.11.

[57] White House, 2002, p.22.

[58] Godbeer, 2002, p.339.

[59] N Lesko, *Act Your Age: A Cultural Construction of Adolescence*, Routledge, New York and London, 2001, pp.110-111.

[60] Weeks, 1986, p.36.

[61] Bercovitch, 1978, p.23, author's emphasis.

[62] R Hagelin, 'Debunking the Siren Song of 'Safe Sex,'' 22 July 2005e, viewed on 9 March 2007, <http://www.heritage.org/Press/Commentary/ed072205a.cfm>

[63] Fox Faith, 'About Fox Faith,' 2006, viewed on 9 March 2007, <www.foxfaith.com>

[64] Diamond, 1998, p.5.

Chapter 12
The Different Functions of Pro-Abstinence Discourses

The previous chapters were devoted to the analysis of the different conservative narratives at the heart of the pro-abstinence discourses produced by authors coming from a continuum of religious and political perspectives. Contrary to the emphasis on similarity displayed there, the coming chapter will focus on understanding the potential differences between the subtexts underlying the two major types of pro-abstinence discourses studied here.

In the first part of this book, it was underlined that what can be described as the "religious" and "political" pro-abstinence discourses are extremely similar in the narratives they use and the vision of sexuality, the family and social order that they seek to promote. However, beneath these apparent similarities lie significant differences in the subtexts implied by these discourses. This chapter focuses on understanding the implications of pro-abstinence rhetoric for conservative Christians as well as the Bush administration. It analyses the function of the blurring of boundaries between the religious and the political operated through pro-abstinence discourses and attempts to investigate the "hidden agendas" behind the overt one of the promotion of abstinence for youths' sake.

1.   **Abstinence's Increased Visibility at the Beginning of the 21st Century**
Federal funding of abstinence education programmes dates back to the beginning of the 1980s with the AFLA and was significantly strengthened with the welfare reform of 1996. These programmes were supported by conservative Christians as part of a backlash throughout the Reagan era against the feminist and sexual revolutions which had challenged the traditional patriarchal family and initiated greater sexual freedom.

Since then, they have continued to be developed, but it is only with the first G.W. Bush administration that they achieved international visibility. Since the 1980s the opposition to abstinence and abstinence-only education has been rather weak and unsuccessful. In spite of efforts since the mid-1990s from SIECUS, the ACLU, the National Coalition Against Censorship, or congressmen/women like Representative Henry Waxman, as well the American Medical Association, the American Public Health Association, and the American Academy of Pediatrics, government funding of abstinence programmes kept increasing. However, changes began to occur at the end of the Bush presidency. The Democratic majority in Congress started demanding more accountability regarding the funding of abstinence-only programmes, and mitigated to frankly negative evaluations of abstinence programmes were published. A growing number of states began reconsidering their support to abstinence-only programmes, as reports of inefficiency and scientific flaws were flowing in and as the Department of Health and Human Services was narrowing its requirements for funding through the CBAE extension of 2006.

Judith Levine accounts for the (to that point feeble) opposition of sexual liberals in the following terms. In the past two decades, she argues

> large, well-funded national conservative organizations with a loyal infantry of volunteers marched through school district after school district, firing at teachers and programmes that informed students about their bodies and their sexual feelings, about contraception and abortion. These attacks met with only spotty resistance. Sex ed was a political backwater to begin with; hardly anyone paid attention to it. Unlike its opponents, sex ed's champions had a couple of national organizations but no national movement, no coherent cultural-political agenda. As the sociologist Janice Irvine points out, neither feminists nor the political Left rallied to the cause; gays and lesbians joined the fray only in the 1990s, when attacks began to focus more directly and hostilely on them. [...] At the grass roots, the visible forces against sex ed were usually minuscule, often one or two ferocious parents and their pastor. But local defenses were feebler, and the already puny garrisons of comprehensive sexuality education began to fall.[1]

Even if, at first, the AFLA met with some opposition, a majority of states finally accepted funding under its requirements, just as, a little more than a decade later, they would accept the abstinence education section of the welfare reform. Even the prominent sex education organization SIECUS, though it opposed abstinence-only, chose to promote "abstinence-plus," thus supporting abstinence as the healthiest and most desirable choice for teenagers. Levine explains that sex-education advocates were tired, "they were worn down and in some cases financially broken by a decade of furious battering from the organized Christian Right."[2] Sex-education teachers were placed under increasing supervision, exposed to legal suits and dismissal from their jobs. All in all, it seemed more pragmatic to accept teaching abstinence-plus rather than not teaching at all. Levine also suggests that another factor might have influenced this change; by the mid-1990s, sexual liberals had become parents themselves and feared the threat of AIDS for their own children. The idea that the sexual freedom and "carelessness" they had enjoyed in the 1970s could be lethal in the era of AIDS pushed many to see the return to stricter sexual norms in a positive light.

What can account for the relative lack of visibility of abstinence programmes before the Bush presidency? First of all, abstinence programmes as defined by the AFLA were not strictly abstinence-only programmes and as such did not alter significantly the content of sex-education in schools. It is only with the 1996 welfare reform that federally funded abstinence programmes were required to teach abstinence-only thus becoming more of a challenge to comprehensive sexual education. As just mentioned, they met with little opposition and did not generate a national debate at that time.

Abstinence seems to have attracted wider international media attention with G.W. Bush's accession to office and his open support to abstinence education. The 2000 elections and the evangelical faith of the new president motivated many broadcasters abroad to present TV shows on evangelicals and on the most spectacular aspects of conservative Christianity, namely creationism and abstinence. This pattern was progressively strengthened with the strongly religious rhetoric of the Bush administration after 9/11. The model of a "blue" and "red" America promoted by the US media and reinforced by the 2004 elections increased the impression in Europe that indeed half the American population[3] identified as conservative Christians and that this constituency had a great amount of power, especially with one of them at the head of the nation.

The authenticity of G.W. Bush's commitment to his evangelical beliefs is not relevant here, since there are no means to evaluate it with certitude. What is of interest, though, is that throughout his presidency, and before as Texas governor, he was very much involved in the promotion of abstinence education programmes. He mentioned these in numerous speeches and in two of his State of the Union Addresses. In the two decades of abstinence programmes that preceded his election, no president had ever mentioned this issue on such an important occasion. G.W. Bush, on the contrary, by giving it such high visibility, attracted media attention abroad on the issue. It is significant that while he only made a small reference to it in 2006, he devoted a whole paragraph to the topic on January 20, 2004, at the beginning of the Republican primaries deciding which Republican candidate would run for office in 2004.

> To encourage right choices, we must be willing to confront the dangers young people face - even when they're difficult to talk about. Each year, about 3 million teenagers contract sexually-transmitted diseases that can harm them, or kill them, or prevent them from ever becoming parents. In my budget, I propose a grassroots campaign to help inform families about these medical risks. We will double federal funding for abstinence programmes, so schools can teach

this fact of life: Abstinence for young people is the only
certain way to avoid sexually-transmitted diseases.[4]

That on this occasion the President attempted to mobilise the
conservative Christian constituency in and outside of the Republican Party by
mentioning one of their warhorses is clear. However, this explanation does
not account for the full extent of the Bush administration's commitment to
abstinence during his two terms in office. Although he did present a
conservative position on teenage pregnancy around 1995 and 1996, when the
Republican Party won a majority in Congress, Bill Clinton barely mentioned
abstinence in his speeches and when he did, it was never in moral terms.[5]
One can argue that due to his Democratic affiliation and his public *persona*,
using the issue of abstinence was not a relevant strategy. On the contrary
G.W. Bush built his public image around his new-born Christianity, his
opposition to abortion, his condemnation of stem cell research and his
promotion of abstinence. The very strong public religiosity of the President
was noted by many commentators as exceeding that of his predecessors.
Theologian Michael S. Northcott, for instance, noted that President Bush, by
inviting the son of Billy Graham to give a blessing and prayer at his inaugural
ceremony, "went beyond the usual civil religion of such occasions."[6] Jeffrey
Siker, another theologian, commented on the self-identification of G.W. Bush
with Moses, arguing that

> [w]e have had other "religious" presidents, from the
> Sunday school teaching Jimmy Carter, to Ronald Reagan's
> famous courting of the religious right, to Bill Clinton's
> Baptist roots. But no other President has so clearly
> perceived his calling in such epic biblical terms.[7]

He also remarked the particular fluidity between church and state
encouraged by Bush in his support to faith-based initiatives among others.
Newsweek political journalist Howard Fineman also argued forcefully on
these points in an article entitled "Bush and God" in 2003,

> [e]very president invokes God and asks his blessing. Every
> president promises, though not always in so many words, to
> lead according to moral principles rooted in Biblical
> tradition. [...] But it has taken a war, and the prospect of
> more, to highlight a central fact: this president - this
> presidency - is the most resolutely "faith-based" in modern
> times, an enterprise founded, supported and guided by trust
> in the temporal and spiritual power of God.[8]

Some argued that, similar to Reagan, Bush was only paying lip service to these issues, as he did not manage to fulfill conservative Christians' wish for outlawing abortion or making same-sex marriage unconstitutional, for instance. However, even if his administration had little effect on these issues, it undoubtedly contributed by giving such topics an increasing space in political discourses.

2.   Blurring Boundaries Between Political and Religious Discourses
          In spite of the separation of church and state guaranteed by the US constitution, political discourse in the US is far from secular. The "In God We Trust" on dollar bills and the "God Bless America" of politicians can be seen in many cases as rhetorical traditions rather than true signs of religious commitment. However, such formulas, together with the high level of religiosity of the American population, open the door for the inclusion of more religious elements in political discourse. Indeed, surveys show that atheism is not widely accepted in the US. In a 2006 *Newsweek* poll, Americans said they believed in God

> by a margin of 92 to 6 - only 2 percent answered "don't
> know" - and only 37 percent said they'd be willing to vote
> for an atheist for president. (That's down from 49 percent
> in a 1999 Gallup poll - which also found that more
> Americans would vote for a homosexual than an atheist.)[9]

In this, US Americans still follow the idea formulated by John Locke in 1689 that "promises, covenants, and oaths, which are the bonds of human society, can have no hold upon an atheist. The taking away of God, though but even in thought, dissolves all."[10] In a context where lack of religion is still considered by many as a lack of "morals," being religious cannot constitute a handicap for a US president and displaying a belief in God appears to be a necessity.

          Through his support of issues usually associated with the Religious Right, G.W. Bush contributed to an increasing "blurring" of the boundaries between religious and political discourses. As shown in the previous chapters, the discourse of the Bush administration in the matter of abstinence education was directly inspired by conservative Christian rhetoric. The government offered similar arguments and similar educational strategies, albeit in an apparently more secular tone. But in spite of these similarities, did the discourses of the government and these religious discourses imply similar subtexts? Did they include the same meanings under terms like the "family," "sexuality," "body," "gender," "abstinence," etc.? Did their discourses on abstinence attempt to reach the same goals? How did these two types of discourses interact with each other, influence each other? Did they involve the same actors? This is what this chapter seeks to investigate.

It is possible to gather under the category of religious pro-abstinence discourses texts by the LaHayes, Meeker and Hagelin. These different authors, while coming from different backgrounds, openly identify themselves as conservative and Christian and share central views of society, the family and the role of the government. However, it is clear that both the LaHayes and Hagelin are also deeply committed to political activism and therefore merge religious and political discourses. This is also the case of the Heritage Foundation which, while being a political organisation, supports issues that are central to the Religious Right like anti-abortion and anti-gay marriage legislations, abstinence programmes and "pro-family" initiatives as well as the idea of the indispensable nature of religion as a social and moral frame.

In the case of the LaHayes, the religious discourse is clearly dominant. They defend abstinence because they see premarital sex as being "wrong" in God's eyes. Hagelin argues in a similar way that it "is just plain wrong."[11] As for Meeker, while her major argument is a medical one, her rhetoric and personal background clearly approaches that of Hagelin and the LaHayes.

The Heritage Foundation presents a more complex picture. Its members defend abstinence on the base of apparently scientific data. However, their research based on the analysis of surveys from different origins has often been qualified as unscientific, is not peer reviewed and is often contradicted by other studies. While they claim for example that abstinence education significantly delays the initiation of sexual activity, this is not backed by any scientific study. Their reasons for promoting abstinence therefore must be other than reaching this goal as shown by the more personal columns of Hagelin.

Likewise the Bush administration kept promoting abstinence-only in spite of its mitigated results and the potentially negative consequences of the messages such programmes promote with regard to gender, family structures, sexual identity and sexuality as well, as in the face of the opposition of key players in the medical community, like the American Medical Association, the American Public Health Association, and the American Academy of Pediatrics.

The main difference between the discourses of the LaHayes and Hagelin on the one hand and the Heritage Foundation and the Bush administration on the other is that the latter two, in their defense of abstinence, put forward an apparently scientific rationale, thus offering a more secular view. Yet, the way they presented and still present, in the case of the Heritage Foundation, abstinence vs. premarital sex is so coded in "moral" terms that the boundaries between their discourses and the personal columns of Hagelin or the LaHayes' writings appear unclear.

The choice of the Heritage Foundation and even of Hagelin and the LaHayes to "politicise" their discourse through "secularisation" and the recourse to a "scientific" argument is not surprising, as it helps them to promote this issue beyond their own conservative Christian constituency and achieve a higher degree of recognition on the public level. However, what were the gains for the Bush administration in making its discourse on abstinence sound more "religious?"

3.   What Functions Do Pro-abstinence Discourses Play for Conservative Christians?

The previous chapters shed light on the processes through which pro-abstinence discourses help conservative Christians reassert some of the main tenets of their religious and cultural beliefs - creationism, parental rights, the belief in a culture war, etc. The open intent of conservative Christians in promoting a religious discourse on abstinence is to "turn back the clock" to a mythical pre-sexual revolution era when the traditional biblical family and "American values" were respected and when America was living according to Christian codes of morality.

Yet as an oppositional social movement, success in reviving this mythical era would mean for conservative Christians the end of their activism, which would no longer be needed. Therefore, conservative Christian leaders have to maintain their constituency in a permanent state of crisis. As underlined by Sara Diamond

> people within the Christian Right view themselves as outsiders even as they wield political strength disproportionate to their number. The perception among evangelicals that they are underdogs, ignored if not abused by the establishment, is part of a mindset that keeps activists from becoming complacent.[12]

By systematically renewing in their followers the sense that they are in the middle of a culture war for the "hearts and minds" of Americans, conservative Christian leaders strengthen their followers commitment and their own influence over them.

Consequently, getting involved in moral battles that they have little chance of winning reasserts this sense of crisis. This appears clearly in the case of abstinence, which seems to assume a more discursive than practical function, since its lack of efficiency has been scientifically proven. Besides, the apparent impossibility of such a task as curbing teen sexual activity brings to mind the following comment on masturbation by Michel Foucault in his *History of Sexuality*:

> [T]he extraordinary effort that went into the task that was bound to fail leads one to suspect that what was demanded of it was to persevere, to proliferate to the limits of the visible and the invisible rather than disappear for good.[13]

Conservative Christians do not want premarital sex to disappear but to proliferate, thus providing them with an inextinguishable ground for social commitment.

The notion of crisis entertained by conservative Christian leaders fits conveniently with the pre-tribulation dispensational premillenialism of most evangelicals: the belief that before the second coming of Christ, Christians will be raptured and non-believers left to live through a period of "tribulation" ruled by the anti-Christ and culminating in the Armageddon, the fight between good and evil. This belief is strongly tainted by a pessimistic approach to the present, as the second coming of Christ is announced by a period of cultural and moral decline which believers always feel they are in the middle of.

The maintenance of this state of crisis is especially crucial at a point in the 20th and 21st first centuries, when conservative Christians never enjoyed so much cultural power. In the past decades, their influence has been felt in American culture to an extent that can hardly be justified by their number. Indeed, helped by a judicial system, which creates a proliferation of legal suits, conservative Christians even appear superfluous to the maintenance of the moral order they want to prevail. This is especially true concerning issues regarding children, where conservative Christian concerns coincide with the pedophilia panic of the past two decades. The media thus propagate stories of oral sex epidemics and of ever-younger children becoming sexually active, while schools are more and more in tune with conservative sensitivities to avoid lawsuits. An example of this can be found in case of the "freak dancing" phenomenon. In October 2006, the *Los Angeles Times* reported on a movement started by school principals and parents to stop a "sexually explicit" type of dancing, inspired by hip-hop and MTV music videos, taking place at school dances across the nation. The principal of a California school, who subsequently cancelled school dances, described freak dancing as being "one step from events that should be occurring on wedding nights."[14] The *LA Times* provides the reader with the following description of a video featuring freak dancing:

> A teenage boy dances behind his winter-formal date, hands on her hips, thrusting his pelvis against her while she

hitches up her satiny gown and bends at the waist. Another
couple dance facing each other, their bodies enmeshed and
their hips gyrating in a frenzy. A boy approaches a third
couple, nearly sandwiching the girl between himself and
her partner.[15]

The article does not mention the involvement of conservative Christian
organizations in this cancellation of school dances. In one of the cases
mentioned it was caused by the call of a mother to the police after her
daughter felt harassed by the dancing of her partner at a back-to-school party.
However, this example is representative of the way conservative Christian
views on sexuality have come to pervade US culture.

The influence of conservative Christian "moral" concerns is also felt
in the movie industry. In a similar pattern, the studio and director of the
screen adaptation of the British child bestseller trilogy *His Dark Materials* by
Philip Pullman decided to cut out the book's references to the Church and
God due to

> fears of a backlash from the Christian Right in the United
> States. [...] [The director] said that the studio, Nine Line
> Cinema, had expressed concern that *His Dark Materials'*
> perceived anti-religiosity might make "it an inviable project
> financially."[16]

In this case, the "fear" of a Christian Right, which in any case is unlikely to
be very attracted by the screen version of this strongly "left" leaning and
"liberal" book, is enough to prompt self-censorship from the studio. In such
cases it appears that conservative Christian organisations, victims of their
own success, might indeed have become almost superfluous in the fight to
preserve a "family" and "religion-friendly" environment. Hence, the sense of
"threat," of being a minority under "siege," needs to be reasserted in ever
stronger terms in times of "success."

For conservative Christians, the "subtext" or "hidden agenda" of
pro-abstinence discourses is to contribute to the reinforcement of this
permanent state of crisis in order to mobilise their constituency and justify
their struggle. They also repeat and reassert over and over again the meanings
they invest in crucial terms like "family," "body," "sexuality" or
"abstinence." That is the "superiority" of the traditional family cell which is
the only legitimate place where sexuality can be expressed and the idea that
the body is a "member of Christ himself."[17]

4.   What Functions Did Pro-abstinence Discourses Play for the Bush Administration?

The argument most often cited by the media at home and abroad for the vocal support of the Bush administration to abstinence-only was the appeal to conservative Christian voters.[18] However, this constituency, though yielding disproportionate political power, is not extremely numerous and the support for abstinence-only if it can gain conservative Christian electors to Republican candidates might also alienate others.[19] Indeed, polls show that parents overwhelmingly support teaching children about contraception in addition to abstinence.[20] Hence, this is unlikely to account for the whole extent of the position of the Bush administration. The other possible reasons for this support are the object of this section.

For politicians, one of abstinence's appeals at the discursive level is the very emotional nature of this subject, which involves two emotionally charged elements often seen as antagonistic: sex and children. The strategy of privileging an emotional discourse over rational political and economic analysis did not originate in the Bush administration but has been the main political tool of the "new" right, as well as the "new" left - for example in Great Britain with Tony Blair and his New Labour Party[21] - since the Reagan era. This phenomenon dubbed by professor of English Lauren Berlant as "the Reaganite cultural revolution"[22] has had, in her view, several major consequences, which include the increased use by politicians of a "rhetoric of intimacy" in order to manage the growing economic inequalities dividing the US population. She argues that

> [b]y defining the United States as a place where normal intimacy is considered the foundation of the citizen's happiness, the right has attempted to control the ways questions of economic survival are seen as matters of citizenship. This use of intimacy is extremely complicated. First, it helps displace from sustained public scrutiny the relation between congealed corporate wealth and the shifting conditions of labor; second, it becomes a rhetorical means by which the causes of U.S. income inequality and job instability in all sectors of the economy can be personalized, rephrased in terms of individual's capacity to respond flexibly to the new "opportunities" presented to them within an increasingly volatile economy [...].[23]

It is this same dynamic which was observed in Chapter 10 in the case of teenage mothers being held responsible by conservatives for the deficit of the welfare state along with numerous other social "evils," while abstinence and personal self-control were deemed to be the solution to most societal problems.

Seven years after Berlant and in the midst of the heated campaign for the reelection of G.W. Bush, polemical journalist Thomas Frank argued along a similar line in his popular book *What's the Matter with Kansas? How Conservatives Won the Heart of America.* He postulates that contemporary conservative politics are defined by what he calls "The Great Backlash," a form of conservatism that "mobilizes voters with explosive social issues [...] which it then marries to pro-business economic policies." This way, "cultural anger is marshaled to achieve economic ends."[24] For Frank, this strategy constitutes the real achievement of contemporary conservatism and ensures the reelection of Republican presidents regardless of their success or failures in managing the country. Of course, after the victory of Barack Obama in the last presidential election this assertion would have to be mitigated.

But why are abstinence, and sexual issues in general, particularly suited to this kind of displacement and to the stimulation of popular anxieties? As Jeffrey Weeks argued, it is the "chameleon-like"[25] quality of sexuality - the fact that it can be associated with extreme feelings both positive and negative, as well as the way it has come to be defined as a constituting part of our identity as human beings[26] - that makes it a "particularly sensitive conductor of cultural influences, and hence of social and political division."[27]

Another powerful catalyst of social anxiety is the appeal to the protection of children. In her classic essay "Thinking Sex", anthropologist Gayle Rubin noted that "for over a century, no tactic for stirring up erotic hysteria has been as reliable as the appeal to protect children."[28] It is through its association with sexuality that the issue of child protection really appeals to the masses. On the contrary, child poverty and physical mistreatment, though much more widespread and dangerous, rarely stir up mass mobilisation. A revealing example of this can be found in the document *President George W. Bush: A Remarkable Record of Achievement* issued by the White House in August 2004. Under the title "Protecting Children" the achievements listed were in the following order:

- the signature of acts to give "law enforcement new tools to prevent, investigate, and prosecute violent crimes against children and increase punishment for Federal crimes against children;"
- the expansion and coordination of a system to notify "the public about child abductions;"
- the strengthening of laws against child pornography;
- the launching of "Operation Predator, a comprehensive initiative to safeguard children from foreign, national

pedophiles, human traffickers, international sex tourists, and internet pornographers;"
- the signature of legislations "requiring states to conduct criminal background checks on prospective foster and adoptive parents;"
- the doubling of funds for abstinence-only education;
- the development of programmes of adult mentoring for disadvantaged children;
- the defence of the *Children's Internet Protection Act*;
- concluding with the statement that "smoking, drinking, and the use of illegal drugs among teenagers all fell between 2001 and 2003."[29]

No mention of any initiative concerning children's health care, poverty or welfare state assistance was made in this section.

In its association of children and sexuality, two privileged catalysts of social anxiety, abstinence provides an ideal ground on which to build "moral panics." Jeffrey Weeks defines moral panics as

flurries of social anxiety, usually focusing on a condition or person, or group of persons, who become defined as a threat to accepted social values and assumptions. They arise generally in situations of confusion and ambiguity, in periods when the boundaries between legitimate and illegitimate behaviour seem to need redefining or classification. Classic moral panics in the past have often produced drastic results, in the form of moral witch-hunts, physical assault and legislative action. [...] A significant feature in many of them has been the connection that has been made between sex and disease, disease becoming a metaphor for dirt and decay.[30]

Pro-abstinence discourses and the anxiety they stir over the issue of teenage sexuality, display the features of Weeks' moral panics. They target a group of persons as the object of an anxiety generated in a period of "confusion and ambiguity" over sexual behavior - of adults as well as youths - and over traditional boundaries between adults and children, and they subsequently generate numerous legislative actions. Moreover, pro-abstinence discourses over the past twenty years have inscribed teenage sex in a discourse of "danger," "disease," "epidemic" and "moral decay."

The notion of moral panic is even more enlightening in understanding abstinence rhetoric in conjunction with the concept of the "epidemic" as defined by philosopher Linda Singer. Throughout the past decade, various problems that abstinence was supposed to address have been raised to the status of "epidemic" either by the government, conservative Christians or the media: the "teen pregnancy epidemic" addressed by Pillow in her book and Meeker's "STD epidemic", also targeted by the Center for Disease Control (CDC), have been followed by a teenage "oral sex epidemic" all of them being generally encompassed under the more global "teen sex epidemic."

I am indebted to Wanda S. Pillow not only for her brilliant analysis of social policy and teen pregnancy but also for her approach to this phenomenon through the work of philosopher Linda Singer. In this section, I likewise use the work of Singer to analyse the mechanisms of power that constitute the subtext of pro-abstinence discourses through the concept of "epidemic."

In her book *Erotic Welfare: Sexual Theory and Politics in the Age of Epidemic*, Singer uses the theories developed by Foucault as well as the analyses of the "plague" by Albert Camus, to define the AIDS epidemic as "a political construct."[31] Following a tradition inaugurated by Susan Sontag, Singer explains that though the language of epidemic came back in use in the 1980s and 1990s with the AIDS epidemic, AIDS is neither the actual "site of anxiety," nor the only phenomenon being described by a rhetoric of pathological proliferation.[32] She argues that this original epidemic gave birth to a whole discursive process of control that defined different, and generally sexual, phenomena - divorce, single-motherhood, teen pregnancy - as having reached "epidemic" proportions. For an epidemic "is a phenomenon that in its very representation calls for indeed, seems to demand some form of managerial response, some mobilised effort of control."[33]

In her claim that "epidemics" are political constructs, Singer does not imply that these are solely and coherently operated by a specific instance of power, but that they are more confusedly acting at different levels and from numerous, often conflicting, and even sometimes incompatible fronts.[34] Pillow provides here an interesting clarification of Singer's thought through a reference to Foucault:

> Modern regulatory power, as Foucault demonstrated, is "less likely to rely on force, but more likely to be comprised of disciplinary regimes, systems of surveillance, and normalizing tactics"[35] that impact our ideologies and actions just as effectively, perhaps even more effectively. Foucault and others understand that power in this way is not simply located in positional power, but evident as "bio-power" in our everyday practices, and interpreted and reinforced in educational and legal institutions and discursive arena such as the media. Policy enacts and

reinforces modern regulatory power and is more regulatory
when a social problem, like teen pregnancy, is defined as
being of epidemic proportions.[36]

In the case of abstinence, "power" or "bio-power" is enacted and reinforced
through abstinence-curriculum in schools, legislative restriction on abortion,
contraception and sex-education as well as by the media. It is interesting to
note here that accounts of "wild" teen sex and "oral sex" as well as "STD
epidemics", for example, are not only being circulated by "radical" authors
like Meeker, but also by mainstream media figures like TV hosts Oprah
Winfrey and Dr. Phil McGraw.[37]

The concept of the epidemic refers to the idea of a "crisis," of a
phenomenon which has spun out of control and therefore requires a shift in
the modes of action. The epidemic, being defined as a "threat," generates a
"kind of panic logic" - "epidemics" are thus intimately linked to the "moral
panics" defined by Weeks - that justify dramatic containment measures.
These dramatic measures alter the old paradigms defining as acceptable
disciplinary means of control that under normal circumstances would be
considered undemocratic.[38] For instance, a Google search reveals many
occurrences of the expression "terrorism epidemic." Envisaging terrorism
through this lens implies that this phenomenon requires control to an extent
that justifies the implementation of the *Patriot Act* and other infringements
on citizens' right to privacy. Likewise, the discursive construction of teenage
sexuality as an "epidemic" by the government, justifies the exceptional
demand for "abstinence by conservative Christians, the media, as well as in
some cases more liberal instances." These discourses are, for example,
framed in terms of danger, physical or psychological like STDs, depression,
suicide, teen pregnancy and excess like in the case of teen sex orgies and
widespread oral sex among middle-school pupils. Interestingly, Singer
explains, epidemic logic

> depends on certain structuring contradictions, proliferating
> what it seeks to contain, producing what it regulates. The
> logic of epidemic depends upon the perpetual revival of an
> anxiety it seeks to control, inciting a crisis of contagion that
> spreads to ever new sectors of cultural life which, in turn,
> justify and necessitate specific regulatory apparatus which
> then compensate - materially and symbolically - for the
> crisis it has produced.[39]

This remark appears particularly well suited to the case of
abstinence-only, as this drastic measure has proven inefficient in curbing the
different epidemics it sought to address, while at the same time abstinence

discourses perpetually generate anxiety over new forms of sexual dangers menacing American children. Singer argues that concerns about health can justify numerous and radical measures of control over bodies and sexual exchanges. The same can be argued for concerns over children's safety, be it physical or "moral." She adds that because epidemics

> justify and are in fact constructed in order to necessitate a complex system of surveillance and intervention, epidemic situations often provide occasions for the reinstitution of hegemonic lines of authority and control.[40]

In the USA, for example, the anxiety over the AIDS epidemic was used by conservative groups of diverse hues like those of Jerry Falwell or Lyndon Larouche to demand the regulation of sexual practices through limitations of the right to abortion or sexual education as well as, of course, a strict control of special risk populations like gays and drug users. Singer argues that conservative groups have been extremely successful in using epidemic rhetoric for their own ends due to their sharp understanding of these as more than just "medico-bureaucratic problematics."

Taking her inspiration from Camus,[41] she explains that epidemics or "plagues" radically question the societal and moral order:

> [F]aced with a plague one can no longer simply go on with business as usual. [The individual] is forced to call [his/her] habits, values, and pleasures into question, precisely because the world in which [s/he] had a place is in the process of slipping away, disrupted in a way that always feels like an imposition, and seems unjustified, senseless.[42]

The success of conservatives lies in their ability to provide all-encompassing moral certitudes as answers to "plagues," by inscribing these in a process of retribution for the transgression committed since the sexual revolution and the establishment of a non-religious morality. Thus epidemics like AIDS or teen pregnancy are used to market the reestablishment of "family values." Singer writes that in

> the social imagery offered, AIDS is but a symptom of the loss or erosion of authority, i.e., absolutist, religious, paternalistic authority, which was better suited to organize energies for socially useful purposes like reproduction and consumption. The failure to heed that authority, in the name of "liberalization," "tolerance," or "sexual liberation," lies at the root of the crisis as we now suffer the

consequences of sexual proliferation, which threatens not
only our physical well-being, but our spiritual health as
well.[43]

In this quote, AIDS could easily be replaced by STDs, teen pregnancy, or
phenomena that have achieved the status of the "epidemic."
    Defining the phenomena addressed by abstinence as having reached
epidemic proportions is particularly useful for conservatives as it enables
them to frame them in this rhetoric, and the potential for control it generates,
in spite of the fact that these are not necessarily of a medical and infectious
nature. Singer explains that the establishment of

> a connection between epidemic and transgression has
> allowed for the rapid transmission of the former to
> phenomena that are outside the sphere of disease. [...] The
> use of this language marks all of these phenomena as
> targets for intervention because they have been designated
> as unacceptable, while at the same time reproducing the
> power that authorizes and justifies their deployment.[44]

Defining "teenage sexuality" as an "epidemic" enables conservative
Christians, as well as conservative politicians like the members of the Bush
administration, to implement measures of control over teenage sexuality that
contribute to the reassertion of traditional hierarchies. In this they are
supported by the media which, as argued by film theorist Richard Dyer,
constantly manage the contradictions within the dominant ideology in order
to maintain its hegemonic status by occasionally denouncing its negative
aspects to preserve the appearance of objectivity.[45]
    The interest of the government in maintaining traditional hierarchies
especially in times of apparent social inequalities lies in the appeal they
constitute for anxious voters displaying a strong desire for stability.
Philosopher Valerie Daoust explains that it is easier for politicians to keep the
power by grounding their policies on traditional categories, since these are
familiar and acknowledged by all.[46] Hence,

> [t]he idea of the contemporary traditional family, with all
> its contradictions, enables politicians to legitimate a certain
> type of family cell and to apply their policies to established
> institutions. Thus they maintain the structures of the state
> even if reality does not necessarily conform to it.
> Obviously, the effect achieved is to legitimate the
> traditional family where it still fulfills its role of social
> reproduction.[47]

Pro-abstinence discourses contributed to the Bush administration's strategy of maintenance of traditional hierarchies and social status quo as well as to the displacement of citizens' anxieties from economic and social concerns onto "moral panics" or "epidemics." The Bush administration, like conservative Christians, attempted through these discourses to establish its influence over their "voters" or "followers." In spite of the fact that conservative Christians appear to seek to "turn back the clock" to the 1950s, their movement is no more revolutionary than the Republican Party, since success for them would result in purposelessness. Hence, it is as much in their interest to preserve the status quo even though they present it as unsatisfactory and as in a state of crisis. Likewise, the Bush administration, or any government, had little interest in actually eradicating the epidemics it contributed to "create." For instance the Bush administration, which built its politics around the threat of terrorism after 9/11, would not have benefited from the decrease of this menace. On the contrary it maintained its citizens in a state of fear and alert by constantly reasserting the danger constituted by terrorism and with its military intervention in Iraq it strengthened the power of Al-Qaeda as an anti-American force.

By promoting delayed gratification and criticising the oversexualised media and fashion industry, abstinence gives the appearance of being in conflict with the defense of capitalism advocated by the Republican Party, but this impression is only superficial. Conservative Christians like the LaHayes and Meeker might genuinely wish the media and the fashion industry to be censured, but the Heritage Foundation and the Bush administration, while occasionally calling for such a censorship, did not contribute to any change in that direction. In fact, for Rosemary Radford Ruether the "Christian Right" plays an important role in maintaining an unequal capitalist economy. She argues that although the Christian Right

> claims victimization in the struggle against the evil forces of feminism, homosexuality, and "secular humanism," it is in fact thoroughly system-supporting in its pro-capitalist commitment to traditional class hierarchies. Even as it diverts attention by crusading for the reestablishment of sex/gender hierarchy, it plays an integral role in the effort to build a conservative political majority that will ratify the growing concentration of wealth in the upper 20 percent of American society and the impoverishment of working-class and unemployed people.[48]

Besides, abstinence is actually at the source of a lucrative market of Christian merchandising, pedagogic tools, etc.[49] It can also be argued that by being brought into the mainstream, abstinence has been recycled as a marketable minority sexual culture like it has been the case for S&M and other sex-based "life styles."

The goals of conservative Christians and the G.W. Bush administration, although not similar, reached at this historical conjunction a significant level of congruity and required similar means to be achieved. Among these were pro-abstinence discourses. Yet these two groups were far from being mirror images of each other, and this for several reasons. First, the "target audiences" of their discursive strategies were not the same. Conservative Christians' targets are fellow believers and potential converts. They try to achieve influence over mainstream media and public discourses however; they need to constitute an antagonistic group under the tag "liberal" or "secular humanist" to represent the "sinners" against which they can define themselves as "righteous."

On the opposite, the Bush administration, as an elected body, needed to address the population at large or at least present the appearance of doing so. This entailed that the meanings they invested in the major terms of pro-abstinence discourses had to be differentiated from those invested by conservative Christians even though they were used in similar discursive contexts. For instance, under the concept of "body" the Bush administration as a national and secular authority could not include the religious meaning given to it by the LaHayes when they explain that the body is a "member of Christ himself."[50] For a government the bodies of its citizens are "populations," "workforces," resources to be managed through measures of hygiene and public health.[51] For example entering the word "body" in the search engine of the US Department of Health and Human Services at the time when the Bush administration was still in office, would have directed the user to resources, often targeted at women in particular, underlining the role their bodies play in population growth and health, and providing information on issues such as: "reproductive health," "puberty," "getting enough sleep," "grooming and hygiene," "fighting germs" or "eating disorders."[52]

Likewise, "sexuality" is not openly invested with a spiritual meaning, but requires management of its reproductive function to ensure the desired population growth.[53] A similar Internet search would have directed the user to resources dealing with "reproductive issues," "abstinence," "homosexuality," "teen pregnancy," "contraception" or "sexual dysfunction."[54] Searching for abstinence similarly highlighted resources stating that "Safe Sex is No Sex" thus positioning the issue in terms of health - physical and psychological - and not in terms of religious requirement.

The definition of the "family" that followed from the G.W. Bush administration's policies was that of the traditional family, established by marriage, comprising children and both heterosexual parents of opposite sexes. As for the issue of gender within this framework, though the administration had to oppose gender discrimination, it made clear in its support of the traditional Fatherhood Initiative that fathers as males bring a unique component to their children's education. Besides, after a quick web search, girls appeared to be the major target of their abstinence and reproductive health messages. Indeed, while there was a whole website devoted to girls' health, reproductive or not, which also promotes abstinence - www. girlshealth.gov - there was no equivalent for boys, who are referred to general websites - www. 4parents.gov. The vision of the role of the woman as mainly responsible for the management of her reproductive capacities was thus highlighted, as well as the unique role of the male in the family, consequently suggesting an opposition to lesbian or single-parenthood.

This political discourse, though distinct in its meanings from that of conservative Christians, was obviously not entirely incompatible with this latter as they both shared a vision of traditional familial and social structures. The pro-abstinence discourse of the Bush administration appeared in many occurrences to be marked by an ideological ambiguity apparently originating on the one hand in the strong religious commitment of the president and of many of his advisors and on the other hand in an attempt to garner support for conservative Christians. This was particularly visible in the support of the Fatherhood Initiative or to abstinence-only education; the opposition to abortion; to contraception access; stem cell research; to gay marriage or in the support of faith-based organisations. Hence, it is reasonable to assert that the pro-abstinence discourses of the Bush administration, while having different goals and strategies, intersected with and were influenced in a significant manner by those of conservative Christians.

In this case the personal religious choices of a number of members of the Bush administration appear to have influenced the political strategies of the government in a manner which can be deemed excessive or at least unusual, since it generated a non-negligible opposition from many American citizens and civil rights organisations. As the Bush administration gathered self-confidence, this aspect came even more into light through initiatives which appeared devoid of any political relevance and attracted attention to this religious bias. This was witnessed for example in the extension of abstinence-only education programmes to all unmarried persons up to the age of twenty-nine, thus preaching abstinence to an age group more than 90% of which had already had sex.[55] Another instance of this bias can be found in the President's resort to executive orders to increase funding for faith-based organisations involved in foreign aid, after such measures were opposed by Congress which raised concerns about the respect of the separation of church and state.[56]

The question of the personal link between the Bush administration and the conservative Christian community is also particularly complex. Bush himself is a friend of Franklin Graham and of his father and addressed the annual National Day of Prayer, whose main organizer is Shirley Dobson. In 2001 Bush was even heralded by some conservative Christians as the "new leader of the religious right in America."[57] Moreover, it has been often pointed out by the press that he appointed many conservative Christians in his administration, among others his former attorney general John Ashcroft, or the pro-life activist Eric Keroack, former deputy assistant secretary for population affairs at the Department of Health and Human Services or his appointment as Supreme Court justice of pro-life Samuel Alito.[58] In such cases the question of the blurring of boundaries between political and religious discourses became even more problematic, as the possibility to dissociate faith and political action seemed difficult in the case of politicians who displayed such a deep religious engagement on issues with which they had to deal at a political level. This was especially the case when one assumed that they had been chosen especially for this religious commitment.

These individual connections, together with the ideological ambiguities displayed by the Bush administration, contributed to the high level of congruity between religious and political pro-abstinence discourses, in spite of the fact that they used these to fulfill different functions.

Pro-abstinence discourses, while they were used by the Bush administration to reinforce a certain number of conservative narratives and incorporate them into mainstream political discourse, also fulfilled the "hidden" agenda of focusing the population's anxieties onto moral rather than economic issues and displacing its concerns over living conditions onto "moral panics" or epidemics. As explained in the coming chapter, another of the subtexts of pro-abstinence discourses is the discursive "management" of teenage sexuality in order to strengthen traditional hierarchies.

Notes

[1] Levine, 2002, p.91.

[2] ibid., p.103.

[3] Yet this was far from the truth, in 2006, in her book *George W. Bush and the War on Women*, Barbara Finlay estimated the percentage of evangelicals in the US population to be no more than 30%; Finlay, 2006, p.8.

[4] Bush, 2004.

[5] Ashbee, 2007, p.104.

[6] M S Northcott, *An Angel Directs the Storm: Apocalyptic Religion and American Empire*, I. B. Tauris, London, 2004, p.3.

[7] J Siker, 'President Bush, Biblical faith, and the Politics of Religion,' *Religious StudiesNews. SBL edition*, May 2003, 4 (5), viewed on 6 February 2007, <http://www.sbl-site.org/Article.aspx?ArticleId=151>

[8] H Fineman, 'Bush and God,' *Newsweek*, March 10, 2003: 22.

[9] J Adler, 'The New Naysayers,' *Newsweek Online*, 11 September 2006, viewed on 24 March 2009, <http://www.newsweek.com/id/45574>

[10] J Locke, *A Letter Concerning Toleration*, 1689, April 2002, viewed on 8 February 2007, <http://etext.lib.virginia.edu/etcbin/toccer-new2?id=LocTole.xml&images=images/modeng&data=/texts/english/moden g/parsed&tag=public&part=1&division=div1>

[11] Hagelin, 2005b, p.149.

[12] Diamond, 1998, p.5.

[13] M Foucault, *The Foucault Reader: An Introduction to Foucault's Thought*, Paul Rabinow (ed), Penguin Books, London, 1991, p.322.

[14] Quoted in S Mehta, 'Teens' Dancing Is Freaking Out the Adults,' *Los Angeles Times*, 17 October 2006, viewed on 8 December 2006, <http://www.latimes.com/news/local/la-me-freaking17oct17,0,4105810.story?coll=la-home-headlines>

[15] ibid.

[16] S Coates, 'God Is Cut From Film of Dark Materials', *The Times Online*, 8 December 2004, viewed on 14 February 2007, <http://www.timesonline.co.uk/tol/news/uk/article400396.ece>

[17] LaHaye, 1998a, p.23.

[18] Here are several instances of this remark. The Canadian newspaper *Le Devoir* reported in August 2006: "l'administration américaine est accusée d'avoir conçu ce plan pour apaiser sa base républicaine conservatrice pour des raisons politiques, religieuses et morales, ce que démentent de hauts responsables de Washington," (The US government is accused of having devised this plan in order to appease the conservative Republican grassroots, for political, religious and moral reasons. This has been denied by high ranking officials in Washington), *Le Devoir*, 'La stratégie américaine de l'abstinence soulève les critiques,' *Le Devoir*, 15 August 2006, viewed on 8 February 2007, <http://www.ledevoir.com/2006/08/15/115899.html>. The French daily newspaper *Le Monde* observed "en prônant la virginité avant le mariage, M. Bush répond aux vœux de la droite chrétienne," (by promoting virginity, Mr. Bush caters to the needs of the Christian Right), M Fauchier-Delavigne, 'L'abstinence vue par la presse des Etats-Unis,' *Le Monde.fr*, 8 January 2003, viewed on 8 February 2007, <http://www.fsa.ulaval.ca/personnel/vernag/EH/F/cause/lectures/abstinence_ Etats-Unis.htm>. December 9, 2002 Debra Rosenberg a *Newsweek* journalist argued "that's just the kind of response George W. Bush was hoping for. To the White House, abstinence seems like an easy win: it resonates with conservative voters, but doesn't upset pro-choice moderates," D Rosenberg, 'The Battle Over Abstinence,' *Newsweek*, 9 December 2002, 8 February 2007,

<http://209.85.135.104/search?q=cache:8r4Am9U68hwJ:www.indiana.edu/~ llc/Current_Students/q199/battle.pdf+newsweek+human+rights+watch+absti nence+2002&hl=en&ct=clnk&cd=1&gl=de>. A journalist for the British newspaper *The Observer* wrote on April 28, 2002 that "one in four sexually active teenagers contracts a sexually transmitted disease each year. Bush is under fire from his conservative Right over a number of issues, from the Middle East to immigration, and there is no safer place to satisfy it than on moral high ground it holds dear," E Vulliamy, 'Bush Promotes Virgin Values to Curb Teen Sex,' *The Observer*, 28 April 2002, 8 February 2007, <http://observer.guardian.co.uk/bush/story/0,,706578,00.html>. The German weekly *Die Zeit* observed regarding abstinence that "dabei wird die erzkonservative Basis auch jenseits der evangelikalen Propheten mobilisiert," (with this the conservtiave grassroots is mobilized beyond the evangelical prophets), T Schimmeck, 'Der Krieg gegen Sex,' *Die Zeit*, 9 September 2004, viewed on 8 February 2007, <http://www.zeit.de/2004/38/Ami-Keuschheit?page=all>.

[19] On this point I disagree with Edward Ashbee; see introduction of this book.

[20] The *Sex Education in America: General Public/Parents Survey* led by National Public Radio, the Kaiser Family Foundation and the Kennedy School of Government of Harvard, found that 72% of parents of children from grades 7 to 8 and 65% of parents of children from grades 9-12 thought that federal money should "be used to fund more comprehensive sex education programmes that include information on how to obtain and use condoms and other contraceptives," Kaiser Family Foundation, 2004, p.7, and that 72% of parents of children from grades 7 to 8 and 70% of parents of children from grades 9-12 were concerned that "not providing information about how to obtain and use condoms and other contraception might mean more teens will have unsafe sexual intercourse," Kaiser Family Foundation, 2004, p.22.

[21] Bhattacharyya, 2002, p.74)

[22] L Berlant, *The Queen of America Goes to Washington City*, Duke University Press, Durham and London, 1997, p.8.

[23] ibid., p.8.

[24] Frank, 2004, p.5.

[25] Weeks, 1986, p.11.

[26] M Foucault, M., *Histoire de la sexualité: La volonté de savoir*, Éditions Gallimard, Paris, 1976.

[27] Weeks, 1986, p.11.

[28] Rubin, 1984, p.271.

[29] White House, 2004, p.36.

[30] Weeks, 1986, pp.96-97.

[31] L Singer, *Erotic Welfare: Sexual Theory and Politics in the Age of Epidemic*, Routledge, London & New York, 1993, p.27.

[32] ibid., p.27.

[33] ibid., p.27.

[34] ibid., p.27.

[35] W Rushing, 'Sin, Sex, and Segregation: Social Control and the Education of Southern Women.' *Gender and Education*, June 2002, 14 (2), pp.167-179, p.168.

[36] Pillow, 2004, p.19.

[37] See Oprah.com, 'A New Kind of Spin the Bottle: Dr. Phil on Alarming Sexual Behavior Among Children,' 7 May 2002, 12 February 2007, <http://www.oprah.com/tows/pastshows/tows_2002/tows_past_20020507_b.j html>

[38] Singer, 1993, p.28.

[39] ibid., p.29.

[40] ibid., p.31.

[41] See A Camus, *La Peste*, 1947.

[42] Singer, 1993, p.31.

[43] ibid., p.31-32.

[44] ibid., p.118.

[45] R Dyer, *Stars*, British Film Institute, London, 1998, p.2-3.

[46] V Daoust, *De la sexualité en démocratie: L'individu libre et ses espaces identitaires*, Presses Universitaires de France, Paris, 2005, p.97.

[47] Daoust, 2005, p.102, my translation.

[48] Radford Ruether, 2001, pp.177-178.

[49] Hendershot, 2004.

[50] LaHaye, 1998a, p.23.

[51] Foucault, 1976, p.184.

[52] <www.hhs.gov> and <http://www.girlshealth.gov/body/>, viewed 2 July 2007.

[53] Foucault, 1976, pp.191-192.

[54] <www.hhs.gov>, viewed 2 July 2007.

[55] Kaisernetwork.org, 'Federal Guidelines Expand Scope of Abstinence Education Funds To Include People up to Age 29,' 31 October 2006, viewed 11 May 2007, <http://kaisernetwork.org/Daily_reports/rep_repro_recent_reports.cfm?dr_cat =2&show=yes&dr_DateTime=10-31-06#40759>

[56] F Stockman, et al., 'Bush Brings Faith to Foreign Aid,' *The Boston Globe Online*. 8 October 2006, viewed on 14 February 2007, <http://www.boston.com/news/nation/articles/2006/10/08/bush_brings_faith_ to_foreign_aid/>

[57] D Milbank, 'Religious Right Finds Its Center in Oval Office,' *The WashingtonPost.com*, 24 December 2001, viewed on 14 February 2007, <http://www.washingtonpost.com/ac2/wp-dyn/A19253-2001Dec23?language=printer>

[58] For an even more detailed record on the issue of appointments see Finlay 2006.

Chapter 13
A Common Goal: Reinforcing Traditional Hierarchies

I cannot avoid seeing, now, the small tattoo on my ankle. Four digits and an eye, a passport in reverse. It's supposed to guarantee that I will never be able to fade, finally into another landscape. I am too important, too scarce, for that. I am a national resource.[1]

In the previous chapter, several subtexts of pro-abstinence discourses have been made visible: the way these discourses on the one hand enable conservative Christians to feed the feeling of being in the middle of a culture war which ensures its followers' commitment and on the other hand the role they played for the Bush administration in the maintenance of a status quo favorable to its electoral success while focusing the population's attention on emotional issues rather than economic ones. In this chapter the emphasis will be placed on the use of pro-abstinence discourses by both the Bush administration and conservative Christians to maintain a hierarchical dominance over teenagers and the functions of this dominance, while highlighting the symbolical function of teenage sexuality as a "national resource." Not unlike the "handmaid" in Atwood's dystopic north-American religious dictatorship, who spends her existence locked up in a room waiting to be impregnated by a member of the ruling class, teenagers' sexuality in contemporary United States is, discursively at least, locked up, their desire under control and suppressed until marriage when they can be released in a socially productive way.

Sexual-abstinence-only-before-marriage, with the very narrow sexual choices it offers teenagers and the conservative vision of the family it promotes has, in the past decade, raised important ethical concerns that have been pointed out by various organisations, including Advocates for Youth or Human Rights Watch. Some of these concerns are the infringement of youths' rights to information, health care and sexual agency.

Pro-abstinence discourses in their emphasis on the limitation of sexual acts to marriage reassert a system of hierarchy based on the concept of "good sexual citizenship" as defined by sociologist Steven Seidman.[2] They also reinforce a domination over and discrimination against youths by denying the legitimacy of their sexual expression and refusing to give them literally "vital" information.

In his study of gay and lesbian life Seidman defines the good sexual citizen in contemporary America as

> an individual whose sexual behavior conforms to
> traditional gender norms, who links sex to intimacy, love,
> monogamy, and preferably marriage, and who restricts sex
> to private acts that exhibit romantic or caring qualities.[3]

In his view "sexual citizenship establishes social boundaries between insiders (good citizens) and outsiders (bad citizens),"[4] outsiders being defined as "abnormal," "diseased," or "unhealthy"[5] with a potential to infect the rest of the population if not properly managed. This image of the good sexual citizen is, he argues, dominated by "roughly speaking, white, Christian, rich, abled, straight" males.[6] It is promoted in the mainstream culture through the media, literature, the academia, schools, corporations, churches, etc.[7] In this respect, even citizens who have achieved civil rights and public recognition might still be disenfranchised like "blacks, Latinos, Asians, women, the disabled, and gays."[8]

The vision of abstinence applied by conservative Christians fits in this frame of good sexual citizenship. Since many conservative Christians are "white," middle-class and "straight," they can identify as "insiders" and feel legitimated in demanding to be protected from possible infections by sexual deviants such as gays or teenage mothers.

Through its pro-abstinence discourses, the US government also supported this narrow definition of sexual citizenship. This is particularly visible in several of the requirements for abstinence-only programs, which are still valid at the beginning of the Barack Obama's presidency and specify that these programs must teach:

> B - abstinence from sexual activity outside marriage as the
> expected standard for all school-age children; [...]
> D - that a mutually faithful monogamous relationship in the
> context of marriage is the expected standard of sexual
> activity;
> E - that sexual activity outside of the context of marriage is
> likely to have harmful psychological and physical effects;
> F - that bearing children out-of-wedlock is likely to have
> harmful consequences for the child, the child's parents, and
> society; [...]
> H - the importance of attaining self-sufficiency before
> engaging in sexual activity.[9]

This definition, coming as it does from the US government, appears extremely problematic as it excludes from its terms many citizens whose rights it is supposed to protect. Among them are: unmarried youths; gays and lesbians; cohabiting couples; and the poor who might not be able to afford marriage and belong predominantly to racial minorities.

Considering the definition of the good sexual citizen promoted by pro-abstinence discourses, youths find themselves particularly disenfranchised on several grounds. First, because abstinence education reflects a discriminatory attitude defined as "adultism." This concept already used in the context of abstinence by sociologist Jessica Fields, sheds light on questions of hierarchies within pro-abstinence discourses. John Bell, the co-founder of the prominent non-profit organization Youthbuild USA, defines adultism as a global "disrespect of the young."

> In our society, for the most part, young people are considered less important than and inferior to adults. They are not taken seriously and not included as decision makers in the broader life of their communities.[10]

They are also under the influence of their parents and other meaningful adults who tell them what to or what not to wear, eat, listen to, etc.

Since the appearance of this concept in the late 19th century, adolescence has been envisaged as a transitory stage from childhood to adulthood, where time and rights are suspended as youths expect their transformation into adults.[11] Not only are they expected to fulfill the expectations of their parents but also of their peers as they learn "proper" socialisation and norms.[12] The life of youths is conceived as following the predetermined script of studying, getting a job, marrying and having children. However, these traditional scripts no longer account for the experience of the majority of Americans for whom these events might not occur in this order or at all.[13] An important emphasis is also laid on the asexual nature of adolescence as a means of differentiating adults from children. In her book *Act Your Age: A Cultural Construction of Adolescence*, professor of education Nancy Lesko underlines that when youth upset these scripts and act in a sexual way deemed inappropriate for their age group they generate "moral panics" like the one over teen pregnancy.[14] Gayle Rubin also emphasised that

> [t]he law is especially ferocious in maintaining the boundary between childhood "innocence" and "adult" sexuality. Rather than recognizing the sexuality of the young, and attempting to provide for it in a caring and responsible manner, our culture denies and punishes erotic interest and activity by anyone under the local age of consent.[15]

This is especially the case with pro-abstinence discourses, which completely deny the legitimacy of teenage sexuality and go as far as denying youths' access and information on contraception, abortion or sexual diversity while substituting for it scientifically incorrect data. This problem has been pointed to by Human Rights Watch, which stated in 2002 that

> [f]ederally funded abstinence-only programs, in keeping with their federal mandate, deny children basic information that could protect them from HIV/AIDS infection and discriminate against gay and lesbian children. In so doing, these programs [...] interfere with fundamental rights to information, to health and to equal protection under the law.[16]

Likewise, in its emphasis on "parental rights," pro-abstinence discourses appear to exceed in many cases legitimate parental care and fall into "adultism."

Inscribing themselves into the restrictive sexual tradition, pro-abstinence discourses define children as too immature for sexual activity which can only have negative and even lethal consequences like depression, teen pregnancy, STDs or suicide and is considered as a "social problem" rather than part of normal youth development. This "immaturity" of teenagers is used to justify an extended control over their private lives through, for example, the strict dating guidelines evoked in the previous chapter. Under the guise of child protection, parents are encouraged not only by conservative Christian authors, as well as the Bush administration when it was in office,[17] to monitor what their children watch, listen to, wear, whom they socialise with, where they go, what kind of activities they do. Parents are even encouraged by Hagelin to make statements on the choices of other children than their own. She explains proudly that her daughter

> knows, and even warns her friends, that bare bellies and bare upper thighs are not allowed in our house. Period. Often, her friends don't believe her. She's brought home more than one friend who has learned otherwise when I've sent them back upstairs to find something in my closet to cover-up with.[18]

Youths are especially excluded from the concept of good citizenship, since most of its terms are *de facto* unavailable to them. First of all, in many states, due to the various legal "age of consent" laws, they are excluded from a wide range of sexual activity. In the United States the age of consent varies from 14 to 18, with differences for hetero- or homosexual relationships. In many cases they are also excluded from marriage, either by law or simply by their status as dependent on adults for their care. It is also difficult for them to comply with the terms of the definition of good sexual citizenship provided by Seidman like linking "sex to intimacy, [and] love [...] and [...] restrict[ing] sex to private acts."[19] The development of intimacy is always limited for a couple of teens since they live under their parents' roof, a situation which also affects their access to privacy. Jessica Fields notes that youths

> enjoy little privacy, and few have their own "most private of spaces." Instead, most live under the roofs, rules, and regulation of parents, guardians, and educators, most of whom feel (and are) entitled to deny young people any privacy. [...] In order to pursue even the most chaste behaviors, they may need to engage in public expressions of their sexuality - flirting, holding hands, or kissing in the dark of the movie theater or in a quiet corner of a city park.[20]

Their attachments are also routinely dismissed as being immature "puppy love" that they will outgrow, or, if they have a sexual nature, as being "heat" rather than love, in the terms of Tim LaHaye.[21] According to pro-abstinence discourses, since "true love waits" for marriage, what comes before can only be dismissed as being of a "lower" nature. The right of teenagers to explore their sexual identity is also denied to them by the emphasis laid by pro-abstinence discourses on heteronormativity; as well as the legitimacy of the pleasure they feel in their emerging sexuality.[22]

Denying teenagers sexual information and refusing to acknowledge the positive dimension of teens' desires through a "just say no message" might also result in a long lasting lack of sexual agency. As underlined by sexuality researcher Deborah Tolman and law professor Tracy E. Higgins, girls who have not developed clear feelings of their sexual desires might be pushed to give in to sexual advances that they feel they have had a share in motivating. Denying their desires altogether might not empower them in situations of coercion but on the contrary leave unclear the boundaries of what they do or do not desire. For example, they might desire to attract a boy and kiss him, but not more. On the contrary, knowing clearly what she desires apparently enables a girl to put a clear stop to things she does not desire.[23] This is reinforced by the fact that, as pointed by Heather Hendershot, constructing the teenage body as "lacking self-control" and dominated by raging hormones which can only be subdued by abstinence "may encourage boys to be sexually violent and girls to see submission to sexual violence as natural."[24] By constantly reminding girls that "they have the capacity to ignite a boy's sexual passion"[25] by their dress, talk or by just brushing against them and that they are responsible for unleashing male "lust," pro-abstinence discourses, especially coming from conservative Christians, might weaken their capacity to resist sexual abuse by blaming themselves for causing it. Meanwhile by telling boys that they are controlled by their sexual instincts, these discourses might encourage them to see themselves as less in control than they actually are.[26] Thus pro-abstinence discourses contribute to the reinforcement of traditional sexist narratives.

Moreover, in spite of the argument that teens are irrational and impressionable, they are expected to do better than adults in managing and subduing their sexual urges. Trends in abortion, unplanned pregnancies or STD rates are similar for adults and for teens, problems on which as Pillow underlines, the U.S. ranks higher than any other industrialised country.[27] Besides, she adds, given the high US divorce rate as well as the fact that "up to half of married persons admit to having sexual affairs outside of marriage",[28] is it really meaningful and just to hold teens to standards that adults do not manage to respect themselves?

This situation appears particularly unequal in the light of the following remark by Fields on "age of consent" and "parental consent" laws regarding access to contraception and abortion "overall, these laws assign young people the responsibility for managing the risks and costs associated with their sexual activity but deny them any right to sexual privacy, let alone dignity or pleasure."[29]

Like the "pure" Victorian woman or Atwood's dystopic "Handmaid", US teens today, especially girls, can either be innocent or "fallen", and are held to higher standards of sexual behaviour than their more privileged counterparts, especially white male adults. Similar to the pure woman who was to be the moral angel of the nation and the mother of future abiding citizens, teens are held responsible for the "morality" of the nation at large as they symbolise its future. Hence, questions of teenage sexual behavior are invested with a dimension that far exceeds the issue itself and are addressed, through abstinence, at a symbolical rather than practical level. This is particularly striking in the following quote from Elayne Bennett's introduction to Meeker's book *Restoring the Teenage Soul*,

> [a] critical mass of adolescent destructive behavior is threatening the future and the stability of our country. After all, we are talking about the next generation.[30]

Here again, the focus is on the sexual behavior of one disenfranchised part of the population as a means to screen from judgment the similar behavior of the more "dominant" part of the population. It is a similar mechanism to the one at work in the stigmatisation of African-American sexuality, which is also operative in abstinence rhetoric. In such a framework, the less powerful and more dependent are held more accountable for sexual behaviors that they cannot hide as easily as the more privileged can, being under constant surveillance from the family or the state.

Judith Levine astutely observes that, without access to abortion and contraception, teenage sexuality is sent back to another age, denied the benefits of reproductive technology which have achieved so much for women's liberation:

> Without abortion, the narrative of teenage desire is strangely, and artificially, unmoored from modern social reality. Instead of sound policy, the anti-abortion movement has rewritten a premodern parable, in which fate tumbles to worse fate, sin is chastised, and sex is the ruination of mother, child, and society. Gone is premeditation in sex; gone too the role of technology, of safe contraception or "planned parenthood." Gone far away is the relief, even joy, of ending an unwanted pregnancy and women's newfound power to decide what they want to do with their bodies and their lives and when they want to do it.[31]

As I have argued in the previous chapter, the message promoted by abstinence discourses that teenagers need boundaries is not necessarily misled. However, the line between responsible care for children and adultism, or infringements on human rights is sometimes very thin, especially for a group of individuals that considers the family as the only legitimate authority over children, while downplaying the potentially oppressive nature of this institution. Indeed, "research shows that more than half, and some say almost all, of sexual abuse is visited upon children by their own family members or parental substitutes"[32] Moreover, incest with the destruction of trust that it implies, is acknowledged as having much more lasting and destructive consequences than abuse by a stranger.[33] Here again, a discursive displacement is operated to shift focus from an unfortunately widespread behavior to a more marginal one.

Pro-abstinence rhetoric and the way it reinforces hierarchical relationships inside the family can raise concerns. By putting parents in complete control of their children's sexuality, pro-abstinence discourses deny teenagers access to health information and a minimum of sexual agency. Thus it reasserts the family as a hierarchical structure based on adultism that disregards youth as "citizens" entitled to rights, duties and federal protection. As will be explained now, this reinforcement of hierarchies and "disenfranchisement" of children is also supported by an eroticization of child and teen sex by pro-abstinence discourses.

We live in a society, which while claiming loudly to protect children from sexual abuse, constantly eroticises them. As underlined by Judith Levine and James Kincaid, magazines are covered with pictures of teenage models featuring androgynous bodies, and the sexual allure of children is permanently asserted by presenting them as victims of countless sexual predators in and outside the family.[34]

In what can appear as a paradox, pro-abstinence discourses, while advocating sexual self-control and the de-sexualisation of the "culture," display complex and varied strategies to construct teens and children as sexual objects exposed to the gaze, imagination and control of adults. In its wish to control, watch, investigate and question teenage sexuality, pro-abstinence discourses can be considered to obey the power-pleasure dynamic described by Foucault in his *History of Sexuality*. Pro-abstinence discourses, like

> [t]he medical examination, the psychiatric investigation, the pedagogical report, and family controls may have the overall and apparent objective of saying no to all wayward and unproductive sexualities, but the fact is that they function as mechanisms with a double impetus: pleasure and power. The pleasure that comes of exercising a power that questions, monitors, watches, spies, searches out, palpates, brings to light; and on the other hand, the pleasure that kindles at having to evade this power, flee from it, fool it, or travesty it.[35]

While it is not within the scope of this study to analyse how teens might find pleasure in evading parental control, investigating how pro-abstinence discourses eroticise children in order to yield power over them is the focus of this section.

Pro-abstinence discourses eroticise children, and consequently teens, through three major discursive processes. First, by telling or retelling highly sexualised stories in which innocent children are pressured by the "culture" to engage in sexual acts; second, they construct children as irresistible sexual objects for the desires of sexual predators; finally, they describe teenagers as highly sexual creatures dominated by "raging hormones."

In pro-abstinence discourses, the distinction between "children" and "teenagers" is intentionally obscured. Arguably, a teenager is always someone's "child." But this distinction is also blurred at a more significant level. While the concept of abstinence conjures up the image of "sexual" teenagers; "child abuse" on the contrary, as the term implies, conjures up the image of a "child" even if this includes a minor, meaning anyone under eighteen years old. The pro-abstinence discourses studied in this book all raise up the issue of "child sexual abuse." In most cases, they do so to argue that teens today live in an "oversexualised" culture, which needs to be contained as it generates sexual abuse not just by adults but also by "teens" or "children" themselves. As mentioned earlier, in the White House document *President George W. Bush: A Remarkable Record of Achievement* abstinence-only education is listed under the section "child protection" next to numerous other "achievements" concerning the prosecution of pedophiles and the censorship of pornography. Thus, in pro-abstinence discourses the boundaries between the child and the teenager are blurred.

Even under the category of "teenager" itself, the realities covered are extremely varied since it concerns anyone between thirteen and nineteen years old, an age at which one is legally an adult at least regarding sexual matters. Jessica Fields and Celeste Hirschman underline, for example, that by stating that "abstinence from sexual activity outside marriage [is] the expected standard for all school age children" the *Personal Responsibility and Work Opportunity Reconciliation Act of 1996* "reifies adults' authority over youth, reducing all young people to 'children,' and affording youth no role to play in determining the standards guiding their lives."[36] Thus, pro-abstinence discourses reinforce the hierarchy between adults and children by assimilating very different ages under the blanket age category of "minority" that needs to be protected from sexuality and its consequences. As explained in Chapter 1, this enables conservative Christians to further deny teenage sexual desire by subsuming teens under the category of the "innocent" child. But if teenage desire is denied in pro-abstinence discourses, teenage sexuality is often described in almost pornographic details.

The most "extreme" example of erotic description of teen sexuality in the texts studied in this book is provided by Meeker in Chapter 9, "High-Risk Sex," in *Epidemic*, where she offers an example of how our "oversexualised" culture pushes originally "innocent" children towards sexual activity. She opens the chapter with the summary of a PBS TV documentary aired in 1999, which has since then attracted much notice, *The Lost Children of Rockdale County*:[37]

> In 1996, THE SMALL, UPSCALE community of Conyers, Georgia, experienced an epidemic of syphilis. More than 200 teenagers - many as young as 13 and 14 - were infected. When officials and the media investigated, they discovered a community in which teens gathered in large, empty houses for drinking, drugs, and group sex. A small core of teens had had sex with as many as 50 different people in a short span of time (one young girl told health

officials she'd slept with at least 65 people). Some of them
had been holding "study groups," in which they watched,
then re-enacted scenes from The Playboy Channel in their
bedrooms. Preteen girls admitted to participating in an act
they called "the sandwich," in which one girl had oral sex
with a boy while having vaginal sex with another boy and
anal sex with a third boy, all at the same time. The girls had
also had sex with each other.[38]

Though Meeker repeats this example in order to "warn" parents, it is
clear that if her book were to be online it would not pass the internet filters
recommended by Hagelin in her columns for the Heritage Foundation. The
picture she draws from the documentary is one worthy of pornographic
literature and is as titillating as it is appalling in its orgiastic excess. One can
indeed only wonder at the flexibility of teenage bodies as well as at their
sexual endurance. Compared with the transcript of the documentary Meeker
does not exaggerate what the reporters heard of the sexual activities of
Rockdale's "lost children." However, Meeker does mislead her readers since,
according to the transcript of the show, it was not two hundred teens who
were infected but only seventeen, the others having been just exposed to the
disease while only fifty of them "reported being involved in extreme sexual
behavior."[39]

Meeker is not the only commentator to have used the Rockdale
County story. Oprah Winfrey aired a show on the documentary on February
7, 2000, inviting specialists to reveal to the audience that "this new
generation uses casual sex to feel connected - and they're trying everything
from sexual gymnastics to orgies to numerous sexual partners."[40] Hagelin
uses the same device as Meeker in her book *Home Invasion*, where she
quotes a passage from a National Public Radio program aired more than ten
years earlier (in 1993-1994), a fact she does not specify, and reporting on a
"wild" prom night:

A hundred kneeling, teenage boys bring their faces against
the slightly sweaty thighs of their dates, grip multi-colored
garters with their teeth, and drag them off their legs. It's a
shocking and amazing sight. But when I ask teachers about
it later, they all say, "Where have you been? They've done
this for years!" At homecoming apparently, things get even
more explicit.[41]

In passing around these stories, conservative writers are not alone. By
repetition and alteration what might have been factual anecdotes become

"urban legends" reinforcing the sense of threat over teenage/child sexual purity.

It is interesting to compare such stories with a survey of teenage sex life led for NBC NEWS and *People Magazine* by Princeton Survey Research Associates International in 2005. The survey found among other things that

> [t]he vast majority (87%) of teens aged 13 to 16, have not had sexual intercourse. Most (73%) have not been sexually intimate at all. [...] Fifty-five percent of teens hold that it is "very important" to be in love before having oral sex. Somewhat more (68%) say it is very important to be in love before having sexual intercourse. [...] One in 10 (12%) teens have had oral sex. Almost 9 out 10 (88%) teens have not. [...] A statistically insignificant *less* than one-half of a percentage of teens said they had ever been to the now mythological oral sex party. [...] Casual relationships are not uncommon among sexually active teens. Eight percent of 13 to 16 year-olds, which amounts to roughly half of young teens who have had oral sex or sexual intercourse, have been involved in a casual sexual relationship.[42]

The picture drawn by this survey does not reflect the extreme statements of "wild sex orgies" described by Meeker, Hagelin and Oprah. Even the findings about casual sexual relationships, when put in perspective, do not match these "dramatic accounts" of sexual cold-bloodedness and calculation:

> [F]ew young teens have casual relationships exclusively. Only fourteen percent of young teens who have had a casual relationship say they have never been involved in a serious relationship.[43]

As pointed out by Judith Levine, "rates of youthful [sexual] activity are not galloping upward" since the 1950s and most "sexually active teenagers," that is the less than 30% of 13 to 16 year olds mentioned above, are "not very sexually active."[44] After all, having oral sex once in five years is enough to fit in the "sexually active" category, but representing teenage sexuality in such an extreme manner has a particular purpose.

Constructing teen sex as necessarily deviant, extreme and unhealthy due to the negative influence of an oversexualised culture reinforces the appeal of abstinence as a means to moderate these influences and to provide teenagers with a "sex-free" environment more "appropriate" to their age. By picturing such images of debauchery, the shortcomings of the "safe sex" approach to sexual education are clearly targeted. The message sent here is that teenagers should not be allowed to have sex at all, since their immaturity leads them to experiment with sexuality in ways that go against their psychological and physical integrity like in the case of the teens of Rockdale County referred to by Meeker. In such cases condoms and birth control are presented as insufficient to protect "children" from harm.

In his book *Erotic Innocence: The Culture of Child Molesting*, James Kincaid insightfully argues that:

> Our culture has enthusiastically sexualized the child while denying just as enthusiastically that it was doing any such thing. We have become so engaged with tales of childhood eroticism (molestation, incest, abduction, pornography) that we have come to take for granted the irrepressible allure of children.[45]

Abstinence advocates, while denouncing this process, heavily participate in this eroticisation of "children"/ "teenagers" as irrepressibly alluring to predators. This is the case of the Bush administration in the president's *Record of Achievement* as mentioned further above, as well as of Hagelin and the LaHayes.

Hagelin devotes a section of her book to the porn industry and the internet.[46] She starts by stating that "our culture" is

> obsessed with sex. Sexual images are everywhere. And they aren't just of men and women having sex. There are adults with kids, kids with kids, group sex, sex with animals - anything goes.[47]

She goes on explaining that the porn industry, including child pornography, is flourishing, resulting in growing numbers of porn addictions, themselves leading to growing rates of divorces, rape and child molestation.[48] Finally, she warns parents that this danger is threatening their home in the shape of the internet. She argues that children are routinely exposed to pornographic content on the web and are at increased risk of being lured and abducted by pedophiles through chat rooms and instant messaging.[49]

The LaHayes warn parents of similar, and other, dangers in a whole chapter entitled "Protect Your Children From Sexual Abuse."[50] molesters they describe are: Catholic priests; day care providers - adding that these might be involved in an "organized operation of child predators" involved in producing child pornography and selling children;[51] - porn addicts; grown-up victims of past molestations; etc. The LaHayes acknowledge the importance of incest, though pointing out that it is aggravated by the "breakdown of the family" and the "delaying of marriage" which leave too many men single.[52]

Finally, though they refrain from arguing it in this chapter, they warn parents earlier on that many homosexuals are "created" by older males luring children and teens into homosexuality.[53]

Through such descriptions, the Bush administration, Hagelin and the LaHayes present "innocent children" and "teens" as potential victims of a host of predators of various hues insisting on the necessity of "adult" protection. This device enables abstinence proponents to reassert the sexual "innocence" of children and consequently to emphasise the boundaries between children and adults.

Paradoxically, the third means of eroticising teens used by abstinence discourses is to present them, boys in particular, as highly sexual creatures ruled by "raging hormones" and in need of parental control. Throughout pro-abstinence discourses teens are described as in need of strict "dating guidelines" and supervision. 4Parents.gov, the LaHayes and Meeker keep telling parents to monitor what their children read, watch and listen to, to prevent them from being sexually aroused. They also promote a vision of teens as out of control of their sexual urges to such an extent that couples cannot be left without supervision. Sex-education is also presented as easily igniting their sexual drives. Hagelin explains that she is

> amazed at the naivete of those who believe that teen boys actually have the ability to listen to detailed discussions of condom usage and sexual activities in one class, and then concentrate on equally exciting topics, as say, algebra or chemistry, the next.[54]

For her this is impossible, especially since "teenagers' bodies are raging with hormones"[55] or, in Meeker's words, since boys have to cope with "tremendous sexual urges."[56] Though all these authors acknowledge female sexual drives, they always describe male ones as being significantly stronger.

The LaHayes also depict teenage sexuality as easily getting to a point where there is no going back. According to the "law of progression" they describe in their book, teenage sexual drives are so out of control that anything beyond holding hands and light kissing will inevitably lead to intercourse.[57] Consequently, teenagers are considered to require constant surveillance and dating guidelines from their parents to help them subdue their uncontrollable sex drives.

Through these different and sometimes contradicting manners of eroticising children and teens, various agendas of abstinence are systematically reasserted. This eroticisation highlights the need to "purify" an oversexualised society that ignites teenagers' uncontrollable sexual drives and threatens the sexual "innocence" of "children" by exciting molesters of all kind. The apparent contradiction in the combination of the innocent child with the hypersexual teenager is negotiated through the emphasis on the sudden nature of the hormonal changes of adolescence and through the intermediate image of the teenage girl, who because she is not as sexual as her male counterpart can remain suitably "innocent" and vulnerable.

Valerie Daoust notes that youth has long been associated with beauty and sexuality. In spite of the fact that most youths are highly dependent on adults, youth is seen as a time of sexual freedom and experimentation before the inscription of the sexual self in the productive pattern of monogamous heterosexuality. The idea that youths have a more "liberated" sexual life than their parents is reinforced by the apparent liberalization of sexuality in the past four decades. Envied and desired, youths are seen by the older generation as a menace to the status quo and thus to require control and education to be integrated in the preexisting social structure.[58] To come to terms with the menace constituted by youths, adults can choose to objectify them sexually in a symbolic attempt to reassert their domination.

Following the suggestion by Gargi Bhattacharyya that children, like third-world inhabitants, can be a support of erotic "exoticisation"[59], I argue in the following paragraphs that pro-abstinence discourses "exoticise" children and teens in order to solidify boundaries between childhood and adulthood.

For Bhattacharyya exoticisation is above all a question of "power disparity." She explains that learning

> the more worldly pleasure of the body requires recognition that social equity may not feel sexy. [...P]ower relations can be solidified for erotic ends. When the world around us seems to be changing so rapidly, the erotic fantasy of an absolute object can provide consolation for other uncertainties.[60]

Children can easily constitute such an "absolute object" since their "lack of social status and power renders them vulnerable to becoming other, as if childhood is a race apart from humanity."[61] Through highly sexualised stories, narratives of abuse, and the definition of the teen as dominated by "raging hormones," pro-abstinence discourses eroticize and, I argue, "exoticise" children and teenagers by denying them sexual agency while constituting them as sexual objects. In so doing, they reassert the domination of adults over minors. For Bhattacharyya, "relegating children to the role of absolute and vulnerable may reassure anxious adults that they are, in fact, in control."[62]

It can also be argued that teenagers are not the only "objects" exoticised by pro-abstinence discourses. In its focalisation on out-of-wedlock births, and thus implicitly on black teenage mothers and the poor, pro-abstinence discourses can also be considered to resort to a traditional form of exoticisation in the United States, the exoticisation of the black African-American body as well as the exoticisation of the "underclass." Thus it can be argued that pro-abstinence discourses use sexual objectification not only to reassert the boundaries between children and adults, but also between races and classes.

Through this double device of exoticisation and eroticisation pro-abstinence discourses reassert the unique role that can supposedly be fulfilled by abstinence education in maintaining teen sexuality within ordained borders and de-sexualising contemporary culture, while strengthening adult/child hierarchies through the sexual objectification of children and teens.

Through contemporary US pro-abstinence discourses, teenager's sexuality is being used to pursue wider political and moral goals with which it often has little to do itself. The Bush administration and conservative Christians used, and still use the emotionally charged association of children and sexuality to achieve, on the one hand political dominance and on the other hand to ensure its survival as a social movement. In conjunction with these two major functions, pro-abstinence discourses enabled both groups to maintain teenagers inside the hierarchically inferior category of "children" in order to maintain traditional family structures while investing teens with the symbolic weight of the nation's sexual morality. Thus, US teens are objectified, denied sexual legitimacy and agency as well as citizenship like Atwood's fictional handmaid.

Such a conclusion should raise a number of ethical concerns: When does parental authority become abusive? What kind of citizenship are children, teens and other minorities entitled to? Does the high degree of significance that our society has invested in sexuality have the potential to blind us to more important social concerns? Should we seek to go beyond a regime of emotional politics? When does the blurring of boundaries between religious and political discourse become problematic in a supposedly secular state?

Notes

[1] M Atwood, *The Handmaid's Tale*, Anchor Books, New York, (1986) 1998, p.65.
[2] For a more extensive sociological approach to this question see also: J Fields and C Hirschman, 'Citizenship Lessons in Abstinence-Only Sexuality Education,' *American Journal of Sexuality Education*, 2007, 2(2), pp.3-25.
[3] S Seidman, *Beyond the Closet: The Transformation of Gay and Lesbian Life*, Routledge, New York and London, 2002, p.189.

[4] ibid., p.189.

[5] ibid., p.17.

[6] ibid., p.203.

[7] ibid., p.203.

[8] ibid., p.204.

[9] *Personal Responsibility and Work Opportunity Reconciliation Act of 1996.*

[10] J Bell, 'Understanding Adultism,' 1995, 15 February 2007, <http://www.youthbuild.org/atf/cf/%7B22B5F680-2AF9-4ED2-B948-40C4B32E6198%7D/Bell_UnderstandingAdultism.pdf>, p.1.

[11] Lesko, 2001, p.123.

[12] ibid., p.129.

[13] ibid., p.140.

[14] ibid., p.138.

[15] Rubin, 1984, p.290.

[16] R Schleifer, *Ignorance Only HIV/AIDS, Human Rights and Federally Funded Abstinence-Only Programs in the United States*, September 2002, 14 (5) (G), viewed on March 16 2009, <http://eric.ed.gov:80/ERICDocs/data/ericdocs2sql/content_storage_01/0000019b/80/1a/a5/5a.pdf>, p.46.

[17] U.S. Department of Health and Human Services, 2005a, p.4.

[18] R Hagelin, 'America's Little Girls ... or Tramps?,' 4 March 2005c, viewed on 15 February 2007, <http://www.heritage.org/Press/Commentary/ed030405a.cfm>

[19] Seidman, 2002, p.189.

[20] Fields, 2004, p.18.

[21] LaHaye, 1998a, p.163.

[22] The question of the absence of teenage, especially female, desire in sex-education has been studied in a very enlightening way since the 1980s by researchers like psychologist Michelle Fine and sexuality specialist Deborah Tolman, among others. See: M Fine, 'Sexuality, Schooling, and Adolescent Females: The Missing Discourse of Desire,' *Harvard Educational Review*, 1998, 58, pp.29-53, and Tolman, 2002.

[23] D L Tolman and T E Higgins, 'How Being a Good Girl Can Be Bad for Girls,' in N. Bauer Maglin and D. Perry (eds), *"Bad Girls"/"Good Girls": Women, Sex and Power in the Nineties*, Rutgers University Press, New Brunswick, New Jersey, 1996.

[24] Hendershot, 2004, p.93.

[25] LaHaye, 1998a, p.163.

[26] Hendershot, 2004, p.93.

[27] Pillow, 2004, p.181.

[28] ibid., pp.181-183.

[29] Fields, 2004, p.15.
[30] in Meeker, 1999, p.IX.
[31] Levine, 2002, p.126.
[32] ibid., p.28.
[33] ibid., p.28.
[34] Kincaid, 1998; Levine, 2002.
[35] Foucault, 1991, p.324.
[36] Fields and Hirschman, 2007, p.11.
[37] Transcript available at:
<http://www.pbs.org/wgbh/pages/frontline/shows/georgia/etc/script.html>,
viewed on 16 March 2009.
[38] Meeker, 2002, p.143, emphasis in the original.
[39] R D Goodman and B Goodman (dir), *The Lost Children of Rockdale County*, 1999.
[40] Oprah.com, 'The Lost Children of Rockdale County,' 7 February 2000,
viewed on 21 February 2007,
<http://www.oprah.com/tows/pastshows/tows_2000/tows_past_20000207.jht
ml>
[41] quoted in Hagelin, 2005b, p.33.
[42] MSNBC.com, 'Nearly 3 in 10 Young Teens 'Sexually Active,'' *MSNBC News*, 31 January 2005, viewed on 21 February 2007,
<http://www.msnbc.msn.com/id/6839072/>
[43] ibid..
[44] Levine, 2002, pp.XXIV-XXV.
[45] Kincaid, 1998, p.13.
[46] Hagelin, 2005b, pp.36-44.
[47] ibid., p.36.
[48] ibid., pp.38-41.
[49] ibid., p.42.
[50] LaHaye, 1998a, pp.193-202.
[51] ibid., p.195.
[52] ibid., p.193-194.
[53] ibid., p.108.
[54] R Hagelin, 'Teens Can Be Responsible,' 28 April 2004a, viewed on 22 February 2007,
<http://www.heritage.org/Press/Commentary/ed042804a.cfm>
[55] ibid..
[56] Meeker, 2002, p.178.
[57] LaHaye, 1998a, pp.46-47.
[58] Daoust, 2005, pp.135-144.
[59] Bhattacharyya, 2002, pp.115-116.

[60] ibid., p.102.
[61] ibid., p.116.
[62] ibid., p.116.

Conclusion

When, at the beginning of this decade, I became familiar with the issue of premarital sexual abstinence in the context of the United States, my first reaction to the degree of political support it enjoyed was one of puzzlement. Why were middle-aged Congressmen and politicians, who had most likely experienced the sexual freedom of the 1960s and 1970s, promoting such apparently "reactionary" policies? Why were they so concerned with the sex lives of young people when one would expect them to be involved in more "political" issues? At the end of the 20th century and beginning of the 21st century, the idea of abstinence before marriage seemed absurd, unrealistic and even somewhat laughable. I could hardly imagine notoriously unfaithful French presidents defending such ideas and after the "Monicagate" and other sexual scandals, American politicians did not seem to be very credible on the issue either.

Certainly, the link with the Christian Right appeared as a motivation for the promotion of abstinence education, yet this answer was not wholly satisfying and deserved, in my view, more in-depth analysis. Why was premarital abstinence coming back, apparently so unexpectedly? What purpose did it serve, in particular for politicians who were unlikely to be moved by a genuine belief in chastity and Christianity? What was this support hiding?

This book has been an attempt to answer these questions and the many others that arose during my research. In the course of this study I became convinced that abstinence before marriage was not, as some scholars and observers have suggested, a "trivial" issue but that it carried important cultural messages about contemporary US society. Through the analysis of pro-abstinence discourses, this study underlined a number of major points.

Abstinence is an issue which coalesces most of the major conservative Christian agendas. Consequently, pro-abstinence discourses are a privileged vehicle for promoting a conservative Christian worldview. Moreover, abstinence discourses are instrumental in supporting and reinforcing a conservative vision of society based on a network of hierarchic relationships that place certain individuals, practices and values above others. These main relations of domination involve: the domination of men over women and, within the family, of fathers over their wives and children; the domination of adults, especially parents, over children; the moral and social superiority of chaste individuals over promiscuous ones and of traditional heterosexual marriage over cohabitation; the emotional and moral superiority of marital sexuality and marital love over other types of sexual and emotional relationships; the moral inferiority of the "underclass" and finally the superiority of the "traditional American values" of work, family and religious worship over the "liberal" values of the post-1960s era.

The promotion of these hierarchies constitutes the overt "text" of pro-abstinence discourses, but these also include a "subtext" which significantly varies depending on the type of pro-abstinence author involved. For conservative Christians, pro-abstinence discourses reinforce both the sense of being in the middle of a culture war and the menace facing young people's moral and physical health. This sense of permanent crisis contributes to the maintenance of the commitment of conservative Christians to the defense of traditional values and to political activism and lobbying.

For the Bush administration, pro-abstinence discourses, and the epidemics they contributed to, helped maintain the status quo along with traditional lines of hierarchy. Voters, made anxious by the threat of epidemics and moral panics of all kinds, vote for conservative candidates who offer to bring them back from post-modern chaos to a reassuringly familiar system of traditional values and moral absolutes.

Pro-abstinence discourses also raise important ethical concerns regarding the citizenship and human rights of children and the disenfranchisement of teens and other minorities.

1.   The Future of Federally-Funded Abstinence Education in the United States

Government funding of abstinence education programmes flourished during the Bush presidency. However, it is currently under reconsideration with the election of President Barack Obama in November 2009 and previously of a Democratic majority in Congress, as well as to the lack of empirical results of this approach in reducing teen pregnancy and STD rates. Moreover, significant objections have been repeatedly raised by scientists and Congress committees on the scientific reliability of many government-funded abstinence-only programmes. In November 2006, a report from the Government Accountability Office (GAO) uncovered

> a near total absence of oversight to ensure that funded abstinence-only-until-marriage programmes are not providing medically inaccurate information. In fact, according to the report, the Administration for Children and Families (ACF), the division of HHS responsible for the vast majority of the programmes, admitted that no such oversight is in place. This absence of accountability follows almost two years after a report from Congressman Henry Waxman (D-CA) found that more than two thirds of the curricula most commonly used in federally funded abstinence-only-until-marriage programmes contained serious medical inaccuracies, including misinformation about HIV, other STDs, and the effectiveness of condoms.

To date, HHS has made no changes to the reviewed
programmes and, despite the evidence, denies that any
problems with the curricula exist.[1]

Interestingly enough in April 2007, Wade Horn, former president of
the National Fatherhood Initiative, resigned from his job as Assistant
Secretary for Children and Families, where he oversaw abstinence funding, to
join a consulting firm. The prospect of having to account for the money
distributed to inaccurate and inefficient abstinence programmes is likely to
have prompted this resignation.

Since 2005, an increasing number of states have began to refuse
federal money for abstinence-only programmes; this trend accelerated after
the extension of the requirements of CBAE funding to include an even
stricter definition of abstinence-only education in October 2006.[2]

In May 2007 Democratic leaders announced that they would let the
$50 million grant for Title V funding expire in June 2007, since the program
had proven ineffective. Representative John Dingell, chairman of the House
Energy and Commerce Committee, even asserted that "abstinence-only
seems to be a colossal failure."[3] However, the funding was renewed and
later, in July 2008, title V was officially reauthorized for a 12-month
extension and received "$50 million in federal funds for Fiscal Year 2009."
The current authorization will expire on June 30, 2009. Overall, for "Fiscal
Year 2008, the federal government ha[d] allocated $176 million through
three separate funding streams for abstinence-only-until-marriage
programmes."[4]

The demise of Title V would have implied that the definition of
abstinence according to "A-H", on which all abstinence funding is based,
would disappear from the US law. This is very concerning for abstinence
advocates who argue that

> "A-H really defines what abstinence education is in terms
> of federal funding, and it is that criteria that says abstinence
> until marriage is what should be taught with the use of
> these monies," Huber said. "And so if we lose Title V, that
> language dies with Title V. So [with] the other abstinence
> education funding streams, even if they were continued, it's
> going to be really difficult for that discussion."[5]

As a response to these attacks on abstinence, a report on
comprehensive sex-education programmes, requested by Republican senators
Tom Coburn of Oklahoma and Rick Santorum of Pennsylvania was released
on June 14, 2007. The report, fashioned as a systematic answer to the one by
Waxman, concluded that while the comprehensive sex-education

programmes surveyed had some positive results in delaying the initiation of first intercourse and on condom use, they did not emphasise abstinence enough and did not stress the failure rate of condoms sufficiently. The report also underlined that some curricula contained scientifically inaccurate information.[6] This last point was a direct answer to the Waxman report which emphasised that

> over two-thirds of abstinence-only education programmes funded by the largest federal abstinence initiative are using curricula with multiple scientific and medical inaccuracies. These curricula contain misinformation about condoms, abortion, and basic scientific facts.[7]

Abstinence-only proponents gave a lot of importance to the findings of the Coburn-Santorum report. Yet when compared with the Waxman report, it appeared to make a significantly weaker case. For example, it concluded that

> although medical accuracy of comprehensive sex education curricula is nearly 100% - similar to that of abstinence-until-marriage curricula - efforts could be made to more extensively detail condom failure rate in context.[8]

The report failed to find major medical inaccuracies in comprehensive sex-education programmes, but appeared to be itself inaccurate in stating that abstinence-only curricula have a medical accuracy of nearly 100% since the Waxman report underlined that "eleven of the thirteen curricula most commonly used by SPRANS programmes contain major errors and distortions of public health information."[9] Moreover, while the Santorum-Coburn report acknowledged, though mitigating them, the positive results of comprehensive sex-education programmes in delaying sexual activity and encouraging condom use, it failed to underline that abstinence-only programmes have not been proven to achieve that much.

In addition to opposing abstinence-only at home, the Democratic Congress also questioned funding for abstinence programmes abroad as an AIDS prevention strategy. In early July 2007 the House of Representative struck down an amendment to reinstate funding for the promotion of abstinence in Africa. In doing so they challenged the White House, which warned that President Bush would veto any law suppressing abstinence funding.[10]

This unwavering commitment of the Bush administration to abstinence was further reinforced on June 21, 2007, when the Department of Health and Human Services launched a new campaign to encourage parents to "to talk to their pre-teen and teenage children about waiting to have sex" and updating its pro-abstinence website 4parents.gov.[11]

Underlining the opposition of the Democratic Congress to abstinence-only programmes, the United States House of Representatives Committee on Oversight and Government Reform, with Henry Waxman at its head, held on April 23, 2008, a first and very critical hearing on the "effectiveness of federally-funded abstinence-only-until-marriage programmes."[12]

This opposition is now gaining momentum with the beginning of Barack Obama's presidency. Counteracting the stance of the previous administration on reproductive rights, one of Obama's first decisions was to overturn the Mexico City Policy, commonly called the "Global Gag Rule" which had been reinstated by president Bush.[13] As previously mentioned, this rule stated, that "taxpayer funds should not be provided to organisations that pay for abortions or advocate or actively promote abortion, either in the United States or abroad."[14]

On March 11, President Obama signed the first-ever cut in the funding of abstinence-only-before-marriage programmes[15], while on March 17 the Responsible Education About Life (REAL) Act was introduced in Congress. This act, of which President Obama was a cosponsor when he was Senator, would

> create a dedicated funding stream administered by the U.S. Department of Health and Human Services to provide states with money for comprehensive sexuality education that is age-appropriate, medically accurate, and stresses abstinence while also educating young people about contraception.[16]

President Obama also dissociated himself from the Bush administration's support of conservative Christian agendas by "removing barriers to responsible scientific research involving human stem cells"[17] and demanding more "scientific integrity" in the "scientific process informing public policy decisions."[18]

It is likely that these decisions, taken very early in his presidency are only a start and that funding for abstinence-only programmes will progressively be dismantled.

However, if abstinence-only education is not federally funded anymore, the future of abstinence-plus is not necessarily at stake. As noted previously, abstinence, when it is coupled with information on contraception and abortion, is still considered by most American parents the most appropriate form of sex education. Considering this and the lack of support for "permissive" sexual ideology in the United States, it is unlikely that the

Obama presidency will significantly alter the support to abstinence or inaugurate a switch to western European types of sex-education.

2.   Abstinence as a US Phenomenon?

A brief overview of premarital abstinence in the occidental world seems to underline the religious dimension of this choice. Sexual abstinence has been a tendency among gays as a response to AIDS or among individuals who consider themselves as "asexual," but those cases are very different from premarital abstinence. They are motivated either by health reasons or by a lack of sexual drive and therefore entail a completely different relationship to desire, temptation and sexual "legitimacy."

Premarital sexual abstinence, on the contrary, is usually, when it is part of a group movement, motivated by religious beliefs. In Europe for example it is often inspired by US evangelical groups like the French, German or Belgian[19] versions of the US abstinence program True Love Waits of the Southern Baptist Convention.

While in some countries the Catholic Church is very insistent on premarital abstinence, the website of the French Catholic church, for instance, barely mentions the issue and does not make a central agenda of it. Overall, in Western Europe, abstinence appears to be a non-issue on the public scene even for Catholics, and is not considered a sensible public health approach. It is even the object of jokes like the Spanish parody MTV campaign "Amo a Laura: pero esperare hasta el matrimonio"[20] where the channel pretended to support abstinence through a music video featuring a band jokingly called "Los Happiness"[21] in order to ridicule conservative pro-family movements. While some US abstinence groups like the Silver Ring Thing and True Love Waits have developed abroad, they do not reach a wide audience.

Even in a traditionally Catholic Latin-American country like Brazil, abstinence is not supported by the state as sound public health policy. The call of Benedict XVI to Brazilian youths to abstain has been received negatively by the country's officials and parts of the Catholic community; their major argument being that abstinence-only is a dangerous stand in the time of AIDS.[22] While its Catechism clearly highlights the imperative of premarital chastity, the Catholic Church seems to be less successful than Protestant denominations in promoting abstinence among its members, at least in the occidental world. This might be due on the one hand to the less "passionate" and personal relationship of Catholics to their faith and God, and on the other hand to the evolution of religious practices towards a more "pick and choose" attitude, even among the Catholic clergy. This tendency is illustrated by the widespread opposition of many Catholic priests to the prohibition of condom use and the large number of churchmen cohabitating with a sexual partner. One could argue that while prohibitions in the Catholic tradition can be negotiated through the confessional and the relationship to the priest, they are, in the US Protestant tradition, more deeply internalised and mediated through a direct relationship to God, making requirements like abstinence more urgent to respect.

However, many abstinence programmes funded by the federal government in the US were created by Catholics. While it can be argued that this is due to the more conservative nature of American Catholicism, it also suggests that it might not only be religion but also the particular cultural context of the United States which provides a favorable terrain for the promotion of premarital sexual abstinence, making it a uniquely North American phenomenon.

This can be explained first by the particular nature of the sex education debate in the U.S. and the part played in it by conservative Christian lobbies. As explained in Chapter 1, conservative Christians developed through abstinence-only education programmes a unique response to the liberalisation of sex-education. This response found support in the Reagan administration and within congress, and in the past twenty years was consistently supported by the federal government. US political culture thus offered a unique environment in which the fluidity between church and state was sufficient for abstinence-only to flourish with governmental subsidies.

This particular political context was also strengthened by a culture which conjugates an important pornographic industry and with a strong censorship of sexual content and little support for a truly "permissive" sexual ideology. The roots of this ambiguous relationship to representations of sexuality are complex, however, in the past three decades this attitude has been strengthened by two major groups. Levine explains that on one side

> were feminists whose movements exposed widespread rape
> and domestic sexual violence against women and children
> and initiated a new body of law that would punish the
> perpetrator and cease to blame the victim. From the other
> side, the religious Right brought to sexual politics the belief
> that women and children need special protection because
> they are "naturally" averse to sex of any kind.[23]

This particular association intensified the anxiety over children and female sexuality thus favoring the development of abstinence as a desirable response to the potentially negative consequences of early sexual activity like teen pregnancy, STDs and emotional hurt. In addition to this, what Radford Ruether describes as the particular lack of "a critical education on economic and class structures"[24] of the US population enables lobbies and politicians to privilege "moral" solutions to problems that are inherently economic and social ones and are treated as such in other western countries. This tendency

is reinforced and promoted through American religious and cultural
narratives like the narrative of success, or the American dream, as well as the
Puritan narrative and the concept of "traditional American values," which as
Radford Ruether points out, defines

> wealth and poverty primarily in individualistic and
> moralistic terms, as a matter of hard work and personal
> discipline versus laziness and the wrongful expectations of
> "getting something for nothing."[25]

This particular political and cultural context suggests that in contemporary
western societies the promotion of sexual abstinence-only by both
conservative Christian groups and the government, as well as the support of
the population to abstinence, constitutes a uniquely US phenomenon.

However, abstinence is still supported as a socio-cultural
requirement, especially for women, in many non-occidental cultures as well
as in the more eastern parts of Europe. In this regard the more conservative
sexual stance of the US cannot be seen only as representing a minor cultural
tendency but might illustrate a more global norm than the more sexually
liberal stance of European countries. Yet the spread of AIDS has had a
tremendous effect on sexual health policies globally in the past decades and
while in many countries abstinence might still be considered a desirable
norm, pragmatism has led many states to distribute condoms and spread
information regarding sexual health.

3.   Abstinence, Identity and Empowerment.

Having stressed the more "oppressive" nature of pro-abstinence
discourses for teenagers, I would like to conclude this book by considering,
independently from abstinence advocacy and conservative Christian agendas,
the potentially empowering dimension of abstinence as a personal choice.
Indeed, it seems to me important to consider that teenagers are not only
passive "victims" of a conservative agenda that is forced upon them, but can
deliberately choose abstinence as a way to assert their sexual agency.

In *Invented Morality: Sexual Values in an Age of Uncertainty*,
Jeffrey Weeks argues that it is specifically due to its links with "structures of
domination and subordination" that sexuality has been at the center of
struggles for the definition of self and identity. He adds that sexuality, in
Foucault's view, might be a historical construct "but it remains also a key site
for the construction of personal meaning and social location."[26] It is therefore
interesting to envisage sexual abstinence as an important "constituent of
identity"[27] as sociologist Jamie L. Mullaney has done in her study of various
types of abstinence: *Everyone is NOT Doing It*.

In her book, Mullaney argues that the things you choose "not to do" define you as much as the things you do. She cites the example of the early days of sexual education when sexual abstinence was used as a way to differentiate the "civilised" and self-controlled middle-class from the more "savage" and "loose" lower classes.[28]

Referring to sociologist Mary C. Waters, Mullaney argues that in an American culture which constantly emphasises the need for individuals to have "something they can identify with,"[29] abstinence can provide a "relatively cost-free means to the end of gaining some control over the self."[30] To make the decision to abstain from a widespread practice is a deeply personal choice, a way to define oneself as deliberately different from the majority and therefore as a free agent in a world that constructs the practice one abstains from as normative. Abstinence, from sex or any other activity (driving, watching TV, using the internet) or product of consumption (alcohol, meat, cell phones), is also associated with various values and connotations in a particular context. Abstinence from alcohol, in the temperance movement, was seen as a sign of self-control and industry.[31] Vegetarianism is often associated with a particular respect for animal life plus a capacity for self-restraint. As for sexual abstinence, as seen throughout Chapter II, it is usually associated with religion but also, independently from that, valued by conservatives as a sign of self-control, good sense and foresight. Moreover, contrary to other forms of identification, like belonging to the middle-class, or high performance in a given task (athlete, scholar, artist), many types of abstinence are relatively accessible, as remarked by Mullaney, since they do not require any significant financial or time investment and can be within the reach of everyone, regardless of their social background, intellectual or physical capacities. Hence, sexual abstinence can appear as an attractive identity statement for teens, since it is available to all of them, can be performed without parental support or intervention, and asserts to a certain degree their independence from a normative culture.

This last point underlines one of the limits of abstinence-only education as a potential contributor to identity construction, since to be efficient in this regard abstinence has to remain a minority choice. Mullaney remarks that

> [c]urrent efforts to enforce strict abstinence-only programmes [...] may benefit from allowing for a more flexible interpretation of what it means to abstain. In their study of virginity pledges, Bearman and Bruckner[32] found that pledging only works in moderation in that pledges succeed precisely when everyone is not pledging. In short, the somewhat nonnormative character of pledging leads to its effectiveness.[33]

But the ideological context in which abstinence-only programmes are promoted is in complete contradiction with the possibility of allowing for more flexibility, since their very aim is to establish abstinence as a normative practice promoted by parental authority. Consequently, it seems unlikely that sexual abstinence can become a support of identity construction in the context of mandatory school curricula. It might even prompt the opposite reaction of making the practice of sexual activity a minority behavior that constitutes an identity statement.

While sexual abstinence might be more conducive to identity definition by remaining marginal, it can also, in certain communities like those of conservative Christians, be invested with other positive characters that might contribute to Christian teenagers' self-construction. In her study of conservative evangelical media, Heather Hendershot gives some clues as to how this might be the case. She argues that for evangelical teenagers sexual abstinence can be a "potent symbol of their commitment to God."[34] By choosing to postpone sexual activity until marriage, Christian teens affirm the importance of religion in their lives in an autonomous manner and inscribe themselves in a religious tradition that can provide them with a powerful sense of belonging. For Hendershot, it is crucial not to overlook the fact that being part of a religious community that provides them with a clear "rule book" (the Bible) can provide teens with a reassuring sense of stability and order.

> Given the tortuous isolation and feelings of helplessness and despair that many teenagers endure, it is not difficult to see why an ordered belief system and a community of fellow believers would be appealing. The evangelical system, which to outsiders may seem to be all rules and prohibition, offers structure, stability, and community to youths.[35]

Besides, she underscores, it would be unfair to evangelical teens to assume that they follow the abstinence requirement and the evangelical "way of life" blindly, without ever questioning it. She quotes examples where teenagers try to find loopholes and contradictions in the "Biblical chastity mandate"[36] in order to negotiate how far they can go within the boundaries of abstinence.

An argument recurrently mentioned by abstinence proponents is the fact that postponing sexual activity helps protect teens from its potentially negative consequences, like teen pregnancy, STDs or abusive relationships. However, some of these consequences have a completely different impact depending on the age and maturity level of the person involved. Becoming pregnant at thirteen is not the same as becoming pregnant at nineteen, and while younger teens might benefit from being encouraged to abstain, it might be more constructive to emphasise that with their level of maturity increasing, teens, like adults, can develop responsible emotional and sexual relationships.

In the case of teenage girls, postponing sexual activity can also be considered as particularly empowering. As explained by authors like Joan Jacobs Brumberg and Mary Pipher, adolescent girls are today at higher risks than they were forty years ago. In a highly sexualised culture, which defines unreal beauty standards as the norm and promotes consumption as the core of one's identity. teenagers, and particularly girls, are manipulated to boost sales. Such statements echo very interestingly the concerns of Hagelin and Meeker. This similarity is particularly interesting when comparing Meeker's books and Pipher's famous *Reviving Ophelia: Saving the Selves of Adolescent Girls* (1994). The personal tone and medical experience of Pipher as a psychologist, her use of personal stories of teens around which she structures her writing, as well as the arguments she uses suggest that Meeker, who wrote her books several years later, might have been influenced by *Reviving Ophelia*. In a way, Meeker's books can be described as "conservative Christian" and less scientifically grounded versions of Pipher's work.

At puberty (which they now reach at an ever-younger age), girls have to face important bodily changes. They are propelled into a world which, as Pipher claims, breaks their childhood self-confidence by urging them to focus almost exclusively on their outward appearance and its faults, rather than on their unique personalities and qualities. Brumberg and Pipher both argue that girls are pressured by the "culture" and their peers to invest themselves in the "project" of modeling their adolescent body, with its fat and acne, into the unattainable image of digitally-altered top models. While keeping them eternally dissatisfied, this project also focuses them, sometimes almost exclusively, on their image, making them easy targets for publicity and endangering their health dramatically, as in the case of eating disorders.

At school, in the streets, and even sometimes at home, they also face the sexism of a culture in which women are increasingly defined as sexual objects, are victims of sexual assaults in ever higher numbers and are devalued as members of society. Girls are pressured into becoming sexual to fit in, to look sexy even if they are not yet aware of their own sexual desires. Moreover, as has been underlined several times throughout this book, their desire and sexual agency is often negated, to be replaced by the traditional sexual ideology of female sexual passivity and male sexual need. This sexual pressure, as well as the pressure to control their physical appearance, endangers their self-confidence, pushing them to seek appreciation and recognition where they can. Pipher explains that since contemporary culture and our view of adolescence tend to push teenagers away from their parents, this recognition is most of the time sought in peers and boyfriends, often putting girls at even greater risk. As underlined by film studies Professor Kathryn Rowe Karlyn in an article devoted to the representation of girls in teen movies,

> [t]he enduring cultural myths of heterosexual romance [...] highly popular among young women, perpetuate female fantasies of Prince Charming boyfriends who will rescue them. [However] recent work on female adolescence such as Carol Gilligan's [...] explores how coming of age into heterosexual adulthood "kills off" young girls' confidence and strength and suggests how for girls the boyfriend (or desire for a boyfriend) *is* a killer.[37]

The socio-cultural injunction to fulfill heterosexual romantic narratives often leads teenage girls to focus on the search for a boyfriend and, once one is found, to invest themselves overwhelmingly in the relationship rather than in curricular and extra-curricular activities beneficent to their own self-development. The lack of self-confidence created by the "body project" described by Brumberg, sexual pressure, as well as the devaluation of girl's academic achievements often leads them to look for reassurance in sexual activity and weakens their ability to make responsible and healthy choices for themselves.

Considering this, encouraging girls to postpone sexual activity for most of their teen years might be a way to empower them and relieve them from the pressure of heteronormativity. Telling girls that being sexual, either in act or in appearance, is not indispensable to the construction of their identity might relieve the pressure they feel to fashion their bodies in order to be sexually attractive and might enable them to focus on other projects, thus helping them to develop a more positive self-image and more agency.

Likewise, abstinence may also contribute to empowering boys. In a world where social status for men is often equated in the media with sexual performance and seduction, and where boys and men are being told that they are dominated by their sexual drives, sending the message that men do not have to be sexually active to be worthy individuals may also be considered empowering. In this regard, conservative Christian abstinence discourses and the emphasis they lay on the urgency of the male sex drive might actually disempower boys more than the contrary.

However, in these cases, in order for abstinence to be empowering, it would have to be not so much centred on avoiding sexual activity at all costs, but on understanding that at any stage of life, abstaining from sexual activity, temporarily or not, might relieve the individual from the forms of social pressure associated with sex and enable her/him to focus on other goals.

Abstinence, when it is a deliberate and free choice, can provide teens with a significant sense of agency, control, religious commitment and sometimes of belonging to a religious community. Therefore, it would be a mistake to argue that abstinence has no place at all in the sexual education of teenagers. I think that it is important to consider the potentially empowering message of sexual abstinence for the population at large in a western civilization increasingly characterized by a "devoir jouir" (duty of sexual enjoyment).[38] Psychoanalysts, sex therapists, and the media have come to define sexual fulfilment through highly developed sexual techniques as the *sine qua non* condition to happiness, thus leaving many individuals, who either do not have access to sex or might not consider themselves as achieving such standards, feeling disempowered and frustrated.[39] In such a cultural context, temporary or even lifelong sexual abstinence can provide a non-negligible release from this pressure and relevantly question the way we have placed sexuality at the center of our lives and identities.

Notes

[1] SIECUS, 'A New Congress Should Enforce Accountability Over Abstinence-Only Programmes,' 16 November 2006c, viewed on 29 May 2007, <http://www.siecus.org/media/press/press0136.html>

[2] Huffstutter, 2007.

[3] K Freking, 'Funding for Abstinence Likely to Drop,' *WashingtonPost.com*, 16 May 2007, viewed on 29 May 2007, <http://www.washingtonpost.com/wp-dyn/content/article/2007/05/16/AR2007051602298.html>

[4] SIECUS, 'A Brief History of Federal Abstinence-Only-Until-Marriage Funding,' 2008, viewed on 28 March 2009, <http://www.siecus.org/index.cfm?fuseaction=Page.viewPage&pageId=670 &grandparentID=478&parentID=487>

[5] E Roach, 'What if abstinence legislation expires?,' *Baptist Press*, 22 May 2007, viewed on 4 July 2007, <http://www.sbcbaptistpress.net/bpnews.asp?id=25699>

[6] C Wetzstein, 'Study: More 'condoms' than 'abstinence' in sex-ed,' *The Washington Times*, 14 June 2007b, viewed on 24 June 2007, <http://www.washingtontimes.com/apps/pbcs.dll/article?AID=/20070614/N ATION/106140075&SearchID=732851266621455>

[7] Waxman, 2004, p.22.

[8] T Coburn and R Santorum (prepared for), *Review of Comprehensive Sex Education Curricula*, 12 June 2007, viewed on 5 July 2007, < http://www.acf.hhs.gov/programmes/fysb/content/abstinence/06122007-153424.PDF >, p.9.

[9] Waxman, 2004, p.7.

[10] J Thurman, 'House rejects Africa AIDS/abstinence aid,' *The Baptist Press*, 2 July 2007, viewed on 4 July 2007, < http://www.sbcbaptistpress.net/bpnews.asp?id=26002>

[11] U.S. Department of Health and Human Services Administration for Children and Families, 2007.

[12] SIECUS, 'Committee on Oversight and Government Reform Holds First-Ever Hearings on Abstinence Only Until Marriage Programmes,' April 2008, viewed on 28 March 2009, <http://www.siecus.org/index.cfm?fuseaction=Feature.showFeature&featurei d=1144&pageid=483&parentid=478>

[13] White House, 'Memorandum: Mexico City Policy and Assistance for Voluntary Population Planning,' 23 January 2009, viewed on 28 March 2009, < http://www.whitehouse.gov/the_press_office/MexicoCityPolicy-VoluntaryPopulationPlanning/>

[14] White House, 2004, p.38.

[15] SIECUS, 'First Ever Cuts to Abstinence-Only-Until-Marriage Programmes,' 11 March 2009, viewed on 28 March 2009, <http://www.siecus.org/index.cfm?fuseaction=Feature.showFeature&featurei d=1615&pageid=611&parentid=479>

[16] SIECUS, 'SIECUS Applauds the Introduction of the Responsible Education About Life (REAL) Act,' 17 March 2009, viewed on 28 March 2009, <http://www.siecus.org/index.cfm?fuseaction=Feature.showFeature&featurei d=1650&pageid=611&parentid=479>

[17] White House, 'Executive Order: Removing Barriers to Responsible Scientific research Involving Human Stem Cells,' 9 March 2009, viewed on 28 March 2009, < http://www.whitehouse.gov/the_press_office/Removing-Barriers-to-Responsible-Scientific-Research-Involving-Human-Stem-Cells/>

[18] White House, 'Memorandum: Scientific Integrity,' 9 March 2009, viewed on 28 March 2009, <http://www.whitehouse.gov/the_press_office/Memorandum-for-the-Heads-of-Executive-Departments-and-Agencies-3-9-09/>

[19] See for France, AVA, L'Amour Vrai Attend <www.amourvraiattend.com>, viewed 16 March 2009; for Germany, WLW, Wahre Liebe Wartet <www.wahreliebewartet.de>, viewed 16 March 2009; or Belgium, WLW, Ware Liefde Wacht <http://www.wareliefdewacht.be/>, viewed 16 March 2009.

[20] "I love Laura: but I wait until marriage"

[21] For a description of this campaign see Wikipedia: <http://es.wikipedia.org/wiki/Los_Happiness>, viewed on 16 March 2009.

[22] G Dogget, 'Chastity's a Hard Sell For the Pope in Brazil,' *Agence France Presse*, 12 May 2007, viewed on 5 June 2007, <http://www.mg.co.za/articlePage.aspx?articleid=308215&area=/breaking_n ews/breaking_news__international_news/>

[23] Levine, 2002, p.XXIII.

[24] Radford Ruether, 2001, p.192.

[25] ibid., p.192.

[26] Weeks, 1995, p.38.

[27] J L Mullaney, *Everyone is NOT Doing It: Abstinence and Personal Identity*. The University of Chicago Press, Chicago & London, 2006, p.2.

[28] Mullaney, 2006, p.58, and Moran, 2000, p.5,17.

[29] M C Waters, *Ethnic Options: Choosing Identities in America*, University of California Press, Berkeley, 1990, p.155.

[30] Mullaney, 2006, p.174.

[31] ibid., p.12.

[32] Bearman and Brückner, 2001.

[33] Mullaney, 2006, p.179.

[34] Hendershot, 2004, p.88.

[35] ibid., p.102-103.

[36] ibid., p.100.

[37] K Rowe Karlyn, 'Scream, Popular Culture, and Feminism's Third Wave: 'I'm Not My Mother,'' *Genders OnLine Journal*, 2003, 38, viewed on 14 June 2007, <http://www.genders.org/g38/g38_rowe_karlyn.html>, emphasis in the original).

[38] Daoust, 2005, p.142.

[39] ibid., p.97.

Bibliography

Abbott, E., *A History of Celibacy*. Da Capo Press, Cambridge, 2001.

ACGreen.com, 'Abstinence Curriculum'. 2007, viewed on 15 March 2007, <http://www.acgreen.com/default.aspx?pageid=3939>

Adler, J., 'The New Naysayers'. *Newsweek Online*, 11 September 2006, viewed on 8 February 2007, <http://www.msnbc.msn.com/id/14638243/site/newsweek/>

Aikman, D., *A Man of Faith: The Spiritual Journey of George W. Bush*. Thomas Nelson, Nashville, 2004.

Albert, B., 'American Opinion on Teen Pregnancy and Related Issues 2003'. 7 February 2004, viewed 11 May 2007, <https://www.teenpregnancy.org/works/pdf/American_Opinion.pdf>

AMERICAN CIVIL LIBERTIES UNION (ACLU), 'ACLU Applauds Federal Government's Decision to Suspend Public Funding of Religion by Nationwide Abstinence-Only-Until-Marriage Program'. 22 August 2005, viewed on 19 June 2007, <http://64.106.165.214/news/08.22.05%20SilverRing.pdf>

Ammerman, N.T., 'North American Protestant Fundamentalism' in L. Kintz and J. Lesage (eds), *Media, Culture and the Religious Right*. University of Minnesota Press, Minneapolis, 1998.

Ashbee, E., *The Bush Administration, Sex and the Moral Agenda*, Manchester University Press. Manchester and New York, 2007.

Atwood, M., *The Handmaid's Tale*, Anchor Books, New York, 1998.

Barna Group, 'Born Again Christians Just As Likely to Divorce As Are Non-Christians'. 8 September 2004, viewed on 8 March 2006, <http://www.barna.org/FlexPage.aspx?Page=BarnaUpdateNarrow&BarnaUpdateID=216&PageCMD=Print>

Bauer Maglin, N. and D. Perry (eds), *"Bad Girls"/"Good Girls": Women, Sex and Power in the Nineties*. Rutgers University Press, New Brunswick, New Jersey, 1996.

Baumgardner, J. and N. Dépret, 'Le bal de la virginité'. *Glamour* (French Edition), May 2007, 38, pp.50-54.

Bearman, P.S. and H. Brückner, 'Promising the Future: Virginity Pledges and the Transition to First Intercourse'. *American Journal of Sociology*, 2001, 106 (4), pp. 859-912.

Beil, L., 'Abstinence Education Faces an Uncertain Future'. *The New York Times*, 18 July 2007, viewed on 20 August 2007, <http://www.nytimes.com/2007/07/18/education/18abstain.html?ex=1187841 600&en=a6f6061787e7cf9c&ei=5070>

Bell, J., 'Understanding Adultism'. 1995, 15 February 2007, <http://www.youthbuild.org/atf/cf/%7B22B5F680-2AF9-4ED2-B948-40C4B 32E6198%7D/Bell_UnderstandingAdultism.pdf>

Bercovitch, S., *The American Jeremiad*. University of Wisconsin Press, Madison, 1978.

Bergman, J., 'The Effect of Darwinism on Morality and Christianity'. June 2001, viewed on 19 June 2007, <http://www.icr.org/pdf/imp/imp-336.pdf>

Berlant, L., *The Queen of America Goes to Washington City*. Duke University Press, Durham and London, 1997.

Bhattacharyya, G., *Sexuality and Society: An Introduction*. Routledge, London and New York, 2002.

Bird, W.R., 'Evolution in Public Schools and Creation in Student's Home: What Creationist Can Do (Part I)'. 1979a, viewed on 18 June 2007, <http://www.icr.org/article/151/>

Bird, W.R., 'Evolution in Public Schools and Creation in Student's Home: What Creationist Can Do (Part II)'. 1979b, viewed on 18 June 2007, <http://www.icr.org/articles/all/2/>

Blasko, A., 'Reagan and Heritage: A Unique Partnership'. June 7, 2004, viewed on 18 June 2007, <http://www.heritage.org/Press/Commentary/ed060704e.cfm>

Bleakley, A., M. Hennessy and M. Fishbein, 'Public Opinion on Sex Education in US Schools'. *Archives of Pediatrics and Adolescent Medicine*, November 2006, (160), pp. 1151-1156.

Brumberg, J.J., *The Body Project: An Intimate History of American Girlhood*. Vintage Books, New York, 1997.

Buchanan, P.J., 'Republican National Convention Speech'. 17 August 1992, viewed on 5 March 2007, <http://www.buchanan.org/pa-92-0817-rnc.html>

Burns, A. and M.E. Torre, 'Shifting Desires: Discourses of Accountability in Abstinence-only Education in the United States' in A. Harris (ed), *All About the Girl: Culture, Power and Identity*. Routledge, New York and London, 2004.

Bush, G. W., 'Executive Order: Establishment of White House Office of Faith-Based and Community Initiatives'. 29 January 2001, viewed on 18 June 2007, <http://www.whitehouse.gov/news/releases/2001/01/20010129-2.html>

Bush, G.W., 'National Sanctity of Human Life Day, 2002: A Proclamation by the President of the United States of America'. 18 January 2002a, viewed on 17 June 2007, <http://www.whitehouse.gov/news/releases/2002/01/20020118-10.html>

Bush, G.W., 'President Announces Welfare Reform Agenda'. 26 February 2002b, viewed on 18 June 2007, <http://www.whitehouse.gov/news/releases/2002/02/20020226-11.html>

Bush, G.W., 'President Discusses Welfare Reform and Job Training'. 27 February 2002c, viewed on 18 June 2007, <http://www.whitehouse.gov/news/releases/2002/02/20020227-5.html>

Bush, G.W., 'National Sanctity of Human Life Day, 2002: A Proclamation by the President of the United States of America'. 18 January 2002d, viewed on 18 June 2007, <http://www.whitehouse.gov/news/releases/2002/01/20020118-10.html>

Bush, G.W., 'State of the Union Address'. 20 January 2004, viewed on 18 June 2007, <http://www.whitehouse.gov/news/releases/2004/01/20040120-7.html>

Butler, S.M., and K. R. Holmes (eds), *Priorities for the President*. 2001, viewed on 12 June 2007, <http://www.heritage.org/Research/Features/Mandate/upload/Priorities-for-the-President-pdf.pdf>

Butterfield, F., 'This Way Madness Lies: A Fall From Grace to Prison'. *The New York Times*, 21 April 1996, viewed on 15 March 2007, <http://query.nytimes.com/gst/fullpage.html?res=9F02E5D61E39F932A1575 7C0A960958260&sec=health&spon=&pagewanted=all>

Campbell, D.M., 'Forms of Puritan Rhetoric: The Jeremiad and the Conversion Narrative'. February 21, 2006, viewed on 5 March 2007, <http://www.wsu.edu/~campbelld/amlit/jeremiad.htm>

Camus, A., *La Peste*, 1947.

Clinton, W. J., 'The President's Radio Address, May 4th 1996'. 1996, viewed on 18 June 2007, <http://www.presidency.ucsb.edu/ws/index.php?pid=52768>

Clinton, W.J., 'Radio Address of the President to the Nation'. St. Thomas, Virgin Islands, 4 January 1997.

COALITION FOR ADOLESCENT SEXUAL HEALTH, 'Zogby International 2003 Survey on Parents' Reactions To Proposed Sex Education Messages In The Classroom'. 3 February 2003, viewed on 13 May 2005, <www.whatparentsthink.com/pdfs/z_p1_sokfbsdbq.pdf>

Coates, S., 'God Is Cut From Film of Dark Materials.' *The Times Online*, 8 December 2004, viewed on 14 February 2007, <http://www.timesonline.co.uk/tol/news/uk/article400396.ece>

Coburn, T. and R. Santorum (prepared for), *Review of Comprehensive Sex Education Curricula*. 12 June 2007, viewed on 5 July 2007, < http://www.acf.hhs.gov/programs/fysb/content/abstinence/06122007-153424.PDF >

Coltrane, S., 'Marketing the Marriage 'Solution': Misplaced Simplicity in the Politics of Fatherhood'. *Sociological Perspectives*, Winter 2001, 44 (4), pp.347-418.

CONCERNED WOMEN FOR AMERICA, 'Our Core Issues'. January 2007, viewed on 13 March 2007, <http://www.cwfa.org/coreissues.asp>

Coontz, S. and N. Folbre, 'Marriage, Poverty, and Public Policy: A Discussion Paper from the Council on Contemporary Families'. 28 April 2002, viewed on 10 November 2006,

<http://www.contemporaryfamilies.org/subtemplate.php?t=briefingPapers&e
xt=marriagepovertypublicpoli>

Coontz, S., *Marriage, a History: from Obedience to Intimacy or How Love
Conquered Marriage*. Viking Penguin, New York, 2005.

Coontz, S., 'No Sex for You'. 6 November 2006, viewed on 23 March 2007,
<http://www.tompaine.com/articles/2006/11/06/no_sex_for_you.php>

Cooperman, A., 'Bush Leaves Specifics of His Faith to Speculation'. *The
WashingtonPost.com*, 16 September, 2004, viewed on 26 May 2007,
<http://www.washingtonpost.com/wp-dyn/articles/A24634-2004Sep15.html>

Cott, N.F., 'Passionlessness: An Interpretation of Victorian Sexual Ideology,
1790-1850' in N.F. Cott and E.H. Pleck (eds), *A Heritage of Her Own*.
Simon and Schuster, New York, 1979.

Cott, N.F. and E.H. Pleck (eds), *A Heritage of Her Own*. Simon and Schuster,
New York, 1979.

Dailard, C., 'Sex Education: Politicians, Parents, Teachers and Teens'
February 2001, viewed on 5 February 2009,
<http://www.guttmacher.org/pubs/tgr/04/1/gr040109.html>

Daoust, V., *De la sexualité en démocratie: L'individu libre et ses espaces
identitaires*. Presses Universitaires de France, Paris, 2005.

Darroch, J.E., Jacqueline E., S. Singh and J.J. Frost, 'Differences in Teenage
Pregnancy Rates Among Five Developed Countries: The Roles of Sexual
Activity and Contraceptive Use'. *Family Planning Perspectives*,
November/December 2001, 33 (6): pp.244-281.

Davis, M.S., *Smut: Erotic Reality/Obscene Ideology*. University of Chicago
Press, Chicago,1983.

D'Emilio, J. and E.B Freedman, *Intimate Matters: A History of Sexuality in
America*. The University of Chicago Press, Chicago and London, 1997.

Diamond, S., *Not by Politics Alone: The Enduring Influence of the Christian
Right*. The Guilford Press, New York, 1998.

Dixon, K., *Les évangélistes du marché*, Raisons d'Agir Éditions, Paris, 1998.

Dogget, G., 'Chastity's a Hard Sell For the Pope in Brazil'. *Agence France Presse*, 12 May 2007, viewed on 5 June 2007, <http://www.mg.co.za/articlePage.aspx?articleid=308215&area=/breaking_n ews/breaking_news__international_news/>

Durfield, R., 'A Promise with a Ring to It'. *Focus on the Family Magazine*, 1990.

Dyer, R., *Stars*. British Film Institute, London, 1998.

Eager, G.B., *Love, Dating and Sex: What Teens Want to Know*. Mailbox Club Books, Valdosta, 1989.

Edwards, L., *The Power of Ideas: The Heritage Foundation at 25 Years*. Illinois: Jameson Books, Inc., Ottawa, 1997.

Elkind, D., *Ties That Stress: The New Family Imbalance*. Harvard University Press, Cambridge, 1994.

Ellenberg, J., 'Sex and Significance: How the Heritage Foundation cooked the books on virginity'. *Slate.com*. 7 July 2005, viewed on 21 August 2007, <http://slate.com/id/2122093/>

Elwell, W.A., (ed), *Evangelical Dictionary of Theology*. Baker Academic, Grand Rapids, 2001.

Fagan, P.F., 'Marriage and the Family' in HERITAGE FOUNDATION, *Issues 2006: The Candidate's Briefing Book*. 2006, viewed on 18 June 2007, <http://www.heritage.org/research/features/issues/pdfs/BriefingBook2006.pd f>

Faludi, S., *Backlash: the Undeclared War Against American Women*. Anchor Books Doubleday, New York, 1991.

Falwell, J., *Listen America!*. Doubleday, New York, 1980.

Fauchier-Delavigne, M., 'L'abstinence vue par la presse des Etats-Unis'. *Le Monde.fr*, 8 January 2003, viewed on 8 February 2007, <http://www.fsa.ulaval.ca/personnel/vernag/EH/F/cause/lectures/abstinence_ Etats-Unis.htm>

Fields, J., 'Same-Sex Marriage, Sodomy Laws, and the Sexual Lives of Young People.' *Sexuality Research and Social Policy: Journal of NSRC*, September 2004, 1 (3), pp. 11-23.

Fields, J., ''Children Having Children:' Race, Innocence, and Sexuality Education'. *Social Problems*, 2005, 52 (4), pp.549-571.

Fields, J., and D.L. Tolman, 'Risky Business: Sexuality Education and Research in U.S. Schools'. *Research and Social Policy: Journal of NSRC*, September 2006, 3 (4), pp. 63-76.

Fields, J.   and C. Hirschman, 'Citizenship Lessons in Abstinence-Only Sexuality Education'. *American Journal of Sexuality Education*, 2007, 2 (2), pp. 3-25.

Fields. J., *Risky Lessons: Sex Education and Social Inequality*. Rutgers University Press, New Brunswick, New Jersey, and London, 2008.

Fine, M., 'Sexuality, Schooling, and Adolescent Females: The Missing Discourse of Desire'. *Harvard Educational Review*, 1998, 58, pp.29-53.

Fineman, H., 'Bush and God'. *Newsweek*, March 10, 2003: 22.

Finlay, B., *George W. Bush and the War on Women: Turning Back the Clock on Progress*. Zed Books, London and New York, 2006.

Fiorina, M.P., S.J. Abrams and J.C. Pope, *Culture War: The Myth of a Polarized America*. Pearson Longman, New York, 2005.

Foucault, M., *Histoire de la sexualité: La volonté de savoir*. Éditions Gallimard, Paris, 1976.

Foucault, M., *The Foucault Reader: An Introduction to Foucault's Thought*. Paul Rabinow (ed), Penguin Books, London, 1991.

FOX FAITH, 'About Fox Faith'. 2006, viewed on 9 March 2007, <www.foxfaith.com>

Frank, T., *What's the Matter with Kansas? How Conservatives Won the Heart of America*. Metropolitan Books, New York, 2004.

Franklin, B., *The Autobiography and Other Writings*. Penguin Books, London, 2003.

Freking, K., 'Funding for Abstinence Likely to Drop'. *WashingtonPost.com*, 16 May 2007, viewed on 29 May 2007, <http://www.washingtonpost.com/wpdyn/content/article/2007/05/16/AR2007 051602298.html>

Friedan, B., *The Feminine Mystique*. 1963.

Fulton, J., 'Religion and Politics in Gramsci: An Introduction'. *Sociological Analysis*, 1987, 48 (3): 197-216.

Furstenberg, F., 'The Future of Marriage'. *American Demographics*, 1996, 18.

Gates, D., 'Religion: The Pop Prophets'. *Newsweek Online*, 24 May 2005, viewed on 19 June 2007, <http://www.msnbc.msn.com/id/4988269/site/newsweek/>

Gavanas, A., *Fatherhood Politics in the United States: Masculinity, Sexuality, Race, and Marriage*. University of Illinois Press, Urbana and Chicago, 2004a.

Gavanas, A., 'Domesticating Masculinity and Masculinizing Domesticity in Contemporary US Fatherhood Politics'. *Social Politics*, 2004b, 11 (2), pp.247-266.

Ginsberg, M., 'The Politics of Sex Education'. *Educational Law and Policy Forum*, 2005, 1, pp. 1-25.

Godbeer, R., *Sexual Revolution in Early America*. Johns Hopkins University Press, Baltimore and London, 2002.

Gramsci, A., *A Gramsci Reader*. David Forgacs, (ed), Lawrence and Wishart, London, 1999.

Grossberg, L., *We Gotta Get Out of This Place: Popular Conservatism and Postmodern Culture*. Routledge, New York, 1992.

Hagelin, R., 'Parenting II: We're All in This Together'. 3 September 2003, viewed on 7 March 2007, <http://www.heritage.org/Press/Commentary/ed093103a.cfm>

Hagelin, R., 'Teens Can Be Responsible'. 28 April 2004a, viewed on 22 February 2007, <http://www.heritage.org/Press/Commentary/ed042804a.cfm>

Hagelin, R., 'Selling Selfishness to Children'. July 27, 2004b, viewed on 15 February 2007, <http://www.heritage.org/Press/Commentary/ed072704c.cfm>

Hagelin, R., 'The Culture War: A Five-Point Plan for Parents'. 9 August 2005a, viewed on 15 February 2007, <http://www.heritage.org/Press/Commentary/ed080905a.cfm>

Hagelin, R., *Home Invasion: Protecting Your Family In a Culture That's Gone Stark Raving Mad.* Nelson Current, Nashville, 2005b.

Hagelin, R., 'America's Little Girls ... or Tramps?'. 4 March 2005c, viewed on 15 February 2007, <http://www.heritage.org/Press/Commentary/ed030405a.cfm>

Hagelin, R., 'Fashioning a Response to Immodest Clothing'. 23 August 2005d, viewed on 7 March 2007, http://www.heritage.org/Press/Commentary/ed082305a.cfm>

Hagelin, R., 'Debunking the Siren Song of 'Safe Sex''. 22 July 2005e, viewed on 9 March 2007, <http://www.heritage.org/Press/Commentary/ed072205a.cfm>

Hagelin, R., 'Creating a Culture of Belonging'. 1 August 2006, viewed on 15 February 2007, <http://www.heritage.org/Press/Commentary/ed080106b.cfm>

Ham, K., ''Back To Genesis' The Hope For America?'. 7 April 1993, viewed on 15 February 2007, < http://www.icr.org/article/731/>

Harris, A., (ed), *All About the Girl: Culture, Power and Identity.* Routledge, New York and London, 2004.

Harris Interactive, 'Majorities of U.S. Adults Do Not Believe Abstinence Programs are Effective in Preventing or Reducing HIV/AIDS, Unwanted Pregnancies or Extra-Marital Sex'. 11 January 2006, viewed on 23 June 2007, <http://www.harrisinteractive.com/harris_poll/index.asp?PID=629>

Hatlen, B., 'Pullman's *His Dark Materials*, a Challenge to the Fantasies of J.R.R. Tolkien and C.S. Lewis, with an Epilogue on Pullman's Neo-Romantic Reading of *Paradise Lost*,' in M. Lenz and C. Scott (eds), *His Dark Materials Illuminated: Critical Essays on Philip Pullman's Trilogy.* Wayne State University Press, Detroit, 2005.

Hendershot, H., *Shaking the World for Jesus: Media and Conservative Evangelical Culture.* The University of Chicago Press, Chicago and London, 2004.

HERITAGE FOUNDATION, *Issues 2006: The Candidate's Briefing Book.* 2006, viewed on 18 June 2007, <http://www.heritage.org/research/features/issues/pdfs/BriefingBook2006.pdf>

HERITAGE FOUNDATION, 'Issues: Education'. 2007, viewed on 16 March 2007, <http://www.heritage.org/research/education/>

Homeinvasion.org, 'About Rebecca Hagelin'. 2007, viewed on 15 March 2007, <http://www.homeinvasion.org/AboutTheAuthor.cfm>

Howell, M., 'The Future of Sexuality Education: Science or Politics?'. *Transitions*, March 2001, viewed on 26 May 2007, <http://www.advocatesforyouth.org/PUBLICATIONS/transitions/transitions1203.pdf>

Huffstutter, P.J., 'States Abstain From Federal Sex-Ed Funds'. *LATimes.com.* 8 April 2007, viewed on 8 May 2007, <http://www.latimes.com/news/education/la-na-abstinence8apr08,1,1290457,full.story?ctrack=2&cset=true>

HUMAN RIGHTS WATCH, 'Questions and Answers on the UN Special Session on Children'. 2006, viewed on 29 March 2007, <http://www.hrw.org/press/2002/05/unchildrenqa0502.htm>

Hunter, J.D., *Culture Wars: The Struggle to Define America.* Basic Books, New York, 1991.

Independent Sector, *Overview and Executive Summary: Trends Emerging from the National Survey of Volunteering and Giving Among Teenagers.* 2003.

Irvine, J.M., *Talk About Sex: The Battles Over Sex Education in the United States*. University of California Press, Berkeley and Los Angeles, 2002.

Jayson, S., 'Abstinence Message Goes Beyond Teens'. *USAtoday.com*, 31 October 2006, 23 March 2007,
<http://www.usatoday.com/news/washington/2006-10-30-abstinence-message_x.htm>

John Paul II, *Evangelium Vitae*. 25 March 1995, viewed on 26 May 2007,<http://www.vatican.va/holy_father/john_paul_ii/encyclicals/document s/hf_jp-ii_enc_25031995_evangelium-vitae_en.html>

Johnson, E., 'The Emergence of Christian Video and the Cultivation of Videovangelism' in L. Kintz and J. Lesage (eds), *Media, Culture and the Religious Right*. University of Minnesota Press, Minneapolis, 1998.

KAISER FAMILY FOUNDATION, National Public Radio and the Kennedy School of Government, 'Sex Education in America: General Public/Parents Survey'. 2004, viewed on 9 February 2007,
<http://www.kff.org/newsmedia/upload/Sex-Education-in-America-General-Public-Parents-Survey-Toplines.pdf>

KAISER FAMILY FOUNDATION, 'Sexual Health Statistics for Teenagers and Young Adults in the United States'. September 2006, viewed on 11 May 2007, <http://www.kff.org/womenshealth/upload/3040-03.pdf>

Kaisernetwork.org, 'Nearly 150 Advocacy Groups Send Letter to HHS Secretary Criticizing Government Sex Ed Web Site as Biased, Inaccurate'. April 1, 2005a, viewed on 11 May 2007,
<http://www.kaisernetwork.org/daily_reports/rep_index.cfm?DR_ID=29069>

Kaisernetwork.org, 'HHS Abstinence Web Site for Parents of Teens Contains Inaccurate, Misleading Information, Review Says'. July 14, 2005b, viewed on 11 May 2007,
<www.kaisernetwork.org/Daily_reports/rep_index.cfm?DR_ID=31365>

Kaisernetwork.org, 'Federal Guidelines Expand Scope of Abstinence Education Funds To Include People up to Age 29'. 31 October 2006, viewed 11 May 2007,
<http://kaisernetwork.org/Daily_reports/rep_repro_recent_reports.cfm?dr_cat =2&show=yes&dr_DateTime=10-31-06#40759>

Kincaid, J.R., *Child-Loving: The Erotic Child and Victorian Culture.* Routledge, New-York and London, 1994.

Kincaid, J.R., *Erotic Innocence: The Culture of Child Molesting.* Duke University Press, Durham and London, 1998.

Kintz, L., *Between Jesus and the Market: The Emotions that Matter in Right-Wing America.* Duke University Press, Durham and London, 1997.

Kintz, L., 'Clarity, Mothers and Mass-Mediated Soul: A Defense of Ambiguity' in L. Kintz and J. Lesage (eds), *Media, Culture and the Religious Right.* University of Minnesota Press, Minneapolis, 1998.

Kintz, L. and J. Lesage (eds), *Media, Culture and the Religious Right.* University of Minnesota Press, Minneapolis, 1998.

Kirby, D., 'Do Abstinence-Only Programs Delay the Initiation of Sex Among Young People and Reduce Teen Pregnancy?'. October 2002, viewed on 23 March 2007, <http://www.teenpregnancy.org/resources/data/pdf/abstinence_eval.pdf>

LaHaye, B., *The Spirit Controlled Woman.* Harvest House, Irvine, 1976.

LaHaye, B., *Who Will Save Our Children?* Wolgemuth and Hyatt Pub., Brentwood, 1991.

LaHaye, B. *The Desires of A Woman's Heart.* Tyndale, Wheaton, 1993.

LaHaye, B. and J. Crouse, *The Strength of a Godly Woman.* Harvest House Publishers, Eugene, 2001.

LaHaye, T., *The Unhappy Gays: What Everyone Should Know About Homosexuality.* Tyndale, Wheaton, 1978.

LaHaye, T., *The Battle for the Mind*, Revell, Old Tappan, 1980.

LaHaye, T. and B., *Against the Tide: Raising Sexually Pure Kids in an Anything-Goes World.* Mutnomah Publishers, Sisters, 1993.

LaHaye, T. and B., *Raising Sexually Pure Kids: How to Prepare Your Children for the Act of Marriage.* Mutnomah Publishers, Sisters, 1998a.

LaHaye, T. and B., *The Act of Marriage: The Beauty of Sexual Love.* Zondervan, Grand Rapids, 1998b.

LaHaye, T. and J. Jenkins, *Left Behind* (series). Tyndale, Wheaton, 1995-2005.

LaHaye, T. and D. Noebel, *Mind Siege: The Battle for Truth in the New Millennium.* Word Publishing, Nashville, 2000.

Lawson, A. and D.L. Rhode (eds), *The Politics of Pregnancy: Adolescent Sexuality and Public Policy.* Yale University Press, New Haven, 1993.

Lecourt, D., *L'Amérique entre la Bible et Darwin.* Presses Universitaires de France, Paris, 1998.

Le Devoir, 'La stratégie américaine de l'abstinence soulève les critiques.' *Le Devoir,* 15 August 2006, viewed on 8 February 2007, <http://www.ledevoir.com/2006/08/15/115899.html>

Leftbehind.com, 'Dr. Tim LaHaye Bio'. 2007, viewed on 13 March 2007, <http://www.leftbehind.com/channelbooks.asp?pageid=1267&channelID=225>

Lenz, M. and C. Scott (eds), *His Dark Materials Illuminated: Critical Essays on Philip Pullman's Trilogy.* Wayne State University Press, Detroit, 2005.

Lesko, N., *Act Your Age: A Cultural Construction of Adolescence.* Routledge, New York and London, 2001.

Levine, J., *Harmful to Minors: The Perils of Protecting Children from Sex.* University of Minnesota Press, Minneapolis and London, 2001.

Limbert, W.M. and H.E. Bullock, ''Playing the Fool': US Welfare Policy from a Critical Race Perspective'. *Feminism and Psychology,* 2005, 15(3), pp.253-274.

Locke, J., *A Letter Concerning Toleration.* 1689, April 2002, viewed on 8 February 2007, <http://etext.lib.virginia.edu/etcbin/toccer-new2?id=LocTole.xml&images=images/modeng&data=/texts/english/modeng/parsed&tag=public&part=1&division=div1>

Luker, K., *Dubious Conceptions: The Politics of Teenage Pregnancy.* Harvard University Press, Cambridge, 1996.

Luker, K., *When Sex Goes to School: Warring Views on Sex - and Sex Education - Since the 1960s*. Norton & Co, New York and London, 2006.

MacKenzie, D., 'Will cancer vaccine get to all women?'. *NewScientist.com*, 18 April 2005, viewed on 22 June 2007, <http://www.newscientist.com/channel/sex/mg18624954.500>

Mansfield, S., *The Faith Of George W. Bush*. Charisma House, New York, 2004.

Martin, W., *With God on Our Side*. Broadway Books, New York, 1996.

Mathematica Policy Research, Inc., *Impacts of Four Title V, Section 510 Abstinence Education Programs, Final Report*. April 2007, viewed on 8 May 2007, <http://www.mathematica-mpr.com/publications/PDFs/ impactabstinence.pdf>

McKay, A., *Sexual Ideology and Schooling: Towards Democratic Sexuality Education*. State of New York University Press, Albany, 1999.

Medinstitute.org, 'Employment or Internship Opportunities'. 2007, viewed on 13 March 2007, <http://www.medinstitute.org/content.php?name=employment>

Meeker, M., *Restoring the Teenage Soul: Nurturing Sound Hearts and Minds in a Confused Culture*. McKinley and Mann, Traverse City, 1999.

Meeker, M., *Epidemic: How Teen Sex is Killing Our Kids*. LifeLine Press, Washington, D. C., 2002.

Meeker, M., *Strong Fathers, Strong Daughters, 10 Secrets Every Father Should Know*. Regnery Publishing, Washington, D.C., 2006.

Mehta, S., 'Teens' Dancing Is Freaking Out the Adults.' *Los Angeles Times*, 17 October 2006, viewed on 8 December 2006, <http://www.latimes.com/news/local/la-me-freaking17oct17,0,4105810. story?-coll=la-home-headlines>

Milbank, D., 'Religious Right Finds Its Center in Oval Office'. *The WashingtonPost.com*, 24 December 2001, viewed on 14 February 2007, <http://www.washingtonpost.com/ac2/wp-dyn/A19253-2001Dec23?language =printer>

Moran, J.P., *Teaching Sex: The Shaping of Adolescence in the 20th Century.* Harvard University Press, Cambridge and London, 2000.

Morris, H.M., 'The Gospel of Creation and the Anti-Gospel of Evolution'. 1 July 1975, viewed on 19 June 2007, <http://www.icr.org/article/71/>

Morris, H.M., 'All Nations Under God'. October 2002, viewed on 19 June 2007, <http://www.icr.org/pdf/btg/btg-166.pdf>

Morris, J., 'Are Schools Teaching Evolution Well Enough?'. 1 June 1998, viewed on 19 June 2007, <http://www.icr.org/article/1181/>

Moynihan, P., *The Negro Family: The Case For National Action.* Office of Policy Planning and Research, United States Department of Labor Washington D. C., 1965.

MSNBC.com, 'Nearly 3 in 10 Young Teens 'Sexually Active''. *MSNBC News*, 31 January 2005, viewed on 21 February 2007, <http://www.msnbc.msn.com/id/6839072/>

Mullaney, J. L., *Everyone is NOT Doing It: Abstinence and Personal Identity.* The University of Chicago Press, Chicago & London, 2006.

NATIONAL FATHERHOOD INITIATIVE, 'NFI History'. 2007, viewed on March 22 2007, <https://www.fatherhood.org/history.asp>

National Health Information Center, 'Most Americans Favor Comprehensive Sex Education'. *Family Health and Relationships Newsletter*, 20 November 2006, viewed on 8 May 2007, <http://www.healthfinder.gov/newsletters/relation112006.asp>

Nonewmoney.org, 'A Brief History of Abstinence-Only-Until-Marriage Funding'. 2006a, viewed on 22 March 2007, <http://www.nonewmoney.org/history.html>

Nonewmoney.org, 'Harmful Consequences,' 2006b, 23 March 2007, <http://www.nonewmoney.org/harmful.html>

Nonewmoney.org, 'A Brief History of Abstinence-Only-Until-Marriage Funding: Spending for Abstinence-Only-Until-Marriage Programs (1982-2008)'. 2007, viewed 21 June 2007, <http://nomoremoney.org/historyChart.html>

Nonewmoney.org, 'On Our Side: Public Support for Comprehensive Sexuality Education'. 2006c, viewed on 23 March 2007, <http://www.nonewmoney.org/public.html>

Nonewmoney.org, 'A Brief History of Abstinence-Only-Until-Marriage Funding: Spending for Abstinence-Only-Until-Marriage Programs (1982-2008)'. 2007, viewed 21 June 2007, <http://nomoremoney.org/historyChart.html>

Northcott, M.S., *An Angel Directs the Storm: Apocalyptic Religion and American Empire*. I. B. Tauris, London, 2004.

O'Leary, S. D., *Arguing the Apocalypse: A theory of Millennial Rhetoric*. Oxford University Press, New York, 1994.

Oprah.com, 'The Lost Children of Rockdale County'. 7 February 2000, viewed on 21 February 2007, <http://www.oprah.com/tows/pastshows/tows_2000/tows_past_20000207.jht ml>

Oprah.com, 'A New Kind of Spin the Bottle: Dr. Phil on Alarming Sexual Behavior Among Children'. 7 May 2002, 12 February 2007, <http://www.oprah.com/tows/pastshows/tows_2002/tows_past_20020507_b.j html>

Pagels, E., *The Origin of Satan*. Random House, New York, 1995.

Pardue, M.G., R. Rector and S. Martin, 'Executive Summary: Government Spends $12 on Safe Sex and Contraceptives for Every $1 Spent on Abstinence'. 14 January 2004, viewed on 17 June 2007, <http://www.heritage.org/Research/Family/bg1718es.cfm>

Pardue, M.G.,'Waxman Report Is Riddled with Errors and Inaccuracies'. 2 December 2004, viewed on 15 March 2007, <http://www.heritage.org/Research/Abstinence/wm615.cfm>

Phoenix, A., 'The social Construction of Teenage Motherhood: A Black and White Issue?' in A. Lawson and D. L. Rhode (eds), *The Politics of Pregnancy: Adolescent Sexuality and Public Policy*. Yale University Press, New Haven, 1993.

Piccione, J.J. and R.A. Scholle, 'Combatting Illegitimacy and Counseling Teen Abstinence: A Key Component of Welfare Reform'. 31 August 1995, viewed on 19 June 2007, <http://www.heritage.org/Research/Abstinence/BG1051.cfm>

Piekarec, M., 'Droits des enfants: le déni américain'. *Le Devoir*, 8 May 2002, viewed on 29 March 2007, <http://www.ledevoir.com/2002/05/08/376.html#>

Pillow, W. S., *Unfit Subjects: Educational Policy and the Teen Mother.* RoutledgeFalmer, New York and London, 2004.

Pipher, M., *Reviving Ophelia: Saving the Selves of Adolescent Girls.* Grosset Putnam, New York, 1994.

Pontifical Council for the Family, 'The Truth and Meaning of Human Sexuality, Guidelines for Education within the Family'. 8 December 1995, viewed on 19 June 2007, <http://www.vatican.va/roman_curia/pontifical_councils/family/documents/r c_pc_family_doc_08121995_human-sexuality_en.html>

Public Agenda, *Kids These Days '99: What Americans Really Think About the Next Generation.* 1999, viewed on 19 June 2007, <http://www.publicagenda.org/research/pdfs/kids_these_days_99.pdf>

Public Health Institute, 'Regardless of Religion, Politics or Location, New Poll Shows Overwhelming Parental Support for Comprehensive Sex Ed'. 23 May 2007, viewed on 25 May 2007, <http://askmerrill.ml.com/markets_news_story/1,2263,%7B8A40E614-F1C3-47CB-843B-6DEF0E770DC8%7D,00.html>

Pullman, P., *His Dark Materials*: *The Golden Compass: Book I*, 1995; *The Subtle Knife: Book II*, 1997; *The Amber Spyglass: Book III*, 2000; Dell Yearling, New York.

Radford Ruether, R., *Christianity and the Making of the Modern Family.* SCM Press, London, 2001.

Raymo, C., *Skeptics and True Believers.* Walker, New York, 1998.

Rector, R., 'Implementing Welfare Reform and Promoting Marriage'. in S. M. Butler and K. R. Holmes (eds), *Priorities for the President.* 2001, viewed

on   12   June   2007,
<http://www.heritage.org/Research/Features/Mandate/upload/Priorities-for-the-President-pdf.pdf>

Rector, R.,'Abstinence Promotion,' in HERITAGE FOUNDATION, *Issues 2006: The Candidate's Briefing Book.* 2006, viewed on 18 June 2007, <http://www.heritage.org/research/features/issues/pdfs/BriefingBook2006.pdf>

Rector, R. and K.A. Johnson, 'Teenage Sexual Abstinence and Academic Achievement.' 27 October 2005, viewed on 19 June 2007, <http://www.heritage.org/Research/Welfare/upload/84576_1.pdf >

Reisser, P.C., *The Focus on the Family Complete Book of Baby and Child Care.* Tyndale, Wheaton, 1997.

Republican Study Committee, 'Title X Funding and Abstinence Funding'. April 2006, viewed on 8 May 2007, <http://www.house.gov/hensarling/rsc/doc/HC_061306_TitleXvs.Abstinence Funding.doc>

Rezé, M. and R. Bowen, *Key Words in American Life: Understanding the United States.* Armand Colin, Paris, 1998.

Rhode, D.L., 'Adolescent Pregnancy and Public Policy' in A. Lawson and D. L. Rhode (eds), *The Politics of Pregnancy: Adolescent Sexuality and Public Policy.* Yale University Press, New Haven, 1993.

Roach, E., 'What if abstinence legislation expires?'. *Baptist Press*, 22 May 2007, viewed on 4 July 2007, <http://www.sbcbaptistpress.net/bpnews.asp?id=25699>

Rogers Radl, S., *The Invisible Woman: Target of the Religious New Right.* Delacorte Press, New York, 1983.

Rosenberg, D., 'The Battle Over Abstinence'. *Newsweek*, 9 December 2002, 8 February 2007, <http://209.85.135.104/search?q=cache:8r4Am9U68hwJ:www.indiana.edu/~llc/Current_Students/q199/battle.pdf+newsweek+human+rights+watch+abstinence+2002&hl=en&ct=clnk&cd=1&gl=de>

Rowe Karlyn, K., 'Scream, Popular Culture, and Feminism's Third Wave: 'I'm Not My Mother''. *Genders OnLine Journal*, 2003, 38, viewed on 14 June 2007, <http://www.genders.org/g38/g38_rowe_karlyn.html>

Rowling, J. K., *Harry Potter*. Bloomsbury, London, 1997-2007.

Rubin, G., 'Thinking Sex: Notes for a Radical Theory of the Politics of Sexuality,' in C. Vance (ed), *Pleasure and Danger: Exploring Female Sexuality*. Routledge and Kegan Paul, Boston, 1984.

Rushing, W., 'Sin, Sex, and Segregation: Social Control and the Education of Southern Women.' *Gender and Education*, June 2002, 14 (2), pp.167-179.

Rwnetwork.net, 'Rebecca Hagelin'. 2007, viewed 15 March, 2007, <http://www.rwnetwork.net/Rebecca_Hagelin>

Sands, K.M., (ed), *God Forbid: Religion and Sex in American Public Life*. Oxford University Press, Oxford, New York, 2000.

Sands, K.M., 'Public, Pubic, and Private, Religion in Political Discourse,' in K.M. Sands (ed), *God Forbid: Religion and Sex in American Public Life*. Oxford University Press, Oxford, New York, 2000.

Santelli, J., M.A. Ott, M. Lyon, J. Rogers, D. Summers and R. Schleifer, 'Abstinence and Abstinence-Only Education: A Review of U.S. Policies and Programs'. *Journal of Adolescent Health*, 2006, 38 (1), pp. 72-81.

Santorum, R., 'Heritage Lecture: The Necessity of Marriage'. 20 October 2003, viewed on 18 June 2007, <http://www.heritage.org/Research/Family/HL-804.cfm>

Scales, P., 'The Public Image of Adolescents'. *Society*, May 2001, 38 (4), pp. 64-75.

Schimmeck, T., 'Der Krieg gegen Sex'. *Die Zeit*, 9 September 2004, viewed on 8 February 2007, <http://www.zeit.de/2004/38/Ami-Keuschheit?page=all>

Schleifer, R., *Ignorance Only HIV/AIDS, Human Rights and Federally Funded Abstinence-Only Programs in the United States*. September 2002, 14 (5) (G), viewed on March 16 2009, <http://eric.ed.gov:80/ERICDocs/data/ericdocs2sql/content_storage_01/0000 019b/80/1a/a5/5a.pdf>

Schneider, B. and D. Stevenson, *The Ambitious Generation: America's Teenagers, Motivated but Directionless*. Yale University Press, New Haven, 1999.

Seidman, S., *Embattled Eros: Sexual Politics and Ethics in Contemporary America*. Routledge, New York, 1992.

Seidman, S., *Beyond the Closet: The Transformation of Gay and Lesbian Life*. Routledge, New York and London, 2002.

Sessions Stepp, L.,'Study Casts Doubt on Abstinence-Only Programs'. *The WashingtonPost.com*, 14 April 2007, viewed on 8 May 2007, <http://www.washingtonpost.com/wp-dyn/content/article/2007/04/13/AR2007041301003.html?nav=rss_health>

Shell Oil, 'Teens Under Pressure, Coping Well'. *The Shell Poll*, 1999, 1(4), pp.1-3.

SIECUS, ADVOCATES FOR YOUTH, 'Toward a Sexually Healthy America: Roadblocks Imposed by the Federal Government's Abstinence-Only-Until-Marriage Education Program'. 2001, viewed on 13 March 2007, <http://www.advocatesforyouth.org/publications/abstinenceonly.pdf>

SIECUS, 'State Profile 2005: Nevada'. 2006a, viewed on 13 March 2007, <http://www.siecus.org/policy/states/2005/mandates/NV.html>

SIECUS, 'Special Report: It Gets Worse: A Revamped Federal Abstinence-Only Program Goes Extreme'. 2006b, viewed on 23 March 2007, <http://www.siecus.org/policy/SpecialReports/Revamped_Abstinence-Only_Goes_Extreme.pdf>

SIECUS, 'A New Congress Should Enforce Accountability Over Abstinence-Only Programs'. 16 November 2006c, viewed on 29 May 2007, <http://www.siecus.org/media/press/press0136.html>

SIECUS, 'A Brief History of Federal Abstinence-Only-Until-Marriage Funding'. 2008, viewed on 28 March 2009, <http://www.siecus.org/index.cfm?fuseaction=Page.viewPage&pageId=670&grandparentID=478&parentID=487>

SIECUS, 'Committee on Oversight and Government Reform Holds First-Ever Hearings on Abstinence Only Until Marriage Programs'. April 2008,

viewed on 28 March 2009,
<http://www.siecus.org/index.cfm?fuseaction=Feature.showFeature&featurei
d=1144&pageid=483&parentid=478>

SIECUS, 'First Ever Cuts to Abstinence-Only-Until-Marriage Programs'. 11
March 2009, viewed on 28 March 2009,
<http://www.siecus.org/index.cfm?fuseaction=Feature.showFeature&featurei
d=1615&pageid=611&parentid=479>

SIECUS, 'SIECUS Applauds the Introduction of the Responsible Education
About Life (REAL) Act'. 17 March 2009, viewed on 28 March 2009,
<http://www.siecus.org/index.cfm?fuseaction=Feature.showFeature&featurei
d=1650&pageid=611&parentid=479>

Siker, J., 'President Bush, Biblical faith, and the Politics of Religion'.
Religious StudiesNews. SBL edition, May 2003, 4 (5), viewed on 6 February
2007, <http://www.sbl-site.org/Article.aspx?ArticleId=151>

Singer, L., *Erotic Welfare: Sexual Theory and Politics in the Age of
Epidemic*. Routledge, London & New York, 1993.

Stacey, J., *In the Name of the Family: Rethinking Family Values in the
Postmodern Age*. Beacon Press, Boston, 1996.

Stern, S.R., 'Self-Absorbed, Dangerous, and Disengaged: What Popular
Films Tell Us About Teenagers'. *Mass Communication*, 2005, 8 (1), pp. 23-
38.

Stockman, F. et al., 'Bush Brings Faith to Foreign Aid'. *The Boston Globe
Online*. 8 October 2006, viewed on 14 February 2007,
<http://www.boston.com/news/nation/articles/2006/10/08/bush_brings_faith_
to_foreign_aid/>

STOP FAMILY VIOLENCE, 'Press Release: Mothers File International
Complaint Against United States'. 11 May 2007, viewed on 29 May 2007,
<http://stopfamilyviolence.org/ocean/host.php?page=471>

Suskind, R., 'Without a Doubt'. *The New York Times*, October 17, 2004,
viewed on 19 June 2007,
<http://www.nytimes.com/2004/10/17/magazine/17BUSH.html?ex=1255665
600en=890a96189e162076ei=509>

Thurman, J., 'House rejects Africa AIDS/abstinence aid'. *The Baptist Press*,
2 July 2007, viewed on 4 July 2007,
<http://www.sbcbaptistpress.net/bpnews.asp?id=26002>

Timlahaye.com, 'Tim LaHaye Biography'. 2004, viewed on 13 march 2007,
<http://www.timlahaye.cm/about_ministry/index.php3?p=bio&section=Biogr
aphy>

Timlahaye.com, 'Pre-Trib Research Center'. 2004, viewed on 13 March
2007,
<http://www.timlahaye.com/about_ministry/index.php3?p=pretrib&section=
PreTrib%20Research%20Center>

Tolman, D. L. and T. E. Higgins, 'How Being a Good Girl Can Be Bad for
Girls,' in N. Bauer Maglin and D. Perry (eds), *"Bad Girls"/"Good Girls":
Women, Sex and Power in the Nineties*. Rutgers University Press, New
Brunswick, New Jersey, 1996.

Tolman, D.L., *Dilemmas of Desire: Teenage Girls Talk About Sexuality*.
Harvard University Press, Cambridge, 2002.

UNION OF CONCERNED SCIENTIST, *Scientific Integrity in Policymaking: An
Investigation into the Bush Administration's Misuse of Science*. March 2004,
viewed on 23 March 2007,
<http://www.ucsusa.org/assets/documents/scientific_integrity/RSI_final_fullr
eport_1.pdf>

U.S. Congress, Senate, *Abstinence Education: Special Hearing before a
Subcommittee of the Committee on Appropriations of the United States
Senate*, 108th Congress, 2nd sess., 16 February 2004.

U.S. Department of Labor, *Issues in Labor Statistics*. Bureau of Labor
Statistics, Summary 02-06, 2002.

U.S. Department of Health and Human Services, *Parents, Speak Up! Guide
for Discussing Abstinence Sex, and Relationships*. 2005a, viewed on 6 March
2007, <http://www.4parents.gov/downloads/parentguide.pdf>

U.S. Department of Health and Human Services, *Teen Chat: A Guide to
Discussing Healthy Relationships*. 2005b, viewed on 6 March 2007,
<http://www.4parents.gov/downloads/teenchat.pdf>

U.S. Department of Health and Human Services Administration for Children and Families, 'Announcement for Funding Opportunity Under CBAE, Funding Opportunity Number: HHS-2006-ACF-ACYF-AE-0099'. 2006a, viewed on 22 March 2007, <http://www.acf.hhs.gov/grants/pdf/HHS-2006-ACF-ACYF-AE-0099.pdf>

U.S. Department of Health and Human Services Administration for Children and Families, 'FY 2007 Program Announcement, Section 510 Abstinence Education Program'. 2006b, viewed on 27 March 2007, <http://www.acf.hhs.gov/grants/pdf/ACYF-FYSB-AE-01-06updated.pdf>

U.S. Department of Health and Human Services Administration for Children and Families, 'HHS Unveils "Parents Speak Up" National Campaign PSA Campaign, New Web Site Help Parents Talk to Kids About Waiting to Have Sex'. 21 June 2007, viewed on 2 July 2007, <http://www.acf.hhs.gov/news/press/2007/parents_speak_up.htm>

Vance, C., (ed.), *Pleasure and Danger: Exploring Female Sexuality.* Routledge and Kegan Paul, Boston, 1984.

Vineyard, A., 'Protection Teens Are Still Not Getting'. 19 December 2002, viewed on 19 June 2007, <http://www.beverlylahayeinstitute.org/articledisplay.asp?id=2944&department=BLI&categoryid=femfacts&subcategoryid=blicul>

Vulliamy, E., 'Bush Promotes Virgin Values to Curb Teen Sex'. *The Observer*, 28 April 2002, 8 February 2007, <http://observer.guardian.co.uk/bush/story/0,,706578,00.html>

Wallis, J., 'Dangerous Religion'. *Sojourners Magazine*, September-October 2003, viewed on 26 May 2007, <http://www.sojo.net/index.cfm?action=magazine.article&issue=soj0309&article=030910>

The Washington Post, 'Transcript of Roundtable Interview'. *Washington Post.com*. 2 August 2005, viewed on 27 February 2007, <http://www.washingtonpost.com/wp-dyn/content/article/2005/08/02/AR2005080200899_5.html>

Waters, M. C., *Ethnic Options: Choosing Identities in America.* University of California Press, Berkeley, 1990.

Waxman, H.A. (prepared for), *The Content of Federally Funded Abstinence-Only Education Programs*. December 2004, viewed on 22 May 2007, < http://oversight.house.gov/documents/20041201102153-50247.pdf>

Waxman, H.A. (prepared for), *False and Misleading Information Provided by Federally Funded Pregnancy Resource Centers*. July 2006, viewed 26 May 2007,
<http://oversight.house.gov/documents/20060717101140-30092.pdf>

Weeks, J., *Sexuality and its Discontents: Meanings, Myths, and Modern Sexualities*. Routledge and Kegan Paul, London, 1985.

Weeks, J., *Sexuality*. Ellis Horwood Limited, Chichester, 1986.

Weeks, J., *Invented Moralities: Sexual Values in an Age of Uncertainty*. Polity Press, Cambridge, 1995.

West, T.C., 'The Policing of Black Women's Sexual Reproduction,' in K.M. Sands (ed), *God Forbid: Religion and Sex in American Public Life*. Oxford University Press, Oxford, New York, 2000.

Wetzstein, C., 'Unwed Mothers Set a Record for Births'. *The Washington Times*, April 18, 2001.

Wetzstein, C., 'Poll finds majority back birth control; Access sought without 'delay''. *The Washington Times*, June 8, 2007a, viewed on 24 June 2007, <http://www.religiousconsultation.org/News_Tracker/poll_finds_majority_back_birth_control.htm>

Wetzstein, C., 'Study: More 'condoms' than 'abstinence' in sex-ed'. *The Washington Times*, 14 June 2007b, viewed on 24 June 2007, <http://www.washingtontimes.com/apps/pbcs.dll/article?AID=/20070614/NATION/106140075&SearchID=73285126621455>

White House, *Working Toward Independence*. 2002, viewed on 16 February 2009, < http://georgewbush-whitehouse.archives.gov/news/releases/2002/02/welfare-reform-announcement-book.pdf>

White House, *President George W. Bush: A Remarkable Record of Achievement*. August 2004, viewed on 24 March 2007, <http://www.whitehouse.gov/infocus/achievement/Achievement.pdf>

White House, 'Press Briefing by Scott McClellan'. 26 May 2005, viewed on 25 March 2007, <http://www.whitehouse.gov/news/releases/2005/05/20050526-1.html>

White House, 'Memorandum: Mexico City Policy and Assistance for Voluntary Population Planning'. 23 January 2009, viewed on 28 March 2009, <http://www.whitehouse.gov/the_press_office/MexicoCityPolicy-Voluntary PopulationPlanning/>

White House, 'Executive Order: Removing Barriers to Responsible Scientific research Involving Human Stem Cells'. 9 March 2009, viewed on 28 March 2009, < http://www.whitehouse.gov/the_press_office/Removing-Barriers-to-Responsible-Scientific-Research-Involving-Human-Stem-Cells/>

White House, 'Memorandum: Scientific Integrity'. 9 March 2009, viewed on 28 March 2009, <http://www.whitehouse.gov/the_press_office/Memorandum-for-the-Heads-of-Executive-Departments-and-Agencies-3-9-09/>

Wildermuth, J., 'Welfare reform heading back to Congress next year'. *San Francisco Chronicle*, 4 November 2001, p. A11.

Wolfe, A., *One Nation, After All: What Middle-Class Americans Think About: God, Country, Family, Racism, Welfare, Immigration, Homosexuality, Work, The Right, The Left, and Each Other*. Penguin Books, London, 1999.

Legal Texts

Adolescent Family Life Act of 1981. United States Code /Title 42, The Public Health and Welfare Chapter 6A - Public Health and Service/Subchapter XVIII - Adolescent Family Life Demonstration Project, 97th Congress.

Omnibus Budget Reconciliation Act of 1981. Public Law 97-35, 97th Congress.

Elementary and Secondary Education Act. H.R. 6, Public Law 103-382, 103rd Congress.

Defence of Marriage Act of 1996. H.R. 3396, Public Law 104-199, 104th Congress.

Personal Responsibility and Work Opportunity Reconciliation Act of 1996. H.R. 3734, Public Law No: 104-193, 104th Congress also referred to as *Social Security Act.*

Children's Internet Protection Act. Public Law 106-554, Title XVII, 106th Congress.

Uniting and Strengthening America by Providing Appropriate Tools Required to Intercept and Obstruct Terrorism Act of 2001. Also known as *Patriot Act.* Public Law 107-56, 107th Congress.

Marriage Protection Act of 2003. H.R. 3313, 108th Congress.

Personal Responsibility, Work, and Family Promotion Act of 2003. H.R. 4, 108th Congress.

Unborn Victims of Violence Act of 2004. Also known as *Laci and Conner's Law.* H.R. 1997, Public Law 108-212, 108th Congress.

Child Interstate Abortion Notification Act. H.R. 748, introduced 2005, 109th Congress.

Marriage Protection Amendment. Senate Joint Resolution 1, introduced 2005, 109th Congress.
U.S. District Court for the Middle District of Pennsylvania, *Kitzmiller v. Dover Area School District:*

Memorandum Opinion. 20 December 2005, viewed on 10 June 2007, <http://www.pamd.uscourts.gov/kitzmiller/kitzmiller_342.pdf>

Films

Adamson, A., (dir), *The Chronicles of Narnia: The Lion, the Witch and the Wardrobe,* 2005.

Apted, M., (dir), *Amazing Grace,* 2006.

Goodman, R.D. and B. Goodman (dir), *The Lost Children of Rockdale County,* 1999.

Meeker, M., P.J. Warren and M. Maxwell Billingsly (narrators), *The Rules Have Changed the Teen STD Epidemic.* 2004.